SILENT VIOLENCE

Neoliberalism, Islamist Politics and the AKP Years in Turkey

edited by: Simten Coşar &
Gamze Yücesan-Özdemir

RED QUILL BOOKS

ISBN 978-1-926958-18-7

∞ ☘

Printed on acid-free paper. The paper used in this book incorporates post-consumer waste and has not been sourced from endangered old growth forests, forests of exceptional conservation value or the Amazon Basin. Red Quill Books subscribes to a one-book-at-a-time manufacturing process that substantially lessens supply chain waste, reduces greenhouse emissions, and conserves valuable natural resources.

Library and Archives Canada Cataloguing in Publication

Silent violence: neoliberalism, Islamist politics and the AKP years in Turkey / edited by Simten Coşar & Gamze Yücesan-Özdemir.

Includes bibliographical references.
ISBN 978-1-926958-18-7

1. Neoliberalism—Turkey. 2. Islam and politics—Turkey.
3. Turkey—Politics and government—1980-.
I. Coşar, Simten
II. Yücesan-Özdemir, Gamze

JC574.T8S55 2012   320.5109561   C2012-900787-0

RED QUILL BOOKS

[RQB is a radical publishing house.
Part of the proceeds from the sale of this book will support student scholarships.]

To
Evin, Duru, Aras & Ada
with the hope for a better future...

TABLE OF CONTENTS

LIST OF TABLES

INTRODUCTION

AN ATTEMPT TO UNRAVEL THE ARTICULATION OF NEOLIBERALISM WITH ISLAMIST POLITICS DURING THE AKP YEARS IN TURKEY

Simten Coşar & Gamze Yücesan-Özdemir

The rise of the *Adalet ve Kalkınma Partisi* (Justice and Development Party, AKP) as the victorious political party in the 2011 general elections for the third time since 2002 necessitates a thorough analysis of the party's successful manipulation of neoliberal politics with Islamic sensitivities. Actually, the AKP's political identity has always been a major issue on the agenda of debates regarding Turkish politics. Yet, the debates have so far been built upon established dichotomies such as democracy *versus* authoritarianism, laicism *versus* anti-laicism, secularity *versus* religiosity, and civilian *versus* military politics. These dichotomies are essentially embedded in the modernisation paradigm, which offers a comfortable analytical set—conceptual means, discursive practices, and epistemological arguments—for monopolising the process of explanation in modern polities. Put differently, so long as understanding Turkey's experience with the AKP is tied to the modernisation paradigm, the restriction of research with these dichotomies is unavoidable, leaving out the possibility for an analysis that considers social totality. Therefore, while not denying the importance of the dichotomies noted above, this edited volume takes issue with the economic, political, and ideological structures, in which these dichotomies are rooted. Analysing these structures creates the potential for a comprehensive understanding of Turkish politics, in that it involves the interrogation of the multi-layered articulations among religious politics, democracy, secularism, militarism, and authoritarianism, which circumscribe and horizontally crosscut each other.

Looking at the economic, political, and ideological structures in this way requires a thorough reading of neoliberal capitalism, as it was manifested on Turkish lands. Although a global phenomenon, neoliberal capitalism has evolved with different facets and through varying and at times contradictory alliances from region to region. Aside from the generalised division between the "developed" and the "developing" worlds, it has so far also managed to manipulate the contextual dynamics from within the developing world, thus, working in alternative routes. In this respect, and specifically in the Turkish context, this alternative route has been built upon Islamist politics. Islamism, indeed not an unfamiliar political stance since the foundation of the Turkish Republic (1923), has provided the neoliberal pattern with an appropriate venue to develop in the country. Certainly, in this articulation into neoliberal capitalism, Islamist politics have experienced a decisive transformation in relation to the state, economy, and society, thus, challenging the tension between a modern, capitalist life-world and the Islamist precepts that have persisted throughout the republican history of Turkey.

In turn, this necessitates understanding the juxtaposition of Islamist and capitalist precepts. Yet, this articulation shall also be read within the global political economy frame, thus, challenging the long established tension between the East—perceived as in one way or another *Islamic*—and the West—perceived as essentially *modern*. However, this endeavour to challenge the established tensions creates some of its own, which inevitably cultivate a silent violence. In other words, since the challenges concerned involve a transformation in the state, economic, and ideological structures through the use of political power instruments, the transformation itself is most explicitly revealed in a form of silent violence. Thus, the title of this edited volume is *Silent Violence: Neoliberalism, Islamist Politics and the AKP Years in Turkey.*

While analysing the AKP years in Turkey, the volume prioritises three basic approaches, namely a historical perspective, class perspective, and gender perspective. As for the historical perspective, the book considers the 1980 *coup d'état* as the *historical juncture* that marked the structural transformation—concerning the state, society and economy—in Turkey. In this respect, the AKP's rise to power is contextualised by looking at the developments that took place after the 1980 *coup d'état*. Thus, the book offers an alternative reading of contemporary Turkish politics through a comprehensive analysis of the systemic continuities and discontinuities of the past three decades.

Additionally, a reading of the AKP years from a class and gender perspective into the structural dynamics of neoliberal capitalism in Turkey gives voice to other alternative viewpoints on contemporary Turkish politics, which have previously been pushed to the margins. Likewise, these two spheres turn out to be the most accessible from which to observe the reflections of the silent violence of neoliberalism, as it is displayed in the AKP's policies. As for the class perspective, it contributes to the manifestation of the party's fine synthesis between religious conservatism and (neo)liberalism in its pursuit of power politics. Put differently, a class analysis of the AKP's rule, which does not exclude the crosscutting power relationships, reveals the substance and origins of the party's power, which have ultimately worked through capitalist networks.

Furthermore, this perspective goes beyond a *pseudo* photograph of the socio-economic formation that has defined the AKP, and thus, it provides the dynamics for social change and orients the direction of social movements.

The gender perspective specifically contributes to the manifestation of the intertwined nature of seemingly different exploitative structural dynamics. More briefly, the gender policies of the AKP are considered a testament to the fine-tuning of the Islamist political stance with neoliberal requisites, and also of neoliberal policies with Islamist solidarity/charity appeals. This perspective, which crosscuts the edited volume, offers the grounds on which to comprehend the seemingly contradictory coexistence of religious conservative and (neo) liberal policies, especially in terms of a new mode of patriarchy in Turkey's current phase of neoliberalism.

Anchored in the frame above, this book is organised into three main parts: *State, Law, and Society; Social Policy, Citizenship, and Gender;* and *Global Interfaces: Politics, Economy, and International Relations.* In Part I, *State, Law and Society*, Yalman offers a critical analysis of the political transformation that Turkey has underwent during the AKP's rule in Chapter 1, *Politics and Discourse under the AKP's Rule: The Marginalisation of Class-Based Politics, Erdoğanisation, and Post-Secularism.* Yalman focuses on the predominance of the discourse among the academic, media, and political circles through which the recent changes in state-society relations have been presented as the *sine-qua-non* of Turkey's democratisation project. While analysing the discursive practices that form the basis for the arguments on the *reality* of a transformation in Turkish state-society relations under the AKP's rule (2002-), Yalman particularly interrogates the elimination of the *wars of positions* in terms of its advantage to *post-secularism.* In so doing, he walks through the labyrinths of the political role of Islam; the transformation of the state through discussions on "political *versus* "moderate" Islam; and civil societalisation through personalist politics—thus, *Erdoğanisation*.

Law, being the directly decisive mechanism in the transformation of state-society relations, is the topic of Chapter 2 by Özdemir, *Fragments of Changes in the Legal System in the AKP Years: The Development and Reproduction of Market Friendly Law*. Here Özdemir critically explores the "remarkable fragments of changes in Turkey's legal system," with a view to the legalisation of the neoliberal order. Throughout the chapter, Özdemir deciphers the "discoveries" of the policy-makers in adjusting the legal system to the neoliberal frame through empowering markets against society. In this endeavor, Özdemir takes issue with the constitutional rearrangement of the socio-political space in Turkey under the AKP governments. In doing so, he first focuses on the current structure, composition, and functions of the Constitutional Court of Turkey (CCT). Consequently, while portraying the class-based nature of the legal system through the CCT, he problematises the implications of this legal frame for collective labour rights on two levels: constitutional and social policy. Thus, he ultimately analyses the constitutional rights and restrictions regarding labour and the *Sosyal Sigortalar ve Genel Sağlık Sigortası Yasası* (Social Security and General Health Insurance Law, SSGSS).

Mechanisms of ideology, being the major feature of state-society interfaces, form the frame of Chapter 3, by Coşar: *The AKP's Hold on Power: Neoliberalism Meets the Turkish-Islamic Synthesis*. Coşar develops a critical analysis of the AKP's political identity with a view to the Turkish-Islamic synthesis. Her main argument is based on the decisiveness of neoliberal politics in the adoption of this version of the articulation between Turkish nationalism and Islam. She elaborates that though seemingly contradictory, the Turkish-Islamic synthesis and neoliberal policies and politics have functioned as the seedbed for the AKP. In so doing, she delineates the shifts and relocations in the AKP's discursive practices with a view to the intertwined nature of the international and national policy-making on the basis of three issue areas: the foreign policy dimension, the religious dimension, and the ethnic dimension.

The ideological aspect of neoliberalisation in Turkey has so far been overwhelmingly concentrated on the *rhetoric* of democratisation, which is questioned in Chapter 4, *Islamist Bourgeoisie and Democracy under the AKP's Rule: Democratisation or Marketisation of Politics?* by Yılmaz. Problematizing the mainstream approaches that argue for an almost organic connection between embourgeoisment and democratisation, Yılmaz questions the rhetorical tributes to democracy in the Islamist bourgeois discourse. Employing a theoretical framework, which challenges the mainstream assumptions regarding the bourgeoisie-democracy nexus, Yılmaz considers the position of the Islamist bourgeoisie under the AKP with a view to the intersection of a complex web of power relations involving the state, other social classes, and international economic and geopolitical dynamics.

Part II, *Social Policy, Citizenship, and Gender*, is a follow-up to the first part in two respects. Each chapter problematises a certain issue area—social policy, citizenship, and gender, respectively–so as to rip out the neoliberal stitches of the texture of state, law, and society as formulated in Part I. For instance, Chapter 5, by Yücesan-Özdemir, *The Social Policy Regime in the AKP Years: The Emperor's New Clothes*, investigates the foundational pillars of the AKP's social policy regime–neoliberalism, conservatism, and Islam.Yücesan-Özdemir substantiates her arguments, which are built upon the neoliberal-Islamist conservative nexus, with a view to the implications on everyday life of the AKP's policy preferences with regard to social rights. Thus, she observes that while living under this social policy regime, the labour class goes through two interconnected life experiences: precarious work, and finding themselves at the mercy of social assistance with an Islamic dressing. Yücesan-Özdemir's contribution elaborates that precarious work and social assistance reproduce and legitimise the regime itself.

The citizenship dimension is assessed in Chapter 6, by Soyarık-Şentürk, *The AKP's Citizenisation Project: Where To?* In this, Soyarık-Şentürk focuses on the continuities and discontinuities in the citizenisation project, which have characterised the republican history in Turkey on the basis of policies pursued by the AKP governments. She specifically argues that the party's citizenisation project is imbued with an inconsistent composition of (neo)liberalism, Turkish nationalism, and the prioritisation of Muslimhood. Aside from the identity politics pursued by the AKP in terms of Turkish nationalism and Muslimhood, Soyarık-Şentürk also points at the party's challenge to the republican understanding of citizenship through neoliberal politics, which in the final analysis leads to the exclusion of social rights.

The gender plane, which vividly displays the exclusionary politics of the AKP governments, is the concern of Yeğenoğlu & Coşar's Chapter 7, *The AKP and the Gender Issue: Shuttling between Neoliberalism and Patriarchy.* Yeğenoğlu & Coşar trace the gendered nature of the social, cultural, and political conservatisation in the AKP's governmental practice. The main argument of the authors, that the AKP's reign has been characterised by the emergence of a new mode of patriarchy, is built upon the contention that the conservatisation of Turkey shall not be identified with the pro-Islamist origins of the party. In this respect, the authors point out the transformation in the mode of patriarchy being employed, which is structured within the neoliberal frame, and which reveals itself in the interfaces between Islam, conservatism, and nationalism.

The analysis of the structural transformation in Turkey that is elaborated upon in its various dimensions in Parts I and II is carried to the global level in Part III, *Global Interfaces: Politics, Economy and International Relations*. This section centers upon the argument that the neoliberal transformation that Turkey has experienced since the late 1970s is both informed and also reproduced by the shifts and relocations in the world capitalist economy. In other words, the global capitalist world order has provided the context within which Turkey's participation and role in this order has been determined. Hence, the sociopolitical accomodations, constraints, and challenges offered by global capitalism are rather important for a deeper and more critical understanding of Turkey's experience with neoliberalism. In this respect, Chapter 8, *Turkish Foreign Policy under the AKP Governments: An Interplay of Imperial Legacy, Neoliberal Interests and Pragmatism* by Birgül Demirtaş, offers a critical analysis of the juxtapositions of different and at times contradicting foreign policy preferences of the AKP. Essentially, Demirtaş focuses on the question of whether there has so far been a tendential move from Turkey's traditional Western-oriented (Anglo-American and/or European) stance to a tendency towards its "middle-easternisation," through a neo-Ottomanist agenda.

On a more specific plane, Chapter 9, by Filiz Zabcı, *Internalisation of Dependency: The AKP's Dance with the Global Institutions of Neoliberalism*, carries the analysis of the AKP's foreign policy record to the party's intercourse with global financial institutions. Zabcı directly focuses on the implications of the dominance of the World Bank (WB) and International Monetary Fund (IMF) in the economic, political, and ideological structurations in Turkey. Moreover, the chapter contributes to the unfolding of the themes of the book in that it challenges the AKP's claims that it has introduced a *nouevaux* approach that differentiates it from the previous governments of the post-1980 era. In fact, Zabcı contends that the AKP governments have not displayed a shift from the neoliberal policies that had formed the political parameters of previous governments; rather they have further fuelled the internalisation of dependency that is endemic to neoliberal structures.

Turkey's accession to the European Union (EU), which has been one of the most significant topics in Turkey's articulation into the world capitalist economy since the mid-1960s, is critically analysed in Chapter 10, by Yeşilyurt-Gündüz, *The EU and the AKP: A Neoliberal Love Affair?*. Yeşilyurt-Gündüz offers an assessment of Turkey-EU relations under the AKP governments, which has served as a trial-error process for the AKP's "Western-orientedness," with a view to the EU progress reports for Turkey. By underlining the transformation in the EU social policy regime from a social democratic scope to a neoliberal agenda, she concludes that the interaction between the EU and Turkey is in the end dependent upon the neoliberal world order, which tempts one to presume a neoliberal affair.

All in all, the readers of this volume will find a discussion of the silencing of violence in neoliberalism through Islamist politics in Turkey, a significant but naturally insufficient exploration and asset to the ongoing conversation surrounding Turkey's experiences in the AKP years. And they will, we are convinced, find in this book many questions worthy of thought in this regard.

PART I: STATE, LAW AND SOCIETY

1

POLITICS AND DISCOURSE UNDER THE AKP'S RULE: THE MARGINALISATION OF CLASS-BASED POLITICS, ERDOĞANISATION, AND POST-SECULARISM

Galip Yalman

Introduction

Analysing the state transformation that Turkey has been experiencing under the AKP governments requires a detailed look at the party's skilful manipulation of neoliberalisation with Islamisation in building its hegemonic opposition to the established Republican regime. In the current process, it is possible to note the predominance of discourse through which the changes that have been taking place recently are presented as the *sine-qua-non* of Turkey's democratisation project. The carriers of this discourse in the academic, media, and political circles have also assumed the position of agenda setters. Subsequently, the alternative arguments are also forced into a dialogue within the parameters set by this hegemonic discourse.

Can we assume that the disciplines of political science and economics, or the disciplines of social sciences are separate spheres of research in which one can conduct analysis regardless of the other? In this respect, too, the predominant discourse on democratisation that locks the democratisation process into the TINA (There is No Alternative) argument sets the parameters of how to conduct scientific research, which ultimately results in the bifurcation of social reality: the economist deals with economics, political scientist with politics, and sociologist with sociology. This bifurcation leads to the restriction of the discussion on certain political, social, and economic phenomena to narrow frames, determined separately by these disciplines. Thus, new trends and new schools addressing the nature of the relation between politics and economics have begun to emerge.

Interestingly, *new political economy* trends have been emerging since the last quarter of the twentieth century, which tempts one to presume the re-discovery of the political economy. Yet, the common feature of these newly emerging trends is to approach each and every human sphere through neoclassical lenses, or in other words, on the basis of the individual as an actor, defined in terms of neoclassical economics. In this respect, it is of utmost importance to involve critical tradition in analysing Turkish politics, especially the AKP's terms in office. It is the aim of this chapter to explore such a critical analysis of the discursive practices that form the basis for the arguments on the *reality* of a transformation in Turkish state-society relations under the AKP's rule (2002-).

The New Hegemonic Strategy as the Basis for the AKP's Rule: Elimination of Class-Based Politics

As it is known, the transformation experienced through the process of political restructuration in post-1980 Turkey has two significant features, which are also decisive characteristics of the neoliberal hegemony (Yalman, 2004; Yıldızoğlu, 2008). On the one hand, the state has been restructured in

1: Politics and Discourse under the AKP's Rule:
   The Marginalisation of Class-Based Politics,
   Erdoğanisation, and Post-Secularism

23

accordance with the re-definition of its role in the economic sphere. On the other hand, with the aim of offering a long-term resolution to the crisis of hegemony that the bourgeoisie had experienced in the pre-1980 period, democratic rights and liberties of the working class were restricted within the constitutional frame. Therefore, it is apt to define the essence of the new hegemonic strategy, which accompanied the restructuration of the state in the post-1980 period, in terms of *putting an end to the class-based politics* (Yalman, 2004). Putting and end to class-based politics as a strategy is not employed as a means to eliminate class politics. Rather it is employed to marginalise class-based political opposition. The post-1980 neoliberal policies have worked through the marginalisation of class-based politics, and AKP's term in government signified the consolidation of the tehnocratic cum culturalist discourse as the main frame in policy-making.

Thus, an important dimension of the neoliberal restructuration of the state is the manipulation of *identity politics*—nourished by discussions within liberalism, like multi-culturalism—in putting an end to class-based politics. This replacement (of class-based politics) has actually been one of the main achievements of the power bloc in Turkey.[1] This being so, new contradictions, which required the questioning of the decisive feature of the Turkish Republic at the constitutional level, were given way in determining the political agenda. Moreover, such values as democracy, freedom, and equality, which are of utmost importance for leftist politics in defending the rights of the workers, began to be manipulated in terms of identity politics. In other words, these concepts have been accrued with new meanings, as the hegemonic instruments of new politics.

The reasons behind the prioritisation of the restructuration of the state in the contradictory and inconsistent theoretical universe of neoliberalism is that this issue is vital for the maintenance of its ideological hegemony—despite the fact that the process has assumed different routes in different countries. Indeed, the success of the regulations that aim to minimise the political and social costs of structural adjustment is tied to the capacity of the states to carry the reforms regardless of the governmental changes. This phenomenon, which turns neoliberal reforms into a state project, was defined as "different governments, common policy" (BSB, 2007). In other words, the opposition parties, whose objective is governmental power, are required to adjust themselves to the neoliberal frame, and to adopt the hegemonic discourse to a certain extent. Thus, it is apt to define the post-1980 structure in Turkey in terms of a new hegemonic strategy that accompanies state restructuration in accordance with the frame of an authoritarian state. In this context, it is necessary to consider that the foundational parameter of contemporary politics in Turkey is *putting an end to class-based politics*, and furthermore, to question the possibilities for the transition from an authoritarian form of government to a democratic one (for an in-depth analysis of this hegemony construction on the basis of Gramscian "passive revolution"[2] see Tuğal, 2010).

Islam under the AKP's Rule: False Dichotomies as Hegemonic Strategies

More than two decades ago, when the infamous articles of the *Türk Ceza Kanunu* (Turkish Penal Code, TCK) (Articles 141-142 and 163)[3] had not yet been repealed, a prominent student of Turkish political history, Feroz Ahmad, read political dynamics in Turkey as follows: there was a significant rise in the cases filed in *Devlet Güvenlik Mahkemeleri* (State Security Courts, DGMs)[4] against those activities deemed "reactionary"—i.e., those activities that are deemed to aim at eliminating the secular nature of the state—between 1984 and

1987. Besides, under the *Anavatan Partisi* (Motherland Party, ANAP), lead by Turgut Özal, steps were taken to reverse the republican achievements in the spheres of education and scientific progress; religious high schools and Quran courses were fostered. Such developments throughout the 1980s were annoying to observers from the West; news and comments regarding the threat against the secular state in Turkey were gaining frequency in the Western media. This annoyance was nourished by the protests and meetings against the ban on *hijab* as well as by the news on the penetration of fundamentalists into the universities, military schools, and bureaucracy. However, Ahmad has argued that it is inapt to interpret these developments as claims for a shariah state. For him, this would have been impossible since in the same period the Turkish Republic had reached a certain level of capitalism, which automatically negated such a risk. More briefly, according to Ahmad, such an ideology would find social support among ignorant or semi-ignorant, unemployed masses with no hope for the future. The assumption in this reading was that consumer societies would not offer suitable grounds for voicing demands for a shariah state. In other words, there were no material grounds on which to argue the transformation of an advanced capitalist state to an Islamic state. In this respect, one could only note the revolt of the Islamist identity as a cultural phenomenon during the 1980s in Turkey.

Interestingly, Ahmad also argued for a similar assumption in his assessments of the 1950s. He noted that by the *Demokrat Parti*'s (Democratic Party, DP) coming to power in 1950, the laicist approach to Islam was eliminated, but that at the same time this should not be read as the victory of the anti-secularists. On the contrary, he continued, one could talk about the revolt of the Islamist identity as a cultural phenomenon in line with the DP's liberal approach to secularism (Ahmad, 2008). Yet, referring to Islamist identity as a cultural phenomenon connoted different meanings in the analysis of a period when there was no sign of Samuel P. Huntington's "clash of civilizations"—which the current AKP government has adopted in its discursive practices—and when identity politics were not elevated to a decisive position in social struggles (Huntington, 1993). Ahmad's objective in his argument seems to have been to assure that this phenomenon was not so significant as to have a transformative capacity in state-society relations. However, the developments in the past two decades have proved quite the contrary. Islamist identity has increasingly stood as a party to the social struggle, both at the international and national levels—or at least, such a perception has come to be common. The adoption of an "alliance of civilizations" by the United Nations in the aftermath of the September 11 attacks is a manifestation of this perception.[5]

The positioning of culture as the decisive feature in the political struggle in general and specifically in identity politics, which contains demands and claims that go beyond class/national divisions, has also been interpreted as an asset of a postmodern condition in reference to the current state of Islamist politics (Gülalp, 2002). In other words, the term "Islamist" does not connote politics and ideology that interpellate aspirations of the deprived masses for a better past, but it signifies an approach that offers religion as a new social imagination for the generations who opt for better education and life standards (Göle, 2009; Buğra, 2001; 2004). Thus, it is argued that there is no validity to the thesis that Islamist ideology and politics will lose ground due to the requisites of capitalist development. Yet, at this point the discussion gains a new dimension, centered upon the question of how to interpret the adjustment process of Islamist parties and/or movements to the neoliberal globalisation. Remarkably, two tendencies have come to the fore by the insignification of the covert demands for an Islamic state. The first tendency is to discuss the principle and practice of laicism.

The second is the opening of a new space for the mobilisation of political Islam by the persistent implementation of neoliberal economic and social policies (see Yücesan-Özdemir's contribution to this volume).

In this context, one also has to note another theoretical development: the clarification of the insufficiency in adopting those conceptual differentiations such as private/public and state/civil society, which have been absolutised by liberal theoreticians in comprehending and explicating social realities. Briefly, the separation between *the political* and *the economic* so as to overcome the (neo)liberal problem of coming to terms with the public has been reproduced with recourse to the division between the private and the public and to that between the civil society and the state, that had already been ingrained in the original liberal formula. The deficiencies in the original formula aside, in the neoliberal theoretical frame the divisions concerned have so far failed to match with societal realities. In other words, while the neoliberal policy makers held fast to the rationale of individual rights and liberties in their attempts to de-publicise the political sphere they actually communitarianise and/or marketise the latter. This being so, in turn, necessitates the co-existence of two mutually exclusive references—the community and the individual—as the basis for neoliberal formations. All in all, the fallacy of the neoliberal theoretical assumptions in matching with the social reality led to an increase in authoritarian tendencies of the AKP governments.

State under the AKP's Rule: Political Islam or Moderate Islam?

What kind of conceptualisation of state has the AKP adopted? It is certain that the motto–*"state providing services"* - that the party has previously referred to in trying to explain its approach to the state is in compliance with a neoliberal approach:[6]

> The state has to be [restructured] so as to confine
> it to its essential functions, [it has to be] small but
> dynamic and effective; it has to serve as a state that
> is defined, controlled and shaped by its citizen,
> and not as a state that defines, controls and shapes
> its citizen (AK Parti ve Muhafazakar Demokrasi,
> http://www.akparti.org.tr/muhafazakar.doc).

There are arguments stating that a party that has adopted
this understanding cannot be identified with political Islam—
even if it emerged from within an Islamist tradition. At first
sight, it might be thought that it would not be consistent to
impose Islamic rules on a party that has adopted the above
noted definition–a succinct expression of the New Right's
anti-Enlightenment understanding of state. Actually, such a
definition of state is one of the most important reasons behind
the labeling of the AKP as "post-Islamist" (Bayat, 2007). This
designation is mainly related to the AKP's break with the
Islamist *Millî Görüş* (National Outlook) tradition in Turkey.
The term "moderate Islam," which is common in Western
societies, but has not been recognised by the ruling cadres of
the AKP, is a similar way of describing the party. Inherent in
this liberal interpretation of political Islam is the compliance
of Islam with the world capitalist order.

At this point, one has to recall a number of essential
features that define the AKP's discursive practices in a more
comprehensive style: the first feature is related to the ideological function that the neoliberal conceptualisation of state
has so far served for the AKP's political strategy. This is
also one of the junctures between the state-centric–yet anti-
statist–approach and the AKP. In this way, there are attempts
to establish conditionalities between liberalism and Islam.
This endeavor is carried out especially well through laicism.
To put it more briefly, the recent conceptualisation of the state

in Turkey, which has been shaped under the New Right's influence, frequently emphasises that the liberal state shall not prioritise supreme goals over the individuals and that it shall stay neutral in the face of different goals adopted by the individuals. Another way of saying this is that the state is expected not to have an ideology. In this respect, there should be no reason for an unconformity between liberalism, without a normative societal project, and Islam–not as an ideology but as a religion (Erdoğan, 2005; Soli & Sarıkaya, 2005). The AKP's self-definition as a party that would not "impose ideology" underlines this junction (AK Parti ve Muhafazakar Demokrasi). More interestingly, the party has been rendered responsible to cleanse Turkish politics and society from the remnants of the September 12 regime.[7] The commentators as well as the AKP officials who charged the party with such a task seem to perceive the state as an agent that can be abstracted from class contradictions, that dominates politics but that can also be excluded from the political sphere (see, for example, İnsel, 2002). In this respect, they negate the conceptualisation of the state as a historically-specific form of societal relations, independent of social power struggles.

Besides, the common disposition vis-à-vis an omnipotent state that is assumed to impose alternatives to individuals is also important. This disposition has been shared by the proponents of the approach that aims to construct the fundamental axis of contradiction in societal formation in terms of a state/society polarisation—or in Şerif Mardin's particularist reading, a center/periphery polarisation –and by the right wing parties in Turkey since the DP of the 1950s. In this respect, this axis of contradiction, symbolised by the conceptual binary of state/civil society in the 1990s, has been defined under the AKP's terms in government by the conceptual binaries of Kemalist/liberal, laicist/democratic, and statist elites/conservative circles and is worthy of attention. The manipulation of these conceptual binaries in arguing for the desirability of neoliberal socio-economic policies in decreasing the state's influence over society   attest to another dimension of the ideological function (Şen, 2006; Mert, 2007).

The second feature that defines the AKP's discursive practices is the strengthening of political Islam through the course of globalisation. In other words, there seems to be no need to interpret the efforts of a political movement that has been acting as the carrier of a neoliberal globalisation project, attempting to define itself in terms of a break from the Islamist tradition as a qualitative transformation. Actually, if one has to note a transformation within the Islamist movement in Turkey, s/he has to consider the process that started with the *Refah Partisi* (Welfare Party, RP) in the 1990s (Bayat, 2007; Gülalp, 2001; Yavuz, 1999). Thus, Turkey's experience with the AKP calls for an analysis of the way political Islam has adjusted to the neoliberal restructuration process within the globalisation process, rather than an explanation of the party's relation with the *Millî Görüş* movement in terms of breaks/continuities (see Coşar's contribution to this volume).

At this point, the support extended to the AKP government by intellectuals who consider themselves liberals gains meaning. In this the negotiation process between Turkey and the EU until 2005 was effective. It has also been frequently stated that the negotiation process has been instrumental in the transformation of Islamist identity in Turkey, and that this transformation would be a modal example for the other Muslim majority countries so long as the compatibility between Islam and democracy is maintained. Yet, one has to acknowledge that the philosophical roots of such an argument in a liberal tradition go beyond Turkey's borders. For example, it is possible to relate such a stance with the "agonistic" liberalism portrayed in John Gray's works. Or,

one can even observe similar lines of argument in the works
of Jürgen Habermas from Frankfurt School–certainly with no
connections to the liberal tradition. Thus, it is apt to note that
there is a *great consensus* among liberal intellectuals at home
and abroad of eliminating issues of class in the analysis of
Turkey's experience with the AKP. A more recent example of
this consensus is the US-based report on *The Rise of Political
Islam in Turkey* (RAND, 2008), in which it is argued that it is
not possible to note an Islamist ideology imposed on Turkish
society under the AKP's rule. Yet, the same report points at the
increase in the grassroots initiatives, which shape everyday
life according to Islamic principles (cf. Gülalp 2005).

Civil Society under the AKP's Rule:
Erdoğanisation

It is certain that grassroots organising is one factor that shapes
Turkish life, since the RP has been effective both in the coming
to power of the AKP, and in its staying in power (White, 2002).
The same grassroots organisations have also played decisive
roles in putting "neighbourhood pressure"[8] on the people to
conform to the Islamic way of life in everday life. However,
these grassroots organisations can also be thought of as representatives of the futility of the academic attempts to distinguish
civil society from the political society, by utilizing the former
as a protective shield against the presumed omnipotence of the
state in Turkey. This futility is revealed in the observation that
participation in civil societal processes involves simultaneous
articulation with political party organisations and integration
into networks of relationships on the basis of common values
(White, 2002; Yıldızoğlu, 2008).

Here, it should be recalled that civil society has been
an expression of a class society since the first phases of
capitalism. Thus, conflict within society can never be

distant to and/or immune to the contradictions that define
the establishment and/or the state. Yet, one of the most
striking aspects of such discussions in Turkey has been the
dominance of an understanding that presents civil society
as a distinct realm of reality from the political society. This
is certainly related to Turkey's experience with neoliberal
transformation, which involved putting an end to class-
based politics. As is the case with many developed and/
or underdeveloped capitalist countries, which at one time
underwent a hegemonic crisis, in pre-1980 Turkey, too,
the individualist discourse that defines market and/or civil
society as the realm of individual liberties had a critical
function for the bourgeoisie in transcending this hegemonic crisis—and it still does. In other words, putting an
end to class-based politics should be read as a strategy of
the class struggle that the bourgeoisie has adopted in the
neoliberal phase of capitalism.

This model is defined as "Erdoğanisation" (Turkey
and a new vision for Europe, 2007). It is considered the
liberal interpretation of political Islam (Smith, 2005; Öniş,
2009)—i.e., its domestication in terms of its compliance with the world capitalist system. It also connotes
the synthesis of Islamic traditions with the governance
models of the EU, which are primarily based upon Western
liberal and democratic values. This designation is in fact
in congruence with the recent rise in the popularity of
the liberal claim that liberal orders have the potential to
enmesh a pluralist fabric, which can enable the coexistence
of different value and belief systems (Gray, 1995). Actually, this perspective is a means for the rewriting of Turkish
political history—an endeavor nurtured by ever-increasing
international support. It is presented as "normal history"
and to the extent that this presentation is mainstreamed,
it is considered the "objective reference," and ultimately

functions as a means to dominate political thought. In this
frame, Turkey's specific conditions are repeatedly emphasised and issues of identity are historicised as the major
determinants of political parameters in Turkey. It would
be insufficient to describe this style of analysis, which
prioritises identity politics, merely in terms of theoretical
preferences. Here, what is at stake is a discursive construction that works through the repression of reality, both in
its disassembly and deficient representation. In brief, this
construction enables the presentation of the binary oppo-
sitions as the foundational axis of the political struggle
in the formation of the "hegemonic discourse" that now
determines the political horizon of the Turkish society.[9]
One of the clichés that complement this discourse has been
the identification of the AKP's rule with a *revolution* that
is defined on the basis of democracy, peace, and rule of law
(Freely, 2007; Barkey & Çongar, 2007).

In this process of putting an end to class-based politics, ironically, the term "class" is frequently employed in
academic interpretations that overtly or covertly reinforce
the AKP's power. This discursive support, extended by
neoliberal/Islamist/libertarian circles, while shadowing
the class nature of the state, is based on the prioritisation of
"middle classes" It is plural because it is presented as the
new actor of the societal struggle–namely between the old
middle class, which is anxious to preserve its vested interests, and a new middle class. This formulation accrues the
center-periphery metaphor with a new instrumentality. The
fiction of the struggle is now enriched by the identification
of the old middle class–urbanite/educated/laicist - with
the omnipotent state, reduced to a repressive apparatus. It
is further beyond a doubt that such constructions involve
serious illusions about societal struggles and processes of
change.

State-Society Relations under the AKP's Rule: From War of Positions to "Post-Secularism"

The formation of a liberal-Islamic historical bloc[10] was realised by societal Islamisation *via* the new forms of religion-based societal organisations on the one hand,[11] and the maintenance of wars of positions toward the transformation of the "center" on the other hand.[12] In this context, the assessment made on the eve of the 2009 local elections, by a think tank known for its affiliation with the AKP, is exemplary:

> The AK Parti [AKP] is an actor that moves from the periphery to the center and that attempts to transform the center covertly. The party's political journey through which it has reinforced its position by forming the cabinet in the aftermath of July 22 (2007) (general) elections, the election of Abdullah Gül as the President of the Republic, the holding of a referendum on October 21 for the popular election of the President of the Republic and speeding up of the process of the new constitution has not been sufficient to eliminate the antagonism against the AK Parti (Altun, 2009).

Though it is expressed in terms of center-periphery here, the significance of state transformation for the AKP is under-lined. The AKP governments, which appeared to be aiming at a place in the "center," in its first term (2002-2007) (Coşar & Özman, 2004), started to take steps to transform the "center," meaning the state, in the aftermath of 2007 general elections. In the context of the center/periphery problematique that constructs a state/society binary abstracted from social rela-tions, this goal means liberating Turkish political life from bureaucratic tutelage and/or the normalisation of politics. In this respect, the AKP's victory in three subsequent general elections is interpreted as the successful management of the discourse of struggle by the party. This discourse of struggle is formulated especially in relation to the party's disposition vis-à-vis the military's traditionalised political role, which is presented as an indicator of the party's capacity to assume the position of a political actor capable of broadening the political sphere in Turkey (Altun, 2009). This state of affairs renders the AKP oppositionary, yet also hegemonic.

Certainly, the issue of the redefinition of the state-religion interface in Turkey is the most frequently referenced theme in this discourse of struggle. In this respect, the AKP is again attributed with the mission of spearheading the process of transition from the modern laic state structure—which is considered to be essentially inappropriate for Islamic societies—to a "post-secular" establishment (Kalın, 2009). It is expected that in this process the initiatives, which shape everyday life in accordance with Islamic precepts, would also redefine the political society and have a transformative effect on the state on the basis of a "post-secular" understanding. Post-secular connotes the attribution of a subject position to the AKP and a desire to transcend the "center," different from the term post-Islamist, which implies the AKP's aim to have a place in the center. In a nutshell, all the rhetoric of transformation points at the fact that the transformations aimed at and/or realised by political Islam are experienced *without a break, even without necessitating a break*; actually, in Gramscian terms, these transformations are the results of a process of "passive revolution" or "transformismo" (Yıldızoğlu, 2008, p.407; Yıldırım, 2009, p.86).

On the other hand, the anti-statist, state-centric perspective has also been undergoing a critical transformation. The state tradition, which is assumed to represent continuity between the Ottoman Empire and the Turkish Republic, has so far been presented as a distinctive mark of Turkey's social formation, both with respect to the liberal state tradition in the West and the Islamic societies in the proximate regional configuration that surrounds the country (Kazancıgil, 1994). In parallel, Erdoğanisation, or in other words, the new dimension of "Turkey's specificity," is set up as a characteristic that both distinguishes it from Islamic societies and features it as a model for the "political modernization project" for the very same societies (RAND, 2008; Şerif, 2005). The maintenance of this specific model, which attests to the possibility of the coexistence of Islam and democracy, is significant also in terms of Western interests in the region. The success of this model, on the other hand, depends more on domestic factors— i.e., state transformation that would ensure the sustainability of the liberal-Islamist historical bloc.

In sum, in contemporary Turkey, the decisive ingredient of the anti-statist, state-centric epistemological approach, which has assumed hegemonic instrumentality, is the construction of the AKP as the leitmotive behind the country's democratisation process, chiefly through the denial of class reality. It is apt to label this state of affairs in terms of hegemonic opposition. On the one hand, one has to acknowledge the convincing power of this construction in the public. On the other hand, the AKP has so far proved to act oppositionally to what democratisation entails. One recent example is the violence that the AKP government resorted in the workers' protest against the final stage of the privatisation of TEKEL in April 2010. The mission of carrying the democratisation process further aside, the conditions that were attempted to be imposed on the workers and the ensuing constitutional amendment process attest to the fact that the AKP has in fact been a party imposing alternatives –despite wishful presumptions to the contrary. The hegemony is ironically manifested in the invisibility of this dimension of Turkey's experience with the

1: Politics and Discourse under the AKP's Rule: **37**
  The Marginalisation of Class-Based Politics,
  Erdoğanisation, and Post-Secularism

AKP. More briefly, critics of the AKP's non-democratic stance focus more on a discussion of the regime—Republic *versus* democracy—than any recognition of the workers' socio-economic rights, which were actually excluded from the legal reform process that Turkey has been going through for about a decade. Underlying this by-pass is certainly the abstraction of the state from class contradictions, and perceiving it only as an agent that dominates politics, but which still can be pushed out of the political sphere. Approaching the state in these terms connotes the denial or the insignification of the state's indispensable role in the maintenance of capital accumulation—i.e, the reproduction of capitalist relations of production. Thus, it is again functional in the strengthening of the neoliberal hegemonic position.

Concluding Remarks

In its current stage, Turkey's encounter with neoliberalism is managed by the AKP governments. The AKP governments' policy preferences and strategies, on the other hand, have so far sufficiently evinced the transformation in the state structure that would enable the coexistence of communitarian values with neoliberal market rationality. The transformation concerned has been characterised by authoritarianism toward (potential) structural opposition. In the contemporary world, at a time when most of the self-proclaimed socialist regimes no longer exist, the world capitalist system no longer needs to be exclusionary. On the contrary, the dominant discourse points at the necessity of *inclusion*. Inclusion is not limited to defining such countries as Russia and China as the constructive ingredients of the system. It is also related to the argument that liberal democratic values should not be persistently recognised as universal values (Kupchan & Mount, 2009). This state of affairs offers one aspect of the international context in which the AKP's rise to power took place. In parallel, the party's political identity, which has so far been diversified among "conservative democratic," "Islamic," and "neoliberal" titles, has matured along the inevitable dynamics of this international milieu. Actually, if "neo-Ottomanism" (see Demirtaş's contribution to this volume) is one of the *chic* representations of the AKP's foreign policy stance, then the party's almost organicised ties with the international financial institutions provides one with the *sine-qua-non* for its survival. This organic connection is in direct correlation with the party's domestic preferences. In this respect, the AKP has thus far been acting as the new agency in the neoliberal capitalist order. What distinguishes the AKP from its predecessors is the current phase of neoliberal capitalism, which necessitates a fragile interplay between liberal and conservative value sets–in the case of Turkey, the latter corresponds to a certain blend of Turkishness with Muslimhood (see Coşar's contribution to this volume).

REFERENCES

Ahmad, F. (1988). Islamic reassertion in Turkey. *Third World Quarterly*, *10* (2), 750-769.

Ahmad, F. (2008). *From Empire to Republic: Essays on the late Ottoman Empire and modern Turkey. Vol.2.* İstanbul: İstanbul Bilgi University Press.

Altun, F. (2009) Değişim ve statüko kıskacında AK Parti. *Analiz.* (6). Retrieved May 6, 2010 from www.setav.org.

Ayata, S. (1996). Patronage, party, and state: The politicization of Islam in Turkey. *Middle East Journal, 50* (1), 40-56.

Bağımsız Sosyal Bilimciler. (2008). *2008 kavşağında Türkiye.* İstanbul: Yordam Kitap. 2nd Ed.

Bağımsız Sosyal Bilimciler. (2007). *IMF gözetiminde on uzun yıl 1908-2008: Farklı hükümetler, tek siyaset.* İstanbul: Yordam Kitap.

Barkey, H. J. & Çongar, Y. (2007). Deciphering Turkey's elections, the making of a revolution. *World Policy Journal, 24* (3), 63-73.

Bayat, A. (2007). Islamism and empire: The incongruous nature of Islamist anti-imperialism. In Leo Panitch and Colin Leys (Eds.), *Socialist Register 2008: Global flashpoints, reactions to imperialism and neoliberalism* (38-55). London: The Merlin Press.

Buğra, A. (2001). Political Islam in Turkey in historical context. In N.Balkan & S.Savran (Eds.), *The Politics of Permanent Crisis: Class, Ideology and State in Turkey* (pp. 107-144). New York: Nova Science Publishers.

Buğra, A. (2004). Dini kimlik ve sınıf: Bir MÜSİAD – Hak-İş karşılaştırması. In N.Balkan & S.Savran (Eds.), *Sürekli kriz politikaları.* İstanbul: Metis.

Çakır, R. (2007). *Mahalle baskısı,* İstanbul: Doğan Kitap.

Coşar, S. & Özman, A. (2004). Centre-right politics in Turkey after the November 2002 general election: Neo-liberalism with a Muslim face. *Contemporary Politics, 10* (1), 58-74.

Erdoğan, M. (2005). Liberalizm ve İslam. In T. Bora & M. Gültekingil (Eds.), *Modern Türkiye'de siyasî düşünce, Vol. 7: Liberalizm* (pp. 444-451). İstanbul: İletişim.

Erdoğan, N. (December 2008/January 2009). Liberal kişilik nedir? Solla ne derdi vardır?. *Birikim* (236/237), 117-122.

Freely, M. (2007). No bloodless revolution. *The Guardian*, July 24.

Gramsci, A. (1971). Q. Hoare ve G. Nowell Smith (Eds..), *Selections from the prison notebooks* London: Lawrence & Wishart.

Gray, J. (1995). Isaiah Berlin. London: Fontana Press.

Gülalp, H. (2005). The Turkish route to democracy: Domestic reform via foreign policy. In S. Wells & L. Kühnhardt (Eds.), *The Crisis in Transatlantic Relations* (pp. 75-87). Bonn: Center for European Integration Studies, ZEI Discussion Paper, C143.

Gülalp, H. (2002). *Kimlikler siyaseti.* İstanbul: Metis.

Göle, N. (2009). *İç içe girişler: İslam ve Avrupa.* İstanbul: Metis.

Huntington, S.P. (1993). The Clash of Civilisations?. *Foreign Affairs,72* (3), 22-49.

İnsel, A. (2002, November-December). Olağanlaşan demokrasi ve modern muhafazakârlık. *Birikim* (163/164), 21-28.

İnsel, A. (2002). 12 Eylül'den çıkış kapısı. *Radikal-2*, November 10.

Kalın, İ. (2009, March 12). How to engage political Islam (II). *Today's Zaman.*

Kazancıgil, A. (1994). High stateness in a Muslim society: The case of Turkey. In M. Doğan & A. Kazancıgil (Eds.), *Comparing nations* (pp.213-238). Oxford: Wiley-Blackwell.

Kupchan, C. & Mount, A. (2009). The autonomy rule. *Democracy* (12). Retrieved May 10, 2010 from http://www.democracyjournal.org/

Mardin, Ş. (2005). Turkish Islamic exceptionalism yesterday and today: Continuity, rupture and reconstruction in operational codes. *Turkish Studies*, 6 (2), 145–165.

Mert, N. (2007). *Merkez sağın kısa tarihi.* İstanbul: Selis Kitaplar.

Öniş, Z. (2009). Conservative globalism at the crossroads: The Justice and Development Party and the thorny path to democratic consolidation in Turkey. *Mediterranean Politics, 14* (1), 21-40.

Özel, S. & Sarıkaya, A. (2005). Türkiye'de liberalizmin prangaları. In T. Bora & M. Gültekingil (Eds.), *Modern Türkiye'de siyasî düşünce, Vol. 7: Liberalizm* (pp. 452-472). İstanbul: İletişim.

RAND. (2008). *The rise of political Islam in Turkey.* Retrieved from http://www.rand.org

Smith, T.W. (2005). Between Allah and Atatürk: Liberal Islam in Turkey. *The International Journal of Human Rights, 9* (3), 307–325.

Şen, M. (2006). Türk-İslamcılığının neoliberalizmle kutsal ittifakı. In C.Gürkan, O. Türel, Ö. Taştan (Eds.), *Küreselleşmeye Güney'den tepkiler* (221-243). Ankara: Dipnot.

Tuğal, C. (2010). *Pasif devrim: İslami muhalefetin düzenle bütünleşmesi.* İstanbul: Koç Üniversitesi Yayınları.

Turkey and a new vision for Europe. (2007, December 12). Retrieved from http://www.opendemocracy.net/article/democracy_power/future_turkey/europe_new_vision

White, J.B. (2002). *Islamist mobilization in Turkey: A study in vernacular politics.* Seattle: University of Washington Press.

Yalman, G. (2004). Türkiye'de devlet ve burjuvazi: Alternatif bir okuma denemesi. In N.Balkan & S.Savran (Eds.), *Sürekli kriz politikaları* (pp.44-75). İstanbul: Metis.

Yavuz, H. (Ed.). (2006). *The emergence of a new Turkey: Democracy and the AK Parti.* Salt Lake City: The University of Utah Press.

Yavuz, H. (1999). Search for a new contract in Turkey: Fethullah Gülen, Virtue Party and the Kurds. *SAIS Review 19* (1), 114-143.

Yıldırım, D. (2009). AKP ve neoliberal popülizm. In İ.Uzgel & B.Duru (Eds.), *AKP kitabı: Bir dönüşümün bilançosu* (pp.66-107). Ankara: Phoenix.

Yıldızoğlu, E. (2008). *Emperyalizm ve siyasal İslam arasında Türkiye.* İstanbul: Siyah-Beyaz.

2

FRAGMENTS OF CHANGES IN THE LEGAL SYSTEM IN THE AKP YEARS: THE DEVELOPMENT AND REPRODUCTION OF A MARKET FRIENDLY LAW

Introduction

While the AKP governments in Turkey has tactfully appropriated the democratic discourse, embracing democratic society and electoral processes, they have been zealous to monopolise the entire neoliberal legal reform process. Underlying the AKP's commitment to the neoliberal reform agenda is the belief in a direct causal link and/or straight correlation between economic growth and the protection of private property rights together with enforceability of contracts. This ideology is maintained despite the outgrowing income inequalities and poverty in the society. Proposals for legal reforms in Turkey have been developed by commentators judging development (a synonym of capital accumulation in the AKP's jargon) on the basis of an increasing GDP. Law reform is considered to have the sole function of building the framework to the market. Even the *modest* goal of building the institutional framework to market seems to be largely uncompleted. Law enforcement, through a formal system, replaced informal methods of dispute resolution conducted by organised crime and/or by clientalistic-religious networks. However, possible redistributive and indirect economic goals of reforms have never made the agenda. Even though a detailed critique of the failures of the *old establishment* has been developing for at least the past eight years of the AKP's rule, almost the same economic programs as those in the past are being promoted under the auspices of the International Monetary Fund (IMF) and/or other international organisations. Under these conditions, the rule of law and democracy rhetoric does not represent a desire for genuine change.

In its attempt to depoliticise the economic decision making process and restrict the domain of democracy as a means of fostering the smooth implementation of market-based economic reforms, the AKP created and widely benefited from the conditions for the spread of generalised corruption and clientelistic networks. In this respect, the changes the Turkish legal system has witnessed under the rule of the AKP have many things in common with the recent changes observed in *developing* countries and with the policy recommendations of international organisations. Many of the so-called AKP reforms in Turkey's legal system, especially the ones in the realm of social policy, correspond to post-Washington consensus-based attempts aiming at the creation and protection of the institutions supporting market-based allocation of resources. Given the drastic consequences of income inequality, the AKP failed to mitigate the negative consequences of market mechanism by new institutions. Reforms designed to secure neoliberal capitalism in Turkey provoked new problems and crises. As a result, the use of law reform to impose neoliberal rationality undermined the legitimacy of democratic institutions in Turkey.

This chapter investigates remarkable fragments of changes in Turkey's legal system with reference to the *failure* of Turkish policy makers to make a vital distinction between the tools needed for market efficiency and the bases for fostering

2: Fragments of Changes in the Legal System in the AKP   **45**
   Years: The Development and Reproduction of a Market
   Friendly Law

democracy in Turkey. While the policies for fostering democracy required enhancement of public contribution to political decision making by way of bestowing democratic rights to trade unions and to other kinds of organisations (structural forms) designed to enhance collective representation of working people (or of unemployed), the government consciously opted to weaken the rights that are provided mainly by the civil law and the collective labour law. Collective rights were supported only when they were not in contradiction with entrepreneurial (therefore individual) rights and liberties. The right to religion is supported as a right to believe in Islam—but not as a right to believe other religions or to deny the religion at all. While the public share in the production of health and educational services declined enormously, the discussions held by big media groups on the right to education are limited with a focus on the right to wear Islamic vesture in the universities, as well as with an emphasis on social responsibility—social meaning, big capital—to ensure the increase of literacy among girls. In today's Turkey one is free to choose to invest/to consume anything s/he desires. On the other hand, no one is entitled to establish an association (or a union or a foundation etc.) that would opt for a systemic change for the purpose of enhancing the rights (especially the rights other than wages and/or other than narrow economic rights) of working class as a whole. Currently, what the labour front in Turkey needs is a new social form (a new structure) by way of which the entire class of labourers' (the workers, the retired, the unemployed) collective demands are organised into a transformative capacity (capable of effecting the ideological, economic and political aspects of life in Turkish society).

Taking this failure into account, the chapter evaluates currently dominant perceptions regarding the role of law in supporting neoliberal order. Currently dominant perceptions express themselves under the guise of proposals for new constitutional articles and parliamentary laws. The solutions (that is proposals for legal reforms of various kinds) *discovered* by Turkish policy makers to solve the *legal problem* included changing the structure of the court system, entrusting regulatory and law-making capacity to independent bodies not subject to democratic audience, and legitimizing market-based *solutions* in the realm of social policy and of labour law with regard to international prerequisites. The outcome of these *discoveries* was to separate economic decision making from politics by way of empowering markets against society. The *politics* of separating economic decision making from politics is completed by the promotion of a strictly controlled market model, without recourse to legitimation found in democratic political processes. Consequently, the dominant discourses on law, economics, and development failed to make a vital distinction between the tools needed for market efficiency and the bases for fostering democracy in Turkey.

The analysis conducted in this chapter starts with a presentation of the current situation of the Constitutional Court of Turkey (CCT). In the last fifteen years, the decisions of the CCT have been the subject of long and intense political controversy. Being the target of a successful court-packing plan proposed and realised by the AKP, CCT is now the object of a new proposal aiming to transform Turkey's two level judiciary into a three level judiciary by placing the Court (whose members were recently replaced by the new judges elected by AKP controlled institutions) at the top of the hierarchy. Given the fact that the CCT has become the arena of the struggle to change judicial structuring of Turkish state, the changes in its structure and functions are investigated primarily. Secondly, the constitutional situation of collective rights of labour is investigated. The chapter ends with a survey on the social policy reform.

The Constitutional Court

It was through the 1961 Constitution that the CCT was established. Both the 1961 Constitution and the currently operative 1982 Constitution opted for a dedicated system of judicial control and determination of the constitutionality of laws, rather than granting general courts the necessary powers to determine the constitutionality of parliamentary laws.[13] The 1961 Constitution was itself the product of the Constituent Assembly of 1960, which was established following the military intervention of that year. In this respect, the composition of a new constitution followed the prevailing international trend after the Second World War: Acknowledgement of abstract labour as being the constituent of society (constitutionalisation of labour). The Constituent Assembly accepted that the government and the *Türkiye Büyük Millet Meclisi* (Turkish Grand National Assembly, TBMM) must comply with the superior principles of law that were enunciated in the Constitution, overturning the principle that sovereignty lay with the TBMM. Despite the 1980 military coup and the introduction of a new constitution in 1982, the CCT remained, albeit in a reformed version. Similar to the 1961 Constitution, the 1982 Constitution was a product of a military takeover. Yet, contrary to the 1961 Constitution, that of 1982 was based on the general idea that civil and social rights were open to *misuse* and, for this reason, they could be detrimental to the –neoliberal- order and to the well-being of the society (Tanör, 1998). This general idea was in total conformity with the global process of the de-constitutionalisation of labour which refers to the discourses and practices focused on the denial of the collective rights of labour gained in the so-*called golden age* of post-War capitalism.[14] The erosion in the regulatory powers of protective labour law as a result of the de-constitutionalisation of labour (Hardt&Negri, 1994) first, in the discourses of production, and then, in the regulations on the industrial relations has a correlation with the new case law produced by the reformed version of the CCT under the guise of 1982 Constitution.

The CCT controls legislative actions in various ways but also acts, in part, as a supreme court. First of all, it controls the constitutionality of the parliamentary laws, that is, legislation created by the TBMM. There are two different sets of procedures for this aim: an annulment action[15] and a deferment action.[16] Moreover, the jurisdiction of the CCT encompasses the constitutionality of statutory decrees, the standing orders of the TBMM, and the formal control of the constitutionality of constitutional amendments.

As a general rule, the CCT is not allowed to consider the merits of a constitutional amendment on substantive grounds with one set of clear exceptions, as stipulated in Article 4 of the Constitution. It states that the provisions of Article 1 of the Constitution (establishing the form of the state as a Republic), of Article 2 (on the characteristics of the Republic including secularism, social state, *respect* to human rights, and loyalty to the nationalism of Atatürk), and of Article 3 (integrity of the state, official language, flag, national anthem, and capital city) shall not be amended, nor shall their amendment be proposed. However, if the CCT considers an amendment to be a threat to articles 1-3 then it may rule the amendment unconstitutional. In short, not even the CCT is permitted to raise questions which might lead to the alteration or re-interpretation of these three unchangeable elements of the constitution.

These are the constitutional powers of the CCT. However, the way in which the CCT has applied these powers is a subject of intense controversy. The sources of the conflict can be categorised under two headings: decisions on cultural issues and decisions having a direct effect on income distribution

2: Fragments of Changes in the Legal System in the AKP
Years: The Development and Reproduction of a Market
Friendly Law

49

between and within classes. With regard to cultural issues, Turkish politics are struck by two major sources of social conflict, both of which have been questioning the state's legitimacy and its ideology without attacking the currently existing neoliberal capitalism. These conflicts have been arising from the clash of the two identity claims with the Turkish state mechanism and ideology, namely Islam and the Kurdish question. The clash involves both the issue of cultural rights and enhancing democratisation, and the issue of collective rights and separatism. This situation has come to the fore and acquired new forms in the last twenty years, corresponding to changes in the world system after the demise of the Soviet Bloc. For this reason, each case including cultural rights, party closure, or questions on secularism is of importance for the fragmented Turkish public opinion.[17]

The majority of the decisions made by the CCT on cultural issues have discredited the Court's authority both in Turkish and international public opinion. In its famous May 1, 2007 decision, the CCT declared that the parliamentary election process of the new president must be halted on the grounds that the initiation of the election process had violated the constitutional procedures stated in the standing orders of the TBMM. The ruling AKP used this decision in two ways. Firstly, it reacted to the decision by calling for early general elections. Secondly, it took the initiative to amend the constitution with a referendum to endorse a new procedure for the election of the president by popular vote under the banner of "a new civilian and democratic constitution." Yet the AKP's proposal for this "new civilian and democratic constitution" had not included any change to the unquestionably non-democratic national threshold of 10 percent. In another controversial decision, the CCT rejected the joint proposal by the AKP and the *Milliyetçi Hareket Partisi* (Nationalist Action Party, MHP) for a constitutional amendment aiming to lift the ban on headscarves in higher education on the grounds that the amendment violated the immutable principle of secularism. Then in 2008 (the same year of the decision on headscarves), the CCT passed a judgement that the governing AKP had to be fined due to the fact that it had become the center for anti-secularist activities. Similarly, the CCT decided in 2009 to close the pro-Kurdish *Demokratik Toplum Partisi* (Democratic Society Party, DTP), stating that the party had become the center of activities targeting the unity of the state together with its territory and the nation.

Most recently, on July 7, 2010, the CCT declared that the bill introduced by the ruling AKP to reform the 26 articles of the existing constitution be voted in referendum on September 12, 2010. The two pillars of the reforms approved in referendum restructured the CCT and the *Hakimler ve Savcılar Yüksek Kurulu* (Supreme Board of Judges and Prosecutors, HSYK), which is responsible for managing the judiciary, including the nomination and promotion of judges and prosecutors.[18] Despite repeated calls from civil-society groups and opposition parties to allow for votes on each amendment separately, the AKP's insistence on submitting the entire package to a single "yes/no" vote indicated that the other proposed changes within the reform package were added for democratic window-dressing.[19] These approved amendments are expected to increase the number of seats on the constitutional court and the HSYK. The president and the TBMM hold the necessary powers in the appointment of the new judges to these institutions.

The CCT's decisions having a direct effect on income distribution between and within classes have not been as public as those decisions on cultural matters. Therefore, reactions against this second set of decisions can mainly be followed in the journals, booklets, and press declarations of capital groups. Newspapers and TV channels owned or

2: Fragments of Changes in the Legal System in the AKP   **51**
   Years: The Development and Reproduction of a Market
   Friendly Law

controlled by big capital groups generally criticise the CCT over their decisions on cultural matters. Until its 2006 decision on Social Security and General Health Insurance Law numbered 5510, the CCT referred to the immutable principle of social state in the majority of its decisions as having a direct effect on income distribution.[20] It is important to note that in the Decision No. 2006/112 dated October 15, 2006, the CCT made no reference to the principle of social state, a principle which had been referred to many times before in the case law of the Court dealing with the constitutional assessment of laws relating to social security. However, the slow (but dense) market-friendly track change in the decisions of the CCT did not stop the anger of the Turkish bourgeoisie, which was suspicious of the CCT that it tended to restore/ revitalise its former statist and social democratic stance.

Conversely, the CCT decision on the neoliberal pension reform bill (No. 4447), enacted in 1999, did refer to the principle of a social state. The bill was to be the very first stage of a larger reform to neoliberalise the system. Further, the main goal of the 1999 reform was to shorten the benefit collection period for the purpose of supporting the private security companies in search for new customers. For this purpose, the minimum entitlement age was elevated to 58 (for females)/60 (for males). In February 2001, the CCT ruled that the bill's scheme for gradual increases in the entitlement age during the transition period violated the principles of equality and social state and hence the constitutional rights of workers in certain age groups. As a result, the transition period was extended until 2020 in order to increase the entitlement age roughly by one year annually, seriously reducing the effectiveness of the initially planned age increase scheme.

Besides the principle of social state, the CCT has also used the European Convention on Human Rights (ECHR)[21] to protect collective rights of labour and other social rights in many cases. One of the earliest references to the ECHR can be found in a verdict of the CCT dated 1967, numbered 1967/29. In this instance, upon the urging of the Turkish Labour Party *(Türkiye İşçi Partisi)*, the Court ruled that certain articles of the Trade Unions Act No. 274 were unconstitutional and in contradiction with the right to freedom of peaceful assembly mentioned in Article 11 of EHRC.

The protection of social rights is not limited to the CCT. In an early reference to the ECHR in 1992, the first chamber of the Council of State, upon a question posed by the prime ministry, declared the compatibility of the approval of ILO Conventions No. 87 and 151 with the Turkish Constitution (Decision No. 147). The decision referred to Article 11 of the ECHR, and to the right of individuals to social and economic rights mentioned in the Charter of Paris for a new Europe.

The CCT has always been accused of impeding the process of privatisation. Until the mid-1990s, succeeding Turkish governments attempted to conduct privatisation by way of legal instruments (statutory decrees or decrees having the force of law), empowering the Council of Ministers (CofM) to manage discretionally the privatisation of State Economic Enterprises (SEEs). In the 1990s, the IMF designed the government's accelerated privatisation implementations to meet the objectives set by the IMF for privatisation in Turkey. For this purpose, various statutory decrees were passed in order to accelerate privatisation. In the Turkish system, statutory decrees require empowering laws defining the purpose, scope, principles, and operative period of the statutory decree. The empowering Law No. 3987 was challenged in the CCT in 1994.[22] In its ruling the CCT stated that the process of privatisation could not be conducted on the basis of statutory decrees and urged parliamentary laws to carry out privatisation.

The CCT delivered its verdict on the grounds that Law No. 3987 gave the CofM the authority to issue statutory

2: Fragments of Changes in the Legal System in the AKP
Years: The Development and Reproduction of a Market
Friendly Law

53

decrees with almost no limitations. In addition, the transfer of control over public services that have strategic value (such as telecommunications and electricity) to foreigners was considered to be unconstitutional by the CCT. Furthermore, the CCT stated that the privatisation of natural monopolies would create private monopolies. According to the CCT, when a monopoly was inescapable, it was necessary to show what sort of measures would be undertaken so as to allow the state to exercise oversight and control. Therefore, the CCT revealed a preference for less discretion and higher legal certainty at the executive and administrative levels in the process of privatisation. Their decision urged governments to issue "golden shares" in privatisations, in which the government loses majority control of a strategic enterprise. Such golden shares would give the government a say in and the authority to approve critical decisions related to public services that have strategic value. Another consequence of the decision was related to the necessary measures to hinder the abuse of market power. The decision required a regulatory framework for the privatisation of natural monopolies in order to restrain the abuse of market power.

On November 24, 1994, the Privatisation Law (No. 4046) was enacted under conditions of severe economic crisis. Public propaganda declared SEEs to be the cause of all ills in the Turkish economy, including unemployment and inflation. It was claimed that the privatisation of SEEs was to solve the majority of the economic troubles Turkey had.[23] The Law No. 4046 went through further amendments. Many of its articles were brought before the CCT. The CCT, in a decision annulling some articles of the law, required that the determination of the details of tender and valuation methods should not be entrusted to administrative agencies, but should be specified in the law. The CCT's concerns on privatisation were echoed in the law through the adoption of the Act No. 4232 in 1997.

The legal basis for a *feasible* privatisation policy that is more or less consistent with the constitutional interpretations of the CCT was established by the end of the 1990s. However, the actual processes of privatisation have repeatedly undergone high levels of controversy. The proponents of the CCT have argued that the legal positions of the SEEs that are privatised unlawfully should be re-examined. Succeeding governments and capital groups accused the CCT of protectionism without any solid reference to the actual content of the CCT case law.

Currently, the structure of the CCT is on debate. The government's constitutional proposal to change the membership structure of the CCT so as to enable the TBMM (that is the strongest party in the TBMM) and the president to insert *proper* members into the Court was voted on in the referendum (September 12, 2010) and accepted. The AKP government has argued that expanding the sources for membership to the Court would democratise it. However, the Electoral Law adopted a national quotient (threshold) of 10 percent. This means that any genuine attempt to democratise the Court by way of expanding the sources of membership requires the lowering of the 10 percent threshold, since the proposal states that the TBMM and the president shall appoint respectively two and three members of the CCT from among the candidates sent by various organisations of the state. However, the TBMM nominates the president that is to be elected by the public.[24]

Apart from the benevolent wish that each party leader has of seeing the 10 percent threshold abided by, there appears to be a tacit understanding in the TBMM not to lower the threshold under a certain level. In addition, the Law on Political Parties bestows enormous power to party leaders, disabling party members to act in accordance with their free-will. Currently, the role of party leaders in the selection of parliamentary candidates is decisive. It is no doubt that the

2: Fragments of Changes in the Legal System in the AKP   **55**
   Years: The Development and Reproduction of a Market
   Friendly Law

national threshold and non-democratic nature of the Law on
Political Parties are the real impediments for the establishment of a genuine parliamentary democracy in Turkey. In this
respect, current constitutional amendments can be considered
as means to neoliberalise the CCT under the auspices of the
Turkish bourgeoisie (represented by the AKP), rather than a
proposal for democracy –even- in the narrowest sense.

The Constitutional Situation of
Collective Rights of Labour

The challenging aspects of trade union rights in Turkey rest in
the constitutional formulation of collective rights of labour.[25]
In this subsection, it is argued that the main problem in the
realm of trade union rights rests in the relevant articles of the
Turkish Constitution. Therefore, contrary to the allegations
of the government as stated in the third draft of the national
program,[26] any serious attempt to reform the Law on Trade
Unions should start by way of changing the relevant constitutional articles. In addition, nothing has been done to bring
the country's legislation on workers' and trade union rights
into line with European Union (EU) and/or international standards. Most changes are in draft form only. This is in contrast
to the accommodating situation found in other legal regulations, where changes have been finalised in attempts to hasten
Turkey's possible accession to the EU.

Indeed, since the decision in 1999 on Turkey's candidate
status for EU membership, Turkey has adopted numerous
important constitutional and legal reforms for the alleged
purpose of strengthening democracy, the rule of law, and the
protection of human rights. As Yeşilyurt-Gündüz argues later
in this volume, these reforms were also in compliance with
the advices given by international organisations searching
for ways to protect markets in line with the principles called

as post-Washington consensus. Although there have been numerous constitutional changes and plentiful attempts to change the constitution, neither the governing AKP nor the opposition parties have attempted to challenge the essence of the notorious articles of the constitution on labour law, namely articles 51, 53, 54. Despite recent changes to the Constitution, including some minor amendments to these articles, the main body of the constitutional text on the collective rights of the labour front still holds the institutional design of the 1980 military takeover, which primarily targeted the working class and its allies. Today, the constitutional articles regulating the collective rights of workers have massive discrepancies when compared with the constitutional systems of Western European States (Özdemir, 2006).

Articles 51 through 54 of the 1982 Constitution pertain to collective rights of labour. The right to organise labour unions and the limitations thereof are described in Article 51 of the Constitution. First of all, the definition of "worker" is not included in the article. This is a source of subsequent violations of the right to organise. For instance, governments can interfere with the right to organise, without infringing upon the wording of the Constitution, by way of employing restrictive definitions of *worker* in the relevant parliamentary laws. Currently, what the labour front in Turkey needs is a capacious definition for organising, for instance, the retired and the unemployed, into labour unions. This is an ironic contradiction in the face of Article 90 of the Constitution, which states that Turkey is bound to let international agreements in the realm of human rights prevail over its own parliamentary laws.[27] The ratified UN Declaration, the 1966 twin agreements on human rights, and the European Convention on Human Rights state that everyone has the right to form trade unions to protect his or her collective and personal interests. Currently, and despite court rulings stating otherwise,[28] there

2: Fragments of Changes in the Legal System in the AKP
    Years: The Development and Reproduction of a Market
    Friendly Law

57

is no clear and satisfying reason why a retired worker and/or unemployed person should not have the right to establish and/ or be a member of a trade union.

Furthermore, the first paragraph of Article 51 states that the activities of labour unions should be limited solely to the economic and social interests of their members. This is extremely problematic in that political rights cannot be separated from workers' economic and social rights/interests. Similar to the above noted ironic contradiction, Article 3 of the International Labour Organization (ILO) Convention 87 on freedom of association, which was also ratified by Turkey, states that "workers' and employers' organisations shall have the right to draw up their constitutions and rules," and that "the public authorities shall refrain from any interference which would restrict this right or impede the lawful exercise thereof."[29] Last but not least, labour unions cannot be forced to represent solely their individual members who, under the current situation, are actively working under a labour contract. Labour unions represent, to a certain extent, the working class as a collective entity composed of retired, unemployed, and actively working people under various statutes.

The right to collective bargaining is regulated in Article 53. In the first paragraph of the Article it states that collective bargaining agreements regulate reciprocally in economic and social positions and conditions of work. The third paragraph acknowledges the rights of public servants and public employees to collective bargaining. However, the problem rests in the following paragraphs. Paragraph four clearly announces that in the event that a conflict arises during the negotiations, public officials and other public servants will not be entitled to strike. The only remedy for the holders of these positions is an arbitration tribunal established solely for dealing with conflicts between the government and public servants. Additionally, paragraph four affirms that the arbitration tribunal should be established by the government by way of a parliamentary law. Prior to the 2010 amendments, public servants and public employees had the right to conduct meetings with the relevant administrative body. In the case of disagreement, the only option that trade unions composed of public servants and public employees had was to compose a text which would be dependent upon the sentiments of the CofM, regardless of the nature of the disagreement. Therefore, the novelty of the 2010 amendment to Article 53 rests here. Public servants and public employees are now entitled to apply for an arbitration tribunal whose members shall be elected by the government and who has the power to issue absolute decrees. Finally, the last paragraph of Article 53 furnishes the government with vast discretion in determining the content and scope of the collective bargaining agreements. Furthermore, the paragraph states that the exceptions, beneficiaries, and procedures of the collective bargaining agreement shall be decided by law.

Constitutional Article 54 was meant to regulate the right to strike. First of all, the first paragraph of Article 54 clearly states that workers have no right to strike if the dispute in question does not arise from the collective bargaining process. This clearly means that if the employer decides to waive his obligations arising from the collective agreement, workers will not be entitled to strike on the basis of this violation. The Constitution clearly states that the conclusion of a collective bargaining agreement is distinct from its application. Put differently, Turkish workers can only call for a strike in the event that the dispute arises during the collective bargaining negotiations. Workers cannot go on strike in order to force the employer to keep his word, they cannot go on strike for political reasons, and they cannot go on strike for solidarity (they cannot support other workers by way of strikes), but they can go on strike if a dispute arises during the collective

2: Fragments of Changes in the Legal System in the AKP
    Years: The Development and Reproduction of a Market
    Friendly Law

59

bargaining process. This article clearly repudiates the right to strike rather than regulating the right to strike.

Currently, the law regulating strikes requires the trade union in question to prove it had the necessary majority to start a strike. In the case of an objection, the conflict has to be seen before a court. As a rule of thumb, it takes more than one year to settle such a case. In addition, it is relatively easy in the Turkish legal system to fire a worker. Furthermore, unregistered work, being the main instrument to weaken unionisation, is excessively common (above 50 percent). In sum, the employer has the necessary capacities to fire unionised workers and to subordinate working people in the workplace. Assume that a group of workers manage to start a strike under these conditions. They must be extremely careful. They cannot, according to the second paragraph of the article, use their right "...in a manner contrary to the principle of goodwill to the detriment of society, *or* in a manner damaging national wealth." If they are still determined to strike, the Constitution reminds workers on strike to determine whether or not their strike plans fall within the scope of the law regulating "the circumstances and places in which strikes and lockouts may be prohibited or postponed." If so, "...the dispute shall be settled by the *Yüksek Hakem Kurulu* (Supreme Arbitration Board, YHK) at the end of the period of postponement' and one should not overlook that "the decisions [of the YHK] shall be final and have the force of a collective bargaining agreement." Under these conditions, politically-motivated strikes and lockouts, solidarity strikes and lockouts, the occupation of work premises, labour go-slows, and other forms of obstruction become illegal.

This is particularly regrettable because in recent years, despite the very limited progress in EU negotiations, Turkey has achieved no significant progress in the field of collective labour rights. Moreover, case law has become more hostile to collective rights of labour than it was before the 2001 crisis. The AKP's 'flexible' Labour Law of 2003 (No. 4857) eroded the rights of labour in the realm of the technical division of labour. It is very clear that Turkish labour legislation is not in line with the already weak international standards. More than that, the implementation on the ground appears to continue to be extremely problematic (Eroğul, 2005; Sabuncu, 2007). Given the fact that unions are still being thwarted in their organising efforts, and/or by massive lay-offs of their members and dubious court cases and arrests of their leaders we cannot speak of the constitutional protection of trade union rights in Turkey. To reach to an acceptable level of protection, the rights to organise, to strike and to bargain collectively need to be brought –at least- in line with EU standards and ILO conventions. Therefore, the necessity of the elimination of main obstacles over the right to organise and over the right to free collective bargaining seems to be vital for even a modest positive change in industrial relations in Turkey. Only after the elimination of legal restrictions it is possible to expect the organised voice of the workers to have a say in the political processes. In other words, if the trade unions are organisations that are assumed to organise workers' collective demands into a transformative capacity their delimitation to the rationality of the capitalist system through legal restrictions and/or through forcing them into compromises with the ruling circles reveals their symbolic existence—i.e., as means for capitalist reproduction.

Social Security Reform

Since it came to power in 2002, the AKP has changed irreversibly the fabric of the Turkish social security system. The AKP has introduced constitutional, institutional, and legal changes in social security under the so-called social security reform. Three trends have shaped the social security reform

2: Fragments of Changes in the Legal System in the AKP
Years: The Development and Reproduction of a Market
Friendly Law

61

under the AKP's rule. The state withdrew from welfare provision, employers' flexibility over labour use was increased, and social security tools were refined to shape the role of markets in the production of welfare (Arın, 2002). This reform is not only in conformity with the premises of the neoliberal understanding of social restructuring, but also in conformity with religious conservatism.[30] As Coşar and Yeğenoğlu (2009) explicate in their account on the neoliberal ordering of the social space in terms of gender relations, religious conservatism has been functional in legitimizing the elimination of the collective claims with the identification of charity works with socials services as well as the definition of the family as the main institution of social policy. The AKP, further refreshed in its power after the 2007 general election, thus continued in its its social security reform. In this subsection, the main pillars of social security reform in Turkey are summarised.

By the end of the 1990s, the burden of the deficits created by the ill working social security system on the State Treasury had become a source of legitimisation for government strategies aiming to restore social policies in conformity with the recipes of the IMF (Koray, 2005). The IMF-oriented economic policies have played a significant role in the 'discoveries' of national economic policy makers in search of credits after the 1998 crisis. Given that financial or capital account liberalisation had already been achieved, the pro-market rhetoric became inadequate for the initiation of necessary regulations. Thus, the main axis of the IMF policies, especially after the February 2001 crisis, aimed to reach stabilisation by way of rebuilding market confidence.[31] According to this strategy, Turkey was to undertake the necessary reforms that were designed by the IMF and would be subjected to direct supervision by the same institution on a regular basis (Yeldan, 2006). If, after each regular control, the controllers announced Turkey as successful, then the markets would assess/perceive the country as reliable and the aim of rebuilding market confidence would be considered complete. The expected outcome of this *success* was the decrease of risk margins for international finance capital and a rise in consumption. In the 2004 Letter of Intent to the IMF, Turkey consented to reduce the pension deficit to 1 percent of the GNP in the long term.

The neoliberal pension reform of 1999 had been proposed in response to the significant losses suffered by the social insurance system. The Bill (No. 4447), enacted in 1999, was to be the very first stage of a larger reform to neoliberalise the system.[32] The second stage was to be launched in 2006, with the introduction of the parliamentary bills enacted for the purpose of a shift from a publicly-financed social security system to a capitalisation system. The legislation enabling this second stage was the result of the AKP's efforts[33] beginning in 2003.[34] The 1999 attempt was to be supported when the AKP initiated a neoliberal/conservative action plan for the improvement of informative and operative capacities of the social security system and for the unification of the existing regulations in 2003. This paved the way for 2006 legislations.

The social security reform considered the marketplace to be the main mode of coordination in the production of the services that are financed and provided by the social security system, such as pensions and health. However, the campaign launched for the legitimisation of the reform is based on the equalitarian aspects of social security measures that operate independently of employment status and on the expansion of the total coverage of the social security system. The market-based *egalitarianism* of the new reforms required different employment statutes to be equated under the conditions of the worst position. Under the emerging conditions of severe social conflicts arising out of urban poverty, the social security measures that operate independently of employment status and the expansion in the coverage of social security

2: Fragments of Changes in the Legal System in the AKP   **63**
    Years: The Development and Reproduction of a Market
    Friendly Law

instruments have had a certain level of charm for both the ruling power bloc and for the poor dealing with unregistered work and activities. Yet, the organised labour, including many trade unions and strong interest groups, opposed the so-called reform.[35] The years following 2008 witnessed the increasing discontent of the disappointed, poverty-stricken urban masses,[36] who were largely unable to pay contribution fees and social security premises demanded by the market-friendly health services.

Constructing a new retirement insurance program and establishing a general health insurance system were the two major ends of the reform in social policy. The *Sosyal Sigortalar ve Genel Sağlık Sigortası Yasası* (Social Security and General Health Insurance Law, SSGSS) numbered 5510,[37] was one of the major pillars of the social security reform set. The main body of the act was entered into force on October 1, 2008.[38] It urged significant changes in retirement age, in the contribution period, and in replacement ratios. In conformity with the neoliberal strategy of shortening benefit collection periods and enlarging the contribution period, the act elevated the minimum entitlement age for pensions by introducing a schema that would gradually raise the minimum entitlement age.[39] The Act also brought some new provisions for alleviating social inequalities deriving from different statutes among working people for retirement earnings. However, as mentioned above, the solution provided by the law maker was to weaken the civil servants' legal status and benefits rather than elevating the status and the benefits of workers and of the self employed.[40]

As for health insurance, currently, employed people have limited access to health services, even if they pay their compulsory contributions (obligatory premiums) in due time. The system brought about by the Act has entered into a social environment in which many workers refuse to contribute due to low earnings and the negative impact of registration on their employment capacities.[41] In addition, the Act requires beneficiaries to make an additional payment (contribution payment) besides their compulsory contributions (obligatory premiums) for the health services. In practice, there seems to be no upper limit for the contribution payments. This situation augments class inequalities. Hence, the social security reform introduces private insurance mechanisms and supports the supply of health services by the private sector. The AKP overtly states that the public share in the creation of health services has to decrease significantly. To put it differently, the government aims to widen the coverage of the social security system by way of leaving the production of health services and the finance of the social security system to the market in the long run. In this context, the mechanisms to support the privatisation of health services and insurance schemes form an integral part of the reform and relevant legislation. Accordingly, the "social" in "social security" loses its meaning, and the question of whether this is the beginning of social security's end emerges (Boratav, 2003).

As a result, the interests of the private sector, those who are invited to invest their capital in the health and pension system, come to the fore in the construction of social policies. The interests of capitalists include serious declines in the *production costs*, including raw materials (medicine), in labour costs (the rise in the employment of unskilled and semi-skilled personnel plus long working hours), savings in equipment, and shrinkages in the workplace. In parallel, the marketing activities require increases in the amount of contribution payments and payments by the state as soon as possible. The dominance of profit-seeking activities in the production of health services will end with huge transfers of value from the state to the private sector. In this respect, the state expenditure will increase yet the quality and amount of services

2: Fragments of Changes in the Legal System in the AKP
Years: The Development and Reproduction of a Market
Friendly Law

65

produced will decrease. The new system is designed to limit and ultimately abolish the role of the state in the production of health services. The same is true for the pension system.

Conclusion

Throughout the chapter, certain aspects of changes in the legal system of Turkey are investigated. Currently, dominant perceptions (as revealed in the reform proposals) indicate that the law is considered to be a means to support the neoliberal order. Separation of economic decision making from politics helps governments to empower markets against society. Further, law reforms in Turkey are made to conform to a neoliberal economic rationality, which is fixed to the goal of capital accumulation without regard to the real lives of real people suffering from economic, ideological, and political facets of social inequality and insecurity. When the law is presented as a technical device, law reform helps create an institutional environment that undermines the legitimacy of democratic institutions. What current reform suggestions are likely to achieve is the hardly *unintended* consequence of markets without democracy, if the term "democracy" refers to the social capacity to develop the means to challenge the fundamental economic basis of the whole political system.

REFERENCES

Arın, T. (2002). The poverty of social security: The welfare regime in Turkey. In N. Balkan and S. Savran (Eds.), *The Ravages of Neoliberalism: Economy, Society and Gender in Turkey* (pp. 73-91), New York: Nova.

Bahçe, S., Yücesan-Özdemir, G., Voyvoda, E., Özdemir, A.M.,Candan, M.A., Kurt, İ.H., (2011). *Emek politikaları: Ne oluyor, ne yapmalı?* Ankara: Belediye-İş.

Bahçe, S. and Köse, A. H. (2010). Krizin teğet geçtiği ülkeden krize bakış: Teorinin naifliği, gerçekliğin kabalığı. *Praksis, 1* (22), 9-40.

Boratav, K. (2003). *Türkiye iktisat tarihi 1908-2002.* Ankara: İmge.

Coşar, S. & Yeğenoğlu M. (2009). The neoliberal restructuring of Turkey's social security system. *Monthly Review, 60* (11), 34-47.

Eroğul, C. (2005). *Anatüzeye giriş.* Ankara : İmaj.

Hardt, M.& Negri, A. (1994). *Labour of Dionysus: A Critique of the State Form.* Minneapolis: Minnesota University Press.

Hyman, R. (2004). *An Emerging Agenda for Trade Unions.* Retrieved May 30, 2010 from International Labor Organization website: http://www.ilo.org/public/english/bureau/inst/research/network/hyman.html

Koray, M. (2005). *Sosyal politika.* Ankara: İmge.

Munck, R. (2002). *Globalisation and Labour: The New Great Transformation,* London: Zed Books.

Özdemir, A. M. (2006). Üretimin söylemlerindeki dönüşüm, kolektif hak kavramı ve emeğin hukuku. *Çalışma ve Toplum, 2* (9), 49-59.

Sabuncu, Y. (2007). *Anayasaya giriş.* Ankara: İmaj.

Tanör, B. (1998). *İki anayasa: 1961-1982.* İstanbul: Beta.

Yeldan, E. (2006). Neoliberal global remedies: From speculative-led growth to IMF-led crisis in Turkey. *Review of Radical Political Economics, 38* (2), 193-213.

3

THE AKP'S HOLD ON POWER: NEOLIBERALISM MEETS THE TURKISH-ISLAMIC SYNTHESIS

Simten Coşar

Introduction

The electoral victory of the AKP first in the November 2002 general elections, then in the July 2007, and then once again in the June 2011 general elections, has necessitated the reevaluation of the fragile connection between nationalism and Islam in Turkish politics. The initial criticism raised against the party from the laicist blocs centered around the AKP's status as a mainly pro-Islamist political party aiming at the institutionalisation of Islamic codes in political and social spheres.[42] This argument is founded on repetitive references to the outgrowth of the party from within the Islamist *Millî Görüş* (National Outlook Movement) in Turkey, which dates back to the early 1970s. Besides, especially relying on the first AKP government's commitment to Turkey's accession to the European Union (EU), the hawkish nationalist blocs criticised the party for assuming a non-nationalist and/or anti-nationalist political program. On the other hand, there is another perspective that approaches the party with a liberal concern, analysing the AKP governments in relation to the record of military involvement in politics as a traditionalised pattern, which has

marked Turkish political history. The same perspective has
considered the AKP's pronounced adherence to EU credentials
and especially, its preference to decrease the military's role
in politics and state affairs as evidence of the party's liberal-
democratic commitment. Likewise, from this perspective the
AKP governments' economic policies have also been acknowledged as signs of the party's Western-orientation.

In this respect, the debate among academic and political
circles on the AKP's political identity has mainly revolved
around the party's adherence to Islamist politics *versus* liberal
democracy. This was mainly due to the party's organic links
to the Islamist *Millî Görüş*, which has been the most significant representative of political Islam in Turkey since the
early 1970s. Considering that all the political parties of the
Millî Görüş,[43] except for the *Saadet Partisi* (Felicity Party,
SP) were closed down either by the Constitutional Court of
Turkey and/or in the aftermath of the military interventions
(1971, 1980, 1997), the AKP's conformity with the basics of
the republican constitution is symbolic. Yet, the AKP as the
ruling party has so far been keen on keeping a fragile discursive balance between its *reformist* policy preferences and the
foundational assets of the republican regime in Turkey (see
Soyarık-Şentürk's contribution to this volume). Here, the
term "reformist" connotes two dimensions: first is that the
AKP's reformism is related to its *Millî Görüş* past. It is no
secret that the party came into being out of a split from within
the *Fazilet Partisi* (Virtue Party, FP). Indeed, the founding
members of the party were among those who called for the
implementation of "democratic credentials both in the party
structure and in the ... (re-)definition of politics" (Coşar &
Özman 2004, p. 62; for a comprehensive comparative analysis
see Yıldız 2003, pp. 187-209). Second, the party's reformism
is related to a series of legal and constitutional amendments
that had already begun by the late 1990s, but which have been

accelerated since the its coming to power in 2002. While this aspect of reformism has been most pronounced in terms of the party's performance in the EU accession process, it is also noteworthy that the legal and constitutional amendments that have been realised so far are driven by the requisites of the neoliberal world economic system (see Özdemir's and Yeşilyurt-Gündüz's contributions in this volume).

More significant has been the fact that the AKP has proved to be a party still in the formation process in its second term in government. This is so despite that the AKP once more emerged as the major political party in the 2007 general election, increasing its votes—compared to the 2002 general election—and receiving the majority of the votes country-wide in 2009 local elections, as well as a significant increase in its votes in the 2011 general election. Likewise, the party had re-ensured the popular support of its administration by successfully managing the referendum for constitutional amendments, held on September 12, 2010. The date of the referendum was symbolic–recalling the September 12, 1980 military *coup d'état*–in underlining the party's claim to stand for civilian politics and democracy *vis-à-vis* the military and statist elite, as well as its promise for a brand new constitution. The AKP's increasing popularity for almost a decade can also be related to its fine-tuning of liberal rhetoric, instilling in it nationalist and religious sentiments. This state of affairs might be linked to the specific intercourse of religion and politics in the Turkish modernisation process throughout the Republican era (1923-). Likewise, the dynamics of the neoliberal age, which have formed the contours of Turkish politics and economics since the 1980s, shall be considered another decisive factor.

In this respect, studying the AKP requires one to search for the connections between seemingly mutually exclusive political identities, cultural policies, and economic preferences. Such distinctive political identities are manifested in the case of the *Millî Görüş* and the Turkish-Islamic synthesis, whereas divergent cultural policies can take the form of cultural conservatism and the discursive defense of women's rights (see Yeğenoğlu & Coşar's contribution to this volume), or in the case of a "liberal" approach to citizenship and periodic references to nationalist sentiments in identity politics (see Soyarık-Şentürk's contribution to this volume). Last, varying economic preferences are offered in the case of staunch adherence to neoliberal policies, as opposed to populist expenditures from the state budget (see Yücesan-Özdemir's contribution to this volume). Briefly, the party employs and synthesises various and at times contradictory socio-political discursive practices into the neoliberal economic and political structure.[44] For example, while the party at times seems to stand for a liberal understanding of citizenship (Yıldız, 2008; see also Soyarık-Şentürk's contribution to this volume and the new Law on Citizenship, Date: May 2009, No.: 5901), its policies in the national education sphere turn out to be distinctly nationalistic.[45] One example in this respect is the AKP governments' National Education projects (see, for example, 17th National Education Council Decisions, 2006. Retrieved June 13, 2006), which evince the coexisting aims of bringing up neoliberal individuals with an emphasis on morality tied fast to Islamic morality—and on nationalistic values. Similarly, while the party disclaims Islamism as a political ideology, its policies in the national education sphere privilege Muslimhood as an integral feature of Turkishness.

However, what differentiates the AKP from the previous agents of neoliberal times in Turkey is that the party has had the highest record of action in the pursuit of a neoliberal agenda in its three terms in office, while at the same time tactly synthesising its conservative nationalist policy preferences with liberal tunes. The (non-)social policy tendencies of the party attest to this preference. Additionally, the Islamic notion of charity fits well into the neoliberal agenda, in that neoliberalism (especially in its Hayekian version) acknowledges the desirability and, at times, necessity of (religious) charity to replace social rights of citizenship (Gamble, 1996, pp. 46ff.). Thus, for example, the AKP spokespersons could comfortably claim that they adopt a social justice perspective in the recently enacted *Sosyal Güvenlik ve Genel Sağlık Sigortası Yasası* (Law on Social Security and General Health Insurance) (No. 5510). Briefly, the new law draws a market, rationality-based understanding of security, essentially holding individuals personally responsible for their health and work security. Yet, the rhetorical reference to "social justice" is contradictory with the Hayekian notion that any assistance in the name of social justice is inacceptable (Gamble, 1996, p.47). The AKP, on the other hand, has called into action populistic policies—and not the social rights of citizens— and social/public charity networks in line with the neoliberal mind. Thus, the dual project of raising the individualist spirit in articulation with moralistic/religious embroidery frames the rights of citizens (Coşar & Yeğenoğlu 2009; see also Yücesan-Özdemir's contribution to this volume), actually eliminating the *social* from the *rights'* context.

This chapter is built on the contention that the reason behind the co-existence of the binary and at times contradictory assessments of the AKP is that the party has formed its discursive identity and policy set with recourse to the neoliberal political frame. In this respect, the chapter involves an analysis of the AKP's political identity within the scope of neoliberal politics in Turkey, and in terms of a certain degree of articulation between Turkish nationalism and Islam—the Turkish-Islamic synthesis. Important in this discussion is that the AKP's political identity stems not only from the

Millî Görüş, which marked the political formation of the party's founding members, but also from the Turkish-Islamic synthesis, which has been forged as the dominant socio-political imagination of the post-1980 period. It is thus argued that the AKP represents one version of the synthesis, which articulates well into the neoliberal frame (Coşar, 2011).

The chapter is composed of three parts. In the first part, I offer a brief account of the Turkish-Islamic synthesis as the socio-political frame that accompanied the rise and consolidation of neoliberalism in the Turkish context. In the second part, I analyse the AKP's discursive practices with reference to three issue areas: the foreign policy dimension, the religious dimension, and the ethnic dimension. In the third and concluding part, I position the AKP's version of the Turkish-Islamic synthesis within the neoliberal frame.

The Reign of the Turkish-Islamic Synthesis: 1980 *Coup D'état* and beyond

The AKP has been and still is a party in the making: it grew out of the *Millî Görüş* movement, yet, has shown no intention of continuing to define itself within the movement. On the contrary, and especially in the early years of the party, they frequently emphasised cutting ties with the *Millî Görüş*. Likewise, the party's willing accomodation of neoliberal policies, evinced not only in its acquiescence toward the IMF and World Bank-directed economic policies (see Zabcı's contribution to this volume), but also in its pro-EU stance (see Yeşilyurt-Gündüz's contribution to this volume), contradicts the "Western philosophy" reading that has dominated the *Millî Görüş*: "Western philosophy is based on domination and hence on power. As a result, it is colonialist and imperialist" (Bahri Zengin quoted in Atacan, 2005, p. 189). Approaching the "Western civilization" as a monolithic phenomenon that is characterised by the will to dominate the "East/Islam and others" (Ibid.), the *Millî Görüş* has proposed "a new civilization" shaped by Islamic moral and spiritual values (Atacan, 2005, p.190). Yet, the AKP's neoliberal diversion from the *Millî Görüş* does not mean that the party has eliminated its moralistic-nationalistic tendencies. On the other hand, the moralistic-nationalistic references in the party's discourse resonate well within the Turkish-Islamic synthesis.

The synthesis springs from a contradictory source, which becomes apparent when the political roots of the bulk of the AKP's members are considered. Above all, the AKP's *Western oriented* face might also seem to contradict with the Turkish-Islamic synthesis. Indeed, it is not possible to trace a direct reference to the synthesis in the discourse of the leading spokespersons and founding members of the party. Still, the argument in this chapter is based on the connections between the AKP as an agent and the Turkish-Islamic synthesis as the basic socio-political ingredient of the post-1980 neoliberal structure in Turkey. As elaborated below, this agency with this structure has been on the agenda since the early 1980s.

From 1960 to 1980, Turkish political history witnessed military interventions in civilian politics almost every decade (1960, 1971, 1980). The political structure that was laid down both by the 1982 Constitution and the military interim regime between 1980 and 1983, prepared the country for a *secure* transformation to a civilian regime, and was based on military concerns for instituting a narrowed down political space (Sunar & Sayari, 1986, pp. 165-186). In drafting the 1982 Constitution, the involved military and the civilian cadres resorted to the civil strife and political violence of the past decade in order to justify the narrowing down of the political sphere. Relatedly, the main point of reference for the military/civilian ruling cadres during and after the interim regime was the desirability of stability and consensus. Both during the three years of military rule and the ensuing civilian governments, there was constant emphasis on pre-empting the risk of falling into *extremist* tendencies–meaning the ideological formations of the previous decade—by prioritizing centre-politics and centrist political discourse (Coşar & Özman, 2007).

The introduction of a neoliberal frame took place almost simultaneously with the 1980 *coup d'état*. As early as January 1980, eight months before the *coup d'état*, there were calls for a stable political system by the technocratic economic policy makers. The January 24, 1980 stabilisation package serves as a case in point. Drafted under the leadership of Turgut Özal, who later would become the founding chairperson of the *Anavatan Partisi* (Motherland Party, ANAP) and prime minister in the 1983 general elections, the package marked the start of the integration of Turkey's economic system with the neoliberal world economic order. The package, like its successors, was anchored in the requisites of the stand-by agreement signed with the IMF (June 1980) and the World Bank's Structural Adjustment Loans. The rejection of everything that resonated with the past two decades also made sense in this respect. For, by the 1970s, the determined place for Turkish economy in the world economic order required its adoption of Import Substituted Industrialisation (ISI). The neoliberal economic structure, on the other hand, entailed policy-making that contrasted with the notion of the ISI (Yalman, 2002, pp. 38ff).

After three years of military rule, which silenced any possible opposition—especially from the Left—and prepared the stage for the implementation of neoliberal economic policies, a new socio-political space was emerging that would meet the neoliberal requisites (Yalman, 2002, pp. 38-46). The Turkish-Islamic synthesis was put on the agenda as a viable

model in this re-making. The initial carrier of the consolidation of the new socio-political structure in Turkey, after the
interim regime, was the ANAP, with Özal as its chairperson.
Aside from the military rulers *making peace* with Islam within
the frame of the synthesis, the ANAP was significant in the
direct implementation of cultural and political policies that
were devised in the same vein (Güvenç *et al.*, 1991). Besides
the structural dynamics of the period, which eased the manipulation of political Islam during the interim regime, the fact
that Özal had been in close contact with the circle that spear-
headed the creation of the Turkish-Islamic synthesis provided
a suitable environment in this respect (Poulton, 1997, pp.
181-187; Mert, 2001, p. 69).

The resulting adoption of the Turkish-Islamic synthesis both
by the military and the ensuing civilian governments marked
a significant turn in the (republican) encounter with Islam.
Since the foundation of the Republic in 1923, the dislocation of
religion—Islam—from the political sphere, and the institutionalisation of state control over Islam in the socio-cultural sphere,
have been the decisive features of the interface between the state
and religion. Briefly, in the early-republican era (1923-1945),
and thenceforth, the official state ideology in Turkey—i.e.,
Kemalism,[46] named after the founder and the first president of
the Turkish Republic, Mustafa Kemal Atatürk—has been built
on the denial of Islam as a reference for political identity. This
was mainly because the dominant republican conceptualisation
of modernisation was devised within the scope of *a* secular
imagination of the nation-state. However, while characterising
the construction of the secular state, this denial has never been
exclusively integrated either into the discursive practices of the
ruling elite nor into the construction of Turkish national identity.
On the contrary, Muslimhood as a leverage for social appeal has
always existed in the discourse of the ruling elite throughout
the Republican era.[47] In a nutshell, what was denied was not

the social force of religion, but the political space that had been accorded to religion in the Ottoman past. Likewise, any claim of authority over religion other than that of the secular state was strictly rejected (Tank, 2005). In this respect, the relation of the republican establishment to Islam has been imbued with an ambivalent nature. An example of this ambivalence can be observed in the dominant definition of Turkishness–a national identity that predates Muslimhood, yet involves Islam as an historical ingredient. Yet, at the policy level one can more easily refer to an occasional overlap between Turkishness and Muslim-hood as evinced in the population exchange between Greece and Turkey, based not only on "national," but also religious identity, and the legal definition of "minorities" in the country solely in relation to religious identity (Yıldız, 2001, pp.132-141). Likewise, the religious instruction in military schools in the early-republican era offers another example of this overlap (Kara, 2007).

What distinguished the post-1980 turn in the state-religion interface was the shift in the official ideology from Islam as a passive ingredient of Turkish national identity to a domi-nant ingredient in the shaping of nationalist discourse. The Turkish-Islamic synthesis was the best available means for such a shift since it provided the grounds for an *Islam-friendly* political identity that was reasonably distant from the shelter of political Islam, which started with the early 1970s under the *Millî Görüş* movement. Manufactured by a group of nationalist intellectuals organised under the name of the *Aydınlar Ocağı* (Intellectuals' Hearth) in 1970, the synthesis envisioned the indivisibility of Turkishness from Muslimhood: "Turkey is one of the countries with the richest cultural heritage. Ultimately then, the Turkish nation is the founder and representative of the syntheses of steppe and Islamic civilisations" (*Türk Kültür Planlama Teşkilâtı Raporu*, quoted in Copeaux, 2006, p.87).

In its formative years and onwards, the circle had organic

connections with the *Milliyetçi Hareket Partisi* (Nationalist Action Party, MHP). The MHP, an extreme nationalist
political party of the late 1960s and 1970s, resorted to Islam
as one of the major features in its definition of the Turkish
nation and nationalism. The *Aydınlar Ocağı* took on the intellectual task of formulating the theory of a synthesis between
Muslimhood and Turkishness. From there, the synthesis was
articulated into the military discourse after the 1980 *coup
d'état*, as well as into the civilian political discourse after
the interim regime (Poulton, 1997, pp.188-187). The conve-
nience of the synthesis for both the military of the time and the
civilian political actors was that it aided in the "construction
of consent" (Harvey, 2005) for the remaking of the socio-
political space along neoliberal requisites.

In fact, the 1980s can be considered a period of the consolidation of the discourse on consensus and synthesis in the
political space. Representing the first civilian governments of
the period, the two ANAP governments (1983-1987; 1987-
1989), under the lead of Özal, based their political credibility
on their novelty in terms of detachment from the political
ideologies of the previous decade. The second central factor
of the ANAP's claim to novelty was related to the party's
synthetic identity: the party formulated its political identity
on the argument for a synthesis among different ideological
stances (Coşar & Özman, 2004, p.59). In doing so, it welcomed
the nationalists, liberals, and religious conservatives into
is ranks (Ergüder, 1991, p.155). This self-definition was a
working formula for the structural dynamics of the period,
since the institutionalisation of the transformation from ISI
capitalism to neoliberal capitalism asked for a stable political
sphere built on the exclusion of ideological cleavages. That
is why as early as January 1980, Özal, then Undersecretary
to the Prime Ministry, asked for a stable political milieu for
the apt implementation of the IMF-led January 24 structural

adjustment package, the first package of Turkey's neoliberal phase. Actually, this demand for stability turned out to be a constant ingredient of centre-right political discourse in the following years, and also offered the grounds for the justification of authoritarian policies (Tünay, 1993, p.21).

Notwithstanding the claim to a break with the past decade, the leading members of the ANAP were from the nationalist and/or Islamist flanks of the 1970s. In this respect, the ANAP can be considered the first post-1980 civilian representative of the Turkish-Islamic synthesis. As Mert elaborates, there was almost a one-to-one correspondence of the nationalist sentimentality of the 1970s with the ANAP's nationalistic face. Likewise, the Turkish-Islamic synthesis was materialised in the discourse of the leading party members, starting with Özal:

> ...ours was a program that had already been in the making. The paper that I had presented to the Nationalists' Assembly, organised by the Intellectuals' Hearth, in 1979 was the basis of our party's program (quoted in Mert 2001, p.69, my translation).

The Turkish-Islamic synthesis was then not an alien formula to the political decision makers or the populace, since it had already been well entrenched in nationalist discourse as an alternative to the formula of the republican establishment (Copeaux, 2006, pp. 79-110). The military regime tactfully made the synthesis its own asset by the exclusion of its original claimant, the MHP, from politics for almost a decade (Copeaux, 2006, p. 90; Bora & Can, 1991, pp. 87-109), and subsequently handed over the social power of the synthesis to the ANAP governments and from there to various combinations of centre-right governments.

Therefore, the Turkish-Islamic synthesis was socially

well established by the end of the 1980s, when the power of the ANAP was in steady decline, and the ban on political activity of political organisations and actors of the previous decade was lifted. Decisive in this context was the educational sphere, which was re-designed in the early-1980s. First, the religious courses in primary and secondary schools were made compulsory. Here, what was meant by religion was Sunni Islam. Second, morality was exclusively defined in religious—i.e., Sunni Islamic—terms. Third, the already existing overemphasis on Turkish nationalism in almost all textbooks and at nearly every rank of the educational system— from the primary to high school level—was revamped with Islam/Muslimhood as a leading cultural ingredient of Turkishness (Kaplan, 2005, pp. 665-679; for the implications of this conservative-nationalistic reconstruction of the educational sphere for the gender plane see Yeğenoğlu & Coşar's contribution to this volume).

The AKP's Turn with the Turkish-Islamic Synthesis

As noted above, the AKP came out of the pro-Islamist *Millî Görüş* movement (which dates back to the early-1970s), and has displayed the portrait of a political party in the making, in a political space where socio-cultural terms had already been shaped with reference to the Turkish-Islamic synthesis. The party has dealt with this contradiction between its origins and the political frame, to which it has been adapting itself, in terms of two strategic objectives: 1. Constantly persuading the republican establishment that it does not have a *radical* Islamist vision, as is the case with the *Millî Görüş* movement and the representative parties of this movement, past and present, but that it is a party of the centre. 2. In so doing, it also has had to keep a tactful balance between its religion-based

electoral backing and its concern for survival in the face of
the risk of termination, which has almost been traditionalised
with the *Millî Görüş* parties.

The foreign policy sphere has offered the most available means for the pursuit of these strategic objectives. One
such instance concerns Turkey's accession to the EU. Especially in its first years in government, the AKP displayed
a persistent commitment to realise the legal amendments
in line with the Copenhagen Criteria, a task that had been
included among the priorities of the Turkish foreign policy
agenda under the coalition government of the *Demokratik Sol
Parti* (Democratic Left Party), the ANAP, and the MHP that
preceeded the AKP government. In terms of its commitment
to the EU accession process, the party can easily be labeled
liberal. Likewise, in its handling of the Cyprus problem, in
its emphasis on "peace and justice" with respect to the Pales-
tinian-Israeli conflict, and in its management of the 2004
US invasion of Iraq, the same political identification can
be used (Dağı, 2006; Robins, 2007). In those instances, the
AKP's foreign policy preferences are shaped by liberal references, and in this respect, they present a stark contrast to the
Millî Görüş discourse, noted above (Yıldız, 2009, pp. 55-56;
Atacan 2005).[48] However, as Yeşilyurt-Gündüz and Demirtaş
delineate in their contributions to this volume, considering
the AKP's foreign policy preferences simply in liberal terms
falls short of understanding the party's ideology. For, while
playing in liberal tunes abroad the AKP governments have
so far managed to translate their foreign policy practices into
domestic politics through an emphasis on Muslimhood, Islam,
and Turkishness that essentialises Turkish identity. Similarly,
the domestic-oriented discourse of the party's chairperson
in times of problematic foreign policy matters has been fed
by a religiously-imbued nationalism. Such shifts are mostly
observed in the case of EU accession process: "Let the nego-

tiations halt, we do not care. We act according to the win-win approach. ... We descend from a civilisation in which there is justice, and not oppression" (Erdoğan quoted in *Vatan*, June 17, 2006; my translation). In this respect, the liberal-democratic principles and consensual foreign policy are staged side by side, with an emphasis on "Turkey's Muslim identity" as grounds for the justification of the party's commitment to the EU accession process:

> We have been walking in this path for 50 years. We entered into a serious process. In the coming years, Turkey, with its Muslim identity, will become an EU country. ... Turkey, with its Muslim identity in the EU, will pursue the relations with Muslim countries on a firmer basis (Abdullah Gül, quoted in "AB şimdi daha yakın," 2003) (my translation).

It is certain that the AKP's terms in government have witnessed a significant change in the style and content of Turkish foreign policy. The party has so far managed to remain at a distance from the survival discourse of the post-1980 establishment, by resorting to the discourse of international cooperation and making Turkey a "regional power" and a "global actor" (Fırat, 2009; see also Demirtaş's contribution to this volume). Decisive in this shift have been the demands of the neoliberal world system, which does not necessarily mandate the demise of nationalisms, and/or hawkish political preferences–most recently exemplified in the US invasion of Iraq - but for their commercialisation. In this respect, as Demirtaş succintly elaborates, the neoliberal world system has hosted the appropriate milieu for the AKP's fine-tuning of the neoliberal requisites into a "neo-Ottomanist" discourse (see Demirtaş's contribution to this volume).[49]

Actually, the AKP's foreign policy experience has so far

proved to be a trial-error process. Lingering between the call for a radical change in the established foreign policy of republican Turkey—from a concern with state security to a concern for cooperation—and the appeal for continuity—in terms of prioritising peace *via* cooperation—by adding the "Ottomanist" dimension, this trial-error process is yet to consolidate. The same trial-error metaphor can also be used for the party's fusion of a zealous commitment to Turkey's EU membership on the one hand, and an interest for strengthening ties with Muslim majority countries on the other hand. Though not necessarily contradictory in themselves, these paths in foreign policy—opening *to Europe and opening to the Islamic world*—were at times used as binary preferences by the party itself.[50] The merger of the two is most recently manifested in the AKP government's uneasy handling of the Blue Marmara conflict with Israel. Actually, the Blue Marmara example evinced the tightrope on which the AKP governments have so far walked: fine-tuning the religion based conservative stance with a liberal discursive set.

The same can also be said for the party's domestic performance. It is hard to argue that the party has been pursuing a neo-Ottomanist route in its domestic policy record. Yet, the shifts that it displays in its discursive practices between a liberal approach to individual rights and liberties on the one hand, and an authoritarian stance in matters concerning the Muslim-Turkish identity politics on the other hand, hint at the resonance between foreign and domestic political spheres. It is no secret that the consolidation of the neoliberal structure in Turkey has helped the party in this instance. Unlike the *Millî Görüş* parties, the AKP was ready to engage itself with the neoliberal rules, which, in turn, brought the party a wider appeal than the religio-conservative electoral support would have provided. This is especially true in the big urbanite capital, known for its distance from religion-based politics. Apart from İstanbul, the "Anatolian tigers," which were nurtured through the interplay of the Turkish-Islamic synthesis with neoliberal policies of the post-1980 period, also proved to be a reliable electoral base for the party.[51]

Apart from paying its tributes to the Turkish-Islamic civilisation, the AKP has also tinkered in the language of individual rights and liberties, and suggested adjustments to the EU requirements as an asset for guaranteeing basic rights and liberties (see Yeşilyurt-Gündüz's contribution to this volume; Özbudun and Hale, 2010, p.97). However, the language of individual rights and liberties has stood short of reflection on such contentious policy spheres as the infamous article 301 of Turkish Penal Code,[52] The Law on Struggle Against Terror,[53] and Law on Foundations, especially in regard to the foundations of the non-Muslim minority (Kurban & Hatemi, 2009, pp. 34-35). More recently, the current AKP government's rather intolerant response to the incidents concerning student protests first against the *Yüksek Öğretim Kurumu* (Higher Education Council, YÖK), and then against the police violence they were subjected to due to their protests in December 2010, further reveals the boundaries of the AKP's liberal stance. In this respect, for the time being, it is possible to designate the AKP liberal abroad, but conservative and authoritarian at home.

Related to this frame is the issue of ethnicity and religion, which is a testing ground for understanding the AKP's version of nationalism. At this point, one shall note that both among political parties, which claim some version of Turkish nationalism, and some prominent scholars (Kalaycıoğlu, 2007; Vergin, 2007) of Turkish politics, the AKP has been regarded a non-nationalist political party. Decisive in this viewpoint is the party's relatively mild discourse on citizenship, as compared to the ethnicist understanding that ruled throughout the republican history (Yıldız, 2009; cf. Coşar, 2011), and the legal reforms that the AKP governments realised within the scope of Turkey's EU accession process. The most recent example in this respect is the new Law on Citizenship (May 2009). As noted above, the new law reveals a liberal understanding of citizenship (see Soyarık-Şentürk's contribution to the volume) that challenges the ethnicist one on the grounds of Turkishness.[54] Yet, as Soyarık-Şentürk elaborates, the international-domestic binary works here, too. In other words, the liberal leaning through legal reforms still awaits projection in practice.

On the other hand, when one looks at the channels through which the notion of citizenship is transferred to Turkish society, it is possible to come up with a different and contradictory picture. Specifically, the mentality that has been maintained in the national education system reveals a continuity with the previous ethnicist understanding of citizenship, and the Turkish-Islamic synthesis version of this understanding, whereby religion occupies not a passive, but a decisive place. As Poulton underlines, "this synthesis aimed at an authoritarian but not an Islamic state where religion was seen as the essence of culture and social control..." (Tapper cited in Poulton, 1997, p. 184). In parallel, the national education system after the 1980 *coup d'état* was modified so as to institutionalise the already running conviction that Islam remains the most fit religion for the Turks on historical grounds. Thus, in the National Culture Plan of the State Planning Organisation in 1983, it was assured that (Güvenç *et al.*, 1991, p. 50):

> The two fundamental pillars of our national culture are [our] "essential values" that descend from Central Asia and Islam. The best fit religion for the character and nature of the Turks is Islam. The Turks could not survive with other religions; those who tried lost their identities.

The AKP governments inherited these priorities in national education, and despite the reforms that have been realised in the realm of national education, the essential features of the Turkish-Islamic synthesis are maintained. The results of two comparative studies on the issue of human rights in textbooks in Turkey, conducted between 2002 and 2004, and 2007 and 2009, substantiate this continuity. Briefly, in both studies, it is revealed that in primary and secondary schools the students are exposed to an essentialist reading of Turkishness, in which Islam is portrayed as an indispensable ingredient (Bora, 2003, pp. 65-89; Bora, 2009, pp. 115-141; Gözaydın, 2009, pp. 167-193). Likewise, in primary and secondary school textbooks, rather than universal moral principles, the Turkish-Islamic credentials are offered as the bastions of the code of conduct (Tüzün, 2009).

Accompanying this discourse is the constant recourse to the vital necessity of an unquestioned loyalty/commitment to the nation and the state (Bora, 2003; 2009). This, one might argue, contradicts with the liberal appearance that the AKP has displayed, especially in relation to the EU accession process. The same contradiction and the endeavour on the part of the party to overcome it can be observed in the gathering of the 17th National Education Council, which convened on 13-17 November 2006, and the decisions agreed upon at the end of that convention. In this respect, while in the concluding decisions of the convention emphasis was put on educating individuals so as to fit into neoliberal times, in between the lines there was frequent recourse to the need to preserve nationalist values (Council Decisions, 2006, p. 10):

In the contemporary world, where a revolution in communication is underway, the world is becoming ever smaller and everything is interconnected, in the processes of globalisation and of membership

to the EU it is necessary that all shareholders of
education be *sensitive* to protecting the national
elements of Turkish national education system.
(emphasis added)(my translation)

Similarly, in the case of the Kurdish issue the party has
followed a double track policy. Among other things, the
Kurdish issue offers a significant ground for the criticisms
of political parties which claim the representative status of
nationalism, and also of the arguments made by some scholars
that the AKP is a non-nationalist political party. It is certain
that the party has displayed a shift in state policy from the
conventional hawkish approach to the Kurdish issue. In fact, it
has been under AKP governments that Kurdish was officially
recognised as a language in Turkey, within the scope of the
individual right to communicate in her/his native language. In
this respect, the opening of a channel (TRT 6),which broad-
casts exclusively in Kurdish is a momentous example. On the
other hand, the AKP's strategy for balancing these liberalising
measures with the nationalist-conservative portion of its electoral base and the hawkish sensitivies of the Turkish Armed
Forces has been contentious, to say the least. Essentially, the
AKP has denied dialogue with the pro-Kurdish *Demokratik
Toplum Partisi* (Democratic Society Party, DTP) (2005-2009)
and its successor, the *Barış ve Demokrasi Partisi* (Peace and
Democracy Party, BDP) (2008-), on the grounds that the party
is a direct extension of the PKK. This argument has been put
into practice in the rather authoritarian policies of the AKP
toward BDP members and followers.

Concluding Remarks

Throughout its life span, the AKP has been frequently
compelled to prove its adherence to the basic principles of
centrist politics. In so doing, it displayed fluctuations in
discourse and policy priorities. These fluctuations can be read
in terms of the two seemingly contradictory ingredients of
the post-1980 socio-political structure—the Turkish-Islamic
synthesis and neoliberalism—into which the party was born
and in which it has developed its political identity. These
ingredients seem mutually contradictory due to the fact that
each proposes radically opposite conceptualisations of the
individual and the state. However, as the post-1980 experience in Turkey has revealed, this contradiction in conceptual
terms can be resolved in practice.

The extension of neoliberal requisites throughout the
world, starting with the 1970s, has followed different political routes in different countries, depending on the countries'
mode of integration to the world capitalist system. This vari-
ance has also been reflected in the "construction of consent"
(Harvey, 2005). In the Anglo-American context, for instance,
the social consent, required for the pre-emption and/or taming
of the opposition, was achieved through the appeal to individual rights and liberties (Harvey, 2005). The same strategy
has been employed in the post-communist countries of
Eastern Europe, with due emphasis on the indispensability of
free market capitalism for democratisation (Klein, 2007, pp.
171-193). On the other hand, in most of the Latin American
context, military dictatorships turned out to be the preferred
route (Harvey, 2005; Klein, 2007). The Turkish context, then,
seems to have witnessed a combination of these two options;
a military regime dissolving the existing socio-political structure and alliances therein, and laying the grounds for a new
structuration. This transition period was followed by civilian

regimes, which called for neoliberal policies in the name of individual rights and liberties, while at the same time appealing to the society through conservative socio-cultural discourse. Thus, in Turkey, the construction of consent has worked on a dual axis: on the one hand, the discourse on individual rights and liberties was devised and put into practice with reference to *homo oeconomicus*, and on the other hand, through conservative socio-cultural measures, the aim has been to revitalise the person in/of the community. However, this duality was not a contradiction in terms, but rather fit well into the neoliberal aspiration to institute the alleged separation of the economic and the political spheres. This state of affairs has been most evident in the reproduction of the Turkish-Islamic synthesis in the national education system throughout the decades, independent of the changes in government administration.

The AKP is an important case in point, especially because what marks the party's terms in office is the consolidation of Turkey's neoliberal order. Thus, throughout the three AKP governments, the main constant variable has been the party's strict adherence to neoliberal policy preferences. Briefly, the AKP governments have been the staunchest followers of neoliberal economic programs—designed in accordance with the IMF packages and World Bank programs (see Zabcı's contribution to this volume)—when compared to the governments of the past three decades. Though the neoliberal structuring of Turkey's economy was launched by the turn of the 1980s and neoliberal discourse has since dominated politics, Turkish governments throughout the decades fell short of the expectations of international financial institutions in the fulfillment of neoliberal requisites. This was particularly so in terms of cutting public expenditure, dismissing populist practices during elections, and failing to institute neoliberal codes in matters related to social rights. In essence, it has been under the AKP governments that this

"lack of commitment" has been overcome by the enactment
of a series of transformative programs in the social sphere
(see Yücesan-Özdemir's contribution to this volume).

A parallel continuity might be observed in the national
education programs throughout the past three decades. What
marks the AKP in this respect is that the party has neither
been the founder nor claimer of the Turkish-Islamic synthesis,
which is by now well embedded in the socio-political structure.
Moreover, even among the party members one can observe a
distance to the Turkish-Islamic synthesis itself. However, it
is certain that the AKP has fed on the synthesis-dominated
social structure in its management of the social consent for
neoliberal policies, or perhaps better put, in its management of
the potential opposition to neoliberal policies. Consequently,
the AKP has adopted the Hayekian suggestion, to turn first
the society and then the state into charity networks within a
moralistic approach formed in Islamic terms, which the party
has initiated in its dislocation of the *social* from the *rights*
discourse (Coşar & Yeğenoğlu, 2009).[55]

All in all, the AKP is a perfect model to illustrate the
search of a pro-Islamist political party to hold onto power in
the neoliberal phase of capitalism. Rejecting both the *Millî
Görüş* tradition and the Turkish-Islamic synthesis in claiming
for itself a political identity at the centre space of the political
spectrum,[56] the party still feeds on Islam's place in Turkish
politics, which was re-defined in the post-1980 period. In
so doing, the party also engages in the language of Turkish
nationalism. As a party in the making, one can tentatively
argue that the AKP's terms in government have thus far
represented a delicate blending of a neoliberal structure with
a *banalised* version of the Turkish-Islamic synthesis.[57]

REFERENCES

AB şimdi daha yakın. (2003). *Türkiye Bülteni*. Retrieved May 10, 2006 from http://turkiyebulteni.net/02/12.htm

Akdoğan, Y. (2004). *Muhafazakâr demokrasi*

Bakırezer, G. & Demirer, Y. (2009). AK Parti'nin sosyal siyaseti. In İ. Uzgel & B. Duru (Eds.), *AKP kitabı: Bir dönüşümün bilançosu* (pp.153-178). Ankara: Phoenix.

Billig, M. (1995). *Banal Nationalism*. London: Sage.

Bora, T. (2009). Ders kitaplarında milliyetçilik: "Siz bu ülke için neler yapmayı düşünüyorsunuz?". In G. Tüzün (Ed.). *Ders kitaplarında insan hakları II: Tarama sonuçları* (pp.115-141). İstanbul: Tarih Vakfı. http://www.tarihvakfi.org.tr/dkih/download/tanil_bora.pdf

Bora, T. (2003). Ders kitaplarında milliyetçilik. In B. Çotuksöken, A. Erzan & O. Silier (Eds.). *Ders kitaplarında insan hakları: Tarama sonuçları* (pp. 65-89). İstanbul: Tarih Vakfı.

Bora, T. and Can, K. (1991). *Devlet, ocak, dergâh: 12 Eylül'den 1990'lara ülkücü hareket*. 2nd ed. İstanbul: İletişim.

Copeaux, E. (2006). *Tarih ders kitaplarında (1931-1993) Türk Tarih Tezinden Türk-İslam sentezine*. İstanbul: İletişim.

Coşar, S. (2011). Turkish nationalism and Sunni Islam in the construction of AKP, BBP, and MHP identities. In A. Kadıoğlu & E. F. Keyman (Eds.), *Symbiotic Antagonisms: Competing Nationalisms in Turkey*. Salt Lake City: Utah University Press.

Özman, A. & Coşar, S. (2007). Reconceptualizing center politics in post-1980 Turkey: Transformation or continuity? In. E. F. Keyman (Ed.), *Remaking Turkey: Globalization, Alternative Modernities, and Democracy* (pp.201-226). Lanham: Lexington Books.

Coşar, S. & Özman, A. (2004). Centre-right politics in Turkey after the November 2002 general elections: Neo-liberalism with a Muslim face. *Contemporary Politics, 10* (1), 57-74

Coşar, S. & Yeğenoğlu, M. (2009). The neoliberal restructuring of Turkey's social security system. *Monthly Review, 60* (11), 34-47.

Dağı, İ. D. (2006). The Justice and Development Party: Identity, politics, and human rights discourse in the search for security and legitimacy. In H. Yavuz (Ed.), *The Emergence of a New Turkey: Democracy and the AK Parti* (pp. 88-106). Salt Lake City: University of Utah Press.

Dik duracağız ama dikleşmeyeceğiz. (June 17, 2006). *Vatan*. Retrieved from http://w9.gazetevatan.com/haberdetay.asp?detay=0&tarih=17.0 6.2006&Newsid=80127&Categoryid=1

Ergüder, Ü. (1991). The Motherland Party, 1983–1989. In M. Heper &
J. M. Landau (Eds.), *Political Parties and Democracy in Turkey* (pp.
152-169). London & New York: I.B. Tauris.

Ermiş, M. (n.d.) Terörle Mücadele Kanunu son değişikliklerin
incelenmesi. Retrieved August 13, 2009 from http://www.
turkhukuksitesi.com/makale_363.htm

Fırat, M. (2009). AKP hükümetinin Kıbrıs politikası. In İ. Uzgel & B.
Duru (Eds.), *AKP kitabı: Bir dönüşümün bilançosu* (pp.439-460).
Ankara: Phoenix.

Gözaydın, İ. (2009). Türkiye'de "Din Kültürü ve Ahlâk Bilgisi ders
kitapları"na insan hakları merceğiyle bakış. In G. Tüzün (Ed.),
Ders kitaplarında insan hakları II: Tarama sonuçları (pp. 167-193).
İstanbul: Tarih Vakfı. http://www.tarihvakfi.org.tr/dkih/download/
tanil_bora.pdf

Gamble, A. (1996). *Hayek: The Iron Cage of Liberty.* Boulder: Westview
Press.

Güvenç, B., Şaylan, G., Tekeli, İ. & Turan, Ş. (1991). *Türk-İslam sentezi
dosyası.* İstanbul: Sarmal.

Harvey, D. (2005). *A Brief History of Neoliberalism.* Oxford: Ozford
University Press.

Kaplan, S. (2005). "Religious nationalism": A textbook case from Turkey.
Comparative Studies of South Asia, Africa and the Middle East, 25 (3),
665-696.

Kalaycıoğlu, E. (2007, July 24). AKP neden kazandı? *Neden?* NTV.

Kara, İ. (2007, October). Cumhuriyet devrinde "Askere din dersleri": İyi
asker iyi müslüman, iyi müslüman iyi asker olur. *Toplumsal Tarih*
(166), 48-53.

Klein, N. (2007). *The Shock Doctrine: The Rise of Disaster Capitalism.*
London: Penguin Books.

Kurban, D. & Hatemi, K. (2009). *Bir 'yabancı'laştırma hikâyesi: Türkiye'de
gayrimüslüm cemaatlerin vakıf ve taşınmaz mülkiyet sorunu.* İstanbul:
TESEV. Retrieved from http://www.tesev.org.tr/UD_OBJS/PDF/
DEMP/AH/TESEV-vakiflar-rapor.pdf

Mert, N. (2001). Türkiye'de merkez sağ siyaset: Merkez sağ politikaların
oluşumu. In Stefanos Yerasimos et.al (Eds.), *Türkiye'de sivil toplum ve
milliyetçilik* (pp. 45-83). İstanbul: İletişim.

Özbudun, E. & Hale, W. (2010). *Türkiye'de İslamcılık, demokrasi ve
liberalizm: AKP olayı.* İstanbul: Doğan Kitap.

Parla, T. (1995). *Kemalist tek parti ideolojisi ve CHP'nin altı oku.* İstanbul:
İletişim.

Poulton, H. (1997). *Top Hat, Grey Wolf and Crescent: Turkish Nationalism and the Turkish Republic*. London: C. Hurst & Company.

Robins, P. (2007). Turkish foreign policy since 2002: between a 'post-Islamist' government and a Kemalist state. *International Affairs, 83* (1), 289-304.

Sönmez, M. (2009). 2000'ler Türkiye'sinde AKP: Hâkim sınıflar ve iç çelişkileri. In İ. Uzgel & B. Duru (Eds.), *AKP kitabı: Bir dönüşümün bilançosu* (pp.179-191). Ankara: Phoenix.

Tank, P. (2005). Political Islam in Turkey: A state of controlled secularity. *Turkish Studies, 6* (1), 3-19.

Tarih Vakfı. (2009). *Ders kitaplarında insan hakları II: Tarama sonuçları*. İstanbul: Tarih Vakfı.

Tünay, M. (1993). The Turkish new right's attempt at hegemony. In A. Eralp, M. Tünay, & B. Yeşilada (Eds.), *The Political and Socioeconomic Transformation of Turkey* (pp.11-30). Westport, Connecticut, London: Praeger.

Vergin, N. (2007, July 24). AKP neden kazandı? *Neden?* NTV.

Yalman, G. (2002). The Turkish state and bourgeoisie in historical perspective: A relativist paradigm or a panoply of hegemonic strategies? In N. Balkan & S. Savran (Eds.), *The politics of permanent crisis: Class, ideology and state in Turkey* (pp. 21-54). New York: Nova.

Yıldız, A. (2009). Problematizing the intellectual and political vestiges: From 'welfare' to 'justice and development'. In Ü. Cizre (Ed.), *Secular and Islamic politics in Turkey: The making of Justice and Development Party* (pp. 41-61). London and New York: Routledge.

Yıldız, A. (2001). *"Ne mutlu Türküm diyebilene": Türk ulusal kimliğinin etno-seküler sınırları (1919-1938)*. İstanbul: İletişim.

17. Millî Eğitim Şurası kararları. (2006). Retrieved June 13, 2007 from http://ttkb.meb.gov.tr/duyurular/17sura/sura.htm.

4

ISLAMIST BOURGEOISIE AND DEMOCRACY UNDER THE AKP's RULE: DEMOCRATISATION OR MARKETISATION OF POLITICS?

Berna Yılmaz

Introduction

The AKP appeared on the Turkish political scene in August 2001 as a result of a split within the Turkish political Islamist movement, and quickly rose to power following the November 2002 general election with 34.3 percent voter support. It increased its electoral support in the following elections (2007, 2011). The rise of a pro-Islamist political party to power and the steady increase in its electoral support marked the beginning of a heated debate on the reasons behind the ideological moderation of the Turkish Islamist movement from which the AKP sprang.[58] On the one hand, skeptics have argued that one should approach AKP's self-styled conservative-democratic identity mainly in strategic terms. They have highlighted the decades-long persecution of Islamists by the secular establishment, reaching peak levels in the late 1990s, and suggested that, under those circumstances, Islamists had no other choice but to moderate to ensure their political survival (Dağı, 2006; Mecham, 2004; Nasr, 2005; Öniş, 2001; Somer, 2004). Others have pointed to the electoral incentives emanating from Turkey's *de facto* majoritarian electoral system, which in the last three decades have encouraged parties of all convictions to occupy the political center if they wanted to maximise votes and have access to executive power (Coşar & Özman, 2004; Mecham, 2004; Özbudun, 2006a, 2006b; Somer, 2004).[59] Finally, some students of Islamic politics have underlined the contributions of the "EU anchor" to the party's ideological moderation (Öniş, 2001, 2006; Robins, 2007; Somer, 2004; Tanıyıcı, 2003). They have argued that Islamists found in the EU a strong external ally to restrain the institutional power of the strictly secularist organs of the Turkish state, and of the military above all. Yet, this new alliance required that the Islamists to denounce their religious integralist goals and embrace, in their stead, liberal democratic ideals. Overall, these strategic arguments have implied that the sustainability of the AKP's commitment to liberal democratic principles is open to questioning due to the supposed preponderance of tactical motives over the decision to be moderate.

Those scholars with more faith in the party's democratic potential, on the other hand, narrate the political Islamists' ideological journey rather differently. This narration testifies to the existence of a genuine value transformation, underlain by a somewhat painful learning process on the part of Islamists (Çınar, 2006; Cizre-Sakallıoğlu & Çınar, 2003; Dağı, 2005; Heper & Toktaş, 2003; Yavuz, 2009). Here, it is important to note that this ideational argument does acknowledge the importance of strategic concerns behind the Turkish Islamists' decision to moderate, especially in reference to the *Fazilet Partisi* (Virtue Party, FP) period (1998-2001) (Cizre-Sakallıoğlu & Çınar, 2003). Yet, they also maintain that the Islamists took heed of their own past, which was characterised by state persecution, and consequently developed a critical stance towards authoritarian political practices. In addition, through their interaction with

4: Islamist Bourgeoisie and Democracy under the AKP's
Rule: Democratisation or Marketisation of Politics?

95

secular oppositional groups, the Islamists came to appreciate the
virtues of a fully democratic regime in which not only the pious
but also the other socially and politically-disadvantaged groups
would be able to find breathing space.

More importantly, however, this "political learning" argument[60] has been reinforced with a parallel argument emphasizing
the changing class composition and value orientations of the
Islamic constituency (Demiralp, 2009; Gümüşçü, 2010; İnsel,
2003; Öniş, 2006; Somer, 2004; Yavuz, 2006a, 2009). Especially
noteworthy is that the Islamic constituency witnessed the emergence of an authentic bourgeoisie among its own ranks, thanks
to the aggressive economic liberalisation policies initiated by
the center-right government of Turgut Özal after his election
in 1983. The Islamic bourgeoisie, reaping large commercial
benefits from the new export-oriented growth policies, quickly
proliferated in numbers and assumed an important place in the
Turkish economy. Initially allying themselves with the Islamist
Refah Partisi (Welfare Party, RP) on the political arena, they
gradually formed the socio-economic backbone of the party's
moderates, which eventually split and formed the AKP. On the
whole, this line of analysis suggests that the right place to look
for the social origins of the Islamists' moderation is the growing
ideological dominance of pro-democratic middle classes inside
the Islamist constituency, which contrasts strongly with the
RP years during which political Islam appeared to be largely a
lower-class phenomenon. In other words, if the AKP opts for
displaying not an Islamist but a pro-liberal democracy party
now, it is because it is no longer a party of marginalised masses
ever-ready for anti-systemic manipulation, but of, by definition, politically moderate and risk-averse middle classes.

This approach has certain merits within the general debate
on Islamic moderation in Turkey. First, it provides a more
powerful endogenous account of the party's ideological repo-
sitioning than the learning-focused arguments mentioned

earlier, thanks to its problematisation of constituency values. As a result, it handsomely avoids getting locked into sterile discussions as to whether the AKP is a "genuine" or "tactical" democratic party because, empirically speaking, there is no way that one can conclusively know what is actually in the minds of the AKP leaders, or as a matter of fact, in the minds of any party leader. Second, it constitutes an invaluable attempt to contextualise the ongoing transformation of political Islamist thought by embedding it in the rapid socio-economic changes of post-1980 *coup d'état* Turkey.

However, the same approach also suffers from a number of shortcomings in its characterisation of the conservative bourgeoisie as the wellspring of democratic energies. The first shortcoming is mainly of a theoretical nature in that most socio-economic accounts of Islamic moderation to date have drawn heavily on the mainstream assumption that the expansion of middle classes is a prerequisite for democratisation. As will be demonstrated shortly, several studies have powerfully challenged this view by demonstrating the historically contingent nature of middle classes' support for democratic institutions, if not its complete absence. Consequently, one of the principal aims of the chapter is to rectify this shortcoming by examining in detail the ideological trajectory of the Muslim bourgeoisie, as reflected in the public pronouncements and reports of *Müstakil Sanayici ve İşadamları Derneği* (Association of Independent Industrialists and Businessmen, MÜSİAD), starting from its foundation in 1991 until the present day by using the analytical tools provided by critical students of the bourgeoisie-democracy nexus mentioned earlier. This ideological trajectory has two distinct phases. The first phase refers roughly the first decade of MÜSİAD's activities during which the association openly supported Islamist forces on the political arena. The second phase, starting in the late 1990s, instead, is

4: Islamist Bourgeoisie and Democracy under the AKP's
Rule: Democratisation or Marketisation of Politics?

97

distinguished from the preceding one by the adoption of a clamorous pro-democratic stance by the Islamic bourgeoisie in place of religious integralism. By discussing the principal elements of the historical conjuncture that made the Islamic bourgeoisie undertake a serious revision of their political preferences in the late 1990s, the chapter aims at a historically-informed contribution to the broader debate on the role of social classes in the emergence and development of liberal democratic regimes. Another problematic feature of the existing socio-economic analyses of Islamic moderation concerns the insufficient attention paid to the impact of the Islamic bourgeoisie's cultural identity on the articulation of its democratic stance. In this respect, the last section of the chapter takes a closer look at the democratisation agenda of MÜSİAD in an attempt to identify the areas in which the Association's "religio-national" (*dinî-millî*) ideological mission, in the words of its founding president Erol Yarar, restricts its notion of democracy by nurturing anti-pluralist attitudes ("Erol Yarar", 2009).

Bourgeoisie and Democracy: Comparative Evidence

The scholarly interest in the relationship between economic and political development dates back to the classical modernisation theory (Huber, Rueschemeyer, & Stephens, 1993; Landman, 2003; Clark, Golder, & Golder, 2008). The modernisation theory argued that traditional societies would eventually become modern ones as a result of technological and economic progress, replicating the historical trajectory of the Western nations (Valenzuela & Valenzuela, 1978). It also suggested that their political structures would undergo a similar transformation from primitive to more complex forms. Then, from this perspective, democracy appears as a natural end-product of (capitalist) economic development (Przeworski & Limongi, 1997).[61]

This contention has inspired several cross-national quantitative studies exploring the linkages between levels of economic and political development (Przeworski & Limongi, 1997).[62] Most of these studies have found a significant, yet imperfect, correlation between the two processes (Huber *et al.*, 1993, Landman, 2003). Could this finding be safely accepted as an empirical validation of the modernisation theory's claim that capitalist development also triggers political progress towards democracy? Highlighting the problematic nature of inferring causation from correlation, critics have argued that the statistical association in question could at most be accepted as an empirical generalisation, and therefore should be "unpacked" to discover the underlying causal mechanisms through careful examination of deviant cases and historical sequences. Guided by these concerns, macro-historical comparative research has pointed to the bourgeoisie, the dominant class created by the advance of the capitalist mode of production, as the missing link between economic development and democracy.[63]

In this respect, one of the earliest and most influential works on the role of the bourgeoisie as the principal agent of democratisation belongs to Barrington Moore (1966). Moore (1966) has argued that the emergence of democracy depends on a unique constellation of historical factors. The presence of *a strong bourgeois* class is one such factor distinguishing the historical trajectory of democratic countries from those that took the fascist and communist routes to modernity. For a country to be able to take the democratic route to modernity, the bourgeoisie had to be strong so that it did not need to ally itself with the crown and/or the upper landed classes against the interests of subordinate classes such as peasants and workers.[64]

Yet, the findings of a new line of historical-comparative

research have challenged Moore's (1966) views on the
centrality of the bourgeoisie as a social class to the emergence of democratic regimes (Bellin, 2000; Harris, 1987;
Huber, Rueschemeyer & Stephens, 1997; Huber & Stephens,
1997; Rueschemeyer, Stephens, & Stephens, 1992; Therborn,
1977). These scholars do concur with Moore that democratisation could not be understood without taking into account
the changes brought about by economic development in the
class structures of modern societies. However, in contrast
to Moore (1966), they argue that it is not the emergence and
expansion of middle classes, but the organisational empowerment of subordinate classes through urbanisation, factory
production, and improvements in communication and transportation that constitutes the most significant of those changes
(Rueschmeyer *et al.*, 1992; Therborn, 1977).

Available historical evidence from both industrialised
and developing countries also challenges the view that the
bourgeoisie characteristically sides with democratic forces in
modernising societies. Huber & Stephens (1997), for instance,
have found that in pre-WWII Europe, large sections of the
bourgeoisie opposed the extension of democracy beyond parliamentary government. In fact, for the leading liberal thinkers
of the time, mass democracy was inherently incompatible
with capitalism due to the dangers it posed to elite interests
(Therborn, 1977). Therefore, what ensured the support of the
propertied classes for democracy after WWII, instead, was a
class compromise. As part of this compromise, labour organisations abandoned their revolutionary ideals, and the business
elites adapted themselves to a high-wage economy underwritten by state welfare policies (Huber & Stephens, 1997).

One encounters a similar picture in the developing world,
too. O'Donnell (1973), for instance, mentions at length the
support given by the Latin American bourgeoisie to the establishment of bureaucratic-authoritarian regimes in the region.

Likewise, Perthes (1994) notes that the fledgling bourgeoisies of the Arab Middle East have shown very little enthusiasm for the liberalisation of authoritarian state structures on which they came to depend for secure markets and high profit levels. Bellin (2000), too, observes in his study of democratisation in late-developing countries that the private sector on the whole has displayed a highly inconsistent attitude towards democratisation over the years ranging from full acquiescence in authoritarian state practices to vocal endorsement of democratic reforms.

On the whole, these studies have contributed to our understanding of the role of social classes and class relations in the birth and development of democratic regimes by showing the absence of a natural disposition on the part of the bourgeoisie towards democratic ideals. They have done this by unearthing the great variation in middle classes' support for democracy both in different countries and across different historical periods. This variation appears to result principally from diverging ways in which democratic reforms factor in the bourgeoisie's calculations of economic and political interests (Bellin, 2000; Huber & Stephens, 1997). These interests in return are never pre-given; they crystallise at the intersection of a number of factors that relate to the distribution of power in society.

Rueschmeyer *et al.* (1992), in this respect, highlight three clusters of power that analysts should take into account while examining the bourgeoisie's attitude towards democracy: class relations, state-society relations, and international power relations. The first cluster refers to the distribution of power among various social classes including both dominant and subordinate elements.[65] Democratic reforms can alter this distribution both against and in favor of the bourgeoisie, for instance, by including non-propertied classes into the decision-making structures or by diminishing the power of land owners. Particularly important in this respect is the relative structural and organisational strength of subordinate classes *vis-à-vis* the economically dominant elements in society. The stronger the lower class mobilisation, the greater the likelihood that the bourgeoisie will align itself with authoritarian political arrangements to thwart challenges to its economic dominance (Bellin, 2000; Huber & Stephens, 1997).

The second power cluster concerns mainly the relations between state structures and social classes. Democratic reforms can restructure state-society relations in ways that are favourable to business interests, for instance, by downsizing the state and redefining its functions especially when state-business relations are antagonistic. Inversely, if the business sector depends primarily, if not exclusively, on the state to expand its economic activities and maintain its profitability, the bourgeoisie is much less likely to support such reforms, as has been the case in many late-developing countries (Bellin, 2000; Harris, 1987).

Finally, transnational power relations, both in their economic and geopolitical dimensions, can affect the bourgeoisie's attitude towards democracy, both by influencing the first two factors and by discrediting, as well as incentivising, certain political options available to these actors. More concretely, both the end of the Cold War and the hegemonic status of free market-oriented policies in global economic relations appear to have rendered business elites generally less apprehensive about democratic governance (Huber *et al.*, 1997). Besides, diplomatic pressures, for the most part, concern themselves with ensuring the procedural minimums of democracy, such as competitive elections and the rule of law, at the expense of more substantial reforms directed towards improving the political representation of socially disadvantaged groups (Huber & Stephens, 1997).

The ensuing section of the chapter will use this threefold

theoretical framework to analyse the evolution of the Turkish conservative bourgeoisie's approach to democracy by focusing on MÜSİAD. MÜSİAD is the principle and, arguably, the most vocal association representing conservative businesses in Turkey.[66] The last section is dedicated to a detailed examination of the MÜSİAD's "democratisation agenda." Here, special attention will be paid to the role of a particular interpretation of Islam in the determination of the generally negative attitude of MÜSİAD towards the protection of workers' rights as well as cultural and minority rights.

The Historical Determinants of the Conservative Bourgeoisie's Support for Liberal Democracy

MÜSİAD was established by a small group of businessmen in May 1990. Its membership basis expanded quickly, from 12 in 1990 to 1153 in 1997,[67] parallel to the rise of the political Islamist movement in Turkey. The Association continued to grow in the 2000s, with the arrival of new members and the opening of new local branches both at home and abroad. According to its website, MÜSİAD currently has more than 3000 members representing approximately 15,000 enterprises. By 2006, the members' contribution to the gross national income reached almost 10 percent.[68] In contrast to the *Türkiye Sanayici ve İşadamları Derneği* (Turkish Industrialists' and Businessmen's Association, TÜSİAD), representing mainly the large-scale businesses, most MÜSİAD members are small and medium-sized enterprises despite the growing number of large business conglomerates among its members. MÜSİAD's geographical reach is also much wider than its secular counterpart, which is mostly concentrated in İstanbul and the adjacent Marmara region.

MÜSİAD excluded democracy promotion from its agenda for approximately the first decade of its existence. Until the publication of the "Constitutional Reform and Democratisation of Government" report in 2000, it hardly ever mentioned, let alone promoted, democracy and human rights. Moreover, it considered liberal democracy a Western imposition (Öniş,1997), and fiercely opposed Turkey's EU bid on the basis of the pressures exerted by the EU on Turkey "towards so-called more democratisation, some sort of political solution to the problem in the South eastern Anatolia, etc. [sic]" in addition to possible concessions regarding the Cyprus issue (MÜSİAD, 1995, p.50). Freedom of religion and expression constituted the only exception for the Association, which was in line with the rest of the Islamist opposition to the secularist regime at the time (Öniş, 1997).

Although the Association never partnered with the Islamist RP officially, its proximity to the RP circles was widely known.[69] During the short-lived coalition government of the RP and *Doğru Yol Partisi* (True Path Party, DYP) (1996-1997), member businesses became regular participants in Premier Necmettin Erbakan's visits to Islamic countries, reportedly making official commitments regarding Turkish foreign trade policy ("MÜSİAD Uzakdoğu'da", 1996). There were even rumors that the coalition government was giving preferential treatment to MÜSİAD members in the allocation of IMF loans (Buğra as cited in Cam, 2006).

The Turkish state and the conservative bourgeoisie

The "February 28 process" constitutes a turning point in the transformation of MÜSİAD's approach to democracy. It refers to a period of a widespread state crackdown, beginning with the National Security Council meeting of February 28, 1997, on perceived nodes of Islamist activity including Islamic businesses.[70] This crackdown, among others, involved the publication of the names of companies allegedly supporting political Islamist networks and the exclusion of such companies from public tenders. Likewise, two consecutive presidents of MÜSİAD were tried by State Security Courts on charges of religious reactionaryism.[71] MÜSİAD, too, at one point risked closure at the hands of these courts on similar charges. All in all, the February 28 process inflicted serious harm on both Islamic businesses and MÜSİAD (which lost 600 members in less than two years), in addition to leading to the collapse of the RP-DYP coalition government and subsequent closure of the RP ("İş dünyasında," 1999).

In reaction to the harsh anti-Islamist measures of the February 28 period, MÜSİAD adopted a strategy of disassociating itself from political Islam. To this end, it tried to underplay the importance of Islamic solidarity in the founding philosophy of MÜSİAD at every occasion by suggesting that money had no religion. Likewise, it initiated an internal investigation process on some of its members allegedly involved in the mismanagement of the financial contributions of religious Turkish workers abroad. Meanwhile, the February 28 measures gave rise to an internal feud inside the FP, the successor of the banned RP.[72] Against hardliner Erbakan loyalists the Association sided with the reformist wing led by Recep Tayyip Erdoğan and his close associates, Abdullah Gül and Bülent Arınç.[73] This reformist faction, unable to seize party leadership after a number of unsuccessful attempts, split and the AKP was formed, immediately denouncing the goal of the establishment of a Sharia-based state and adopting "conservative democracy" as its official ideology.[74]

It was precisely in this atmosphere that MÜSİAD (2000) took its first public stance on democratisation by publishing the report "Constitutional Reform and Democratisation of Government." A cursory look at these proposed reforms reveals that they are an amalgamation of neoliberal themes such as a smaller and less bureaucratic state, the rule of law,

4: Islamist Bourgeoisie and Democracy under the AKP's
Rule: Democratisation or Marketisation of Politics?

105

a stronger civil society, and the administrative decentralisation with other proposals such as the elimination of military influence over civilian politics and full guarantees for individual rights and freedoms. Through a more careful reading, however, one can easily identify the heavy impact of the conflict between the Turkish state and Islamist businesses (which reached its climax during the February 28 process), on the content and scope of MÜSİAD's proposals.

First, the secularist establishment appears to form the principle target of the majority of proposals calling for the reduction of the powers of the military, the presidency, high courts, and the *Yüksek Öğretim Kurumu* (Higher Education Council, YÖK). Second, the report is rather selective in terms of rights that should be better protected by the state. The highest priority is given to the prevention of the violations of the freedom of belief and the right to education in conformity with the Islamist oppositional discourse of the time. Third, the report covertly accuses the state of taking sides with the big capital, at the expense of smaller enterprises. More specifically, it holds the "monopolist and pro-closed economy capital" responsible for state's restrictions of the freedom of enterprise and the right to private property, suggesting that they do not want to share the country's economic resources with Anatolian entrepreneurs (MÜSİAD, 2000, p.27).[75]

The shifting balance of power between the secularist establishment and Islamist opposition forces in the post-1980 period is indispensible to understanding MÜSİAD's strenuous relationship with the Turkish state, as it is reflected in the democratisation report. Following the 1980 *coup d'état*, the military establishment softened the strictly secularist official ideology of the Turkish Republic in favor of a doctrine known as the "Turkish-Islamic synthesis." Aiming to counter the growing influence of left-wing activism in particular and to create political stability in general, this doctrine attempted to reshape Turkish national identity by identifying Muslim-hood and ethnic Turkishness as the main unifying elements of Turkish society (Öniş, 1997; See Coşar's contribution to this volume).[76] Its dissemination, however, paradoxically led to the emergence of a new type of radicalism, this time not based on the left-right cleavage but on religious mobilisation (Birtek & Toprak, 1993). Throughout the late 1980s and early 1990s, the political Islamist movement, represented by the RP, continued to expand its electoral base to such an extent that in the 1995 general election it obtained 21 percent of the votes cast and came to power as the dominant partner in a coalition government.

Conservative businesses largely represented the socially ascendant section of this growing constituency of political Islam. These businesses owed their existence both to the Turkish state's increased political tolerance towards Islamic networks and to its adoption of export-oriented growth strategies in the post-1980 era. Yet, they never came to consider the state as a natural ally to their cause of further capital accumulation. On the contrary, they regarded the Turkish state's economic policies—in terms of subsidies, access to credits and public contracts, and tax reductions—highly discriminatory and inimical to the growth of small and medium-sized enterprises constituting the bulk of conservative business activity.[77]

All in all, the Muslim bourgeoisie's desire to achieve political power, commensurate with its growing economic presence, appears to have considerably influenced its conversion to democracy promotion in the late 1990s. Until then, they had hoped to achieve a greater political presence by allying themselves with the RP, which would have positively discriminated against Muslim businesses once in power. However, following the February 28 process, the bourgeoisie forcibly came to the conclusion that "challenging the secular

4: Islamist Bourgeoisie and Democracy under the AKP's
Rule: Democratisation or Marketisation of Politics?

107

state in Turkey is a dead-end" (Özbudun, 2006a, p.547). And from this conclusion emerged democracy promotion as a new strategy to further their class interests in the political domain.

The post-1980 transformation of capital-labour relations

In the late 1990s, democracy promotion came to dominate the political agendas of all major business organisations in Turkey, including both MÜSİAD and the rival, TÜSİAD (Öniş & Türem, 2001).[78] This state of affairs points to the existence of historical factors that influenced the entire Turkish bourgeoisie, Islamic or not alike, in this period.[79] The first factor is the decrease in the threat perception of the upper classes due to the debilitation of working class organisations following the 1980 military intervention. The second factor, which will be examined in the subsequent paragraphs, concerns the globalisation of the Turkish business elite and their growing exposure to democratising influences, emanating both from international organisations and from Western industrialised countries.

In the case of Turkey, one can safely argue that the propertied classes had very little reason to fear subordinate class empowerment through democratisation in the late 1990s, as the second decade of harsh economic restructuring drew to a close. First, the military junta (1980-1983) inserted several labour-repressive measures into the 1982 Constitution to suppress left-wing activism that had flourished in the past two decades. It introduced restrictions on political freedoms such as freedoms of press, expression, and association, striking severe blows to civic associational life in general and trade union activism in particular. In addition to the selective persecution of many left-wing activists, the junta shut down the most radical of all Turkish trade unions, the *Devrimci İşçi Sendikaları Konfederasyonu* (Confederation of Revolutionary Trade Unions, DİSK), which could resume its operations only in 1992, after a fierce legal and political battle (Buğra, 2003). All of these developments led to an almost 50 percent decrease in union density between 1978 and 2004 (Cam, 2006). Concomitantly, the leftist movement turned into a marginal force in Turkish politics, and never recovered its pre-1980 electoral popularity, particularly after the debacle of real socialism in the late 1980s.

The political debilitation of the subordinate classes has been accompanied by their structural disempowerment due to extensive neoliberal restructuring reforms, which were implemented following the military *coup d'état*. These reforms aimed at dissolving the import-substitution based and state-directed developmental model of the 1970s through privatisation, deregulation, and trade liberalisation in favour of export-based and free market-oriented growth strategies. In fact, the political and economic objectives of the military intervention were quite difficult to disentangle (Cam, 2006). The emphasis placed by the junta on the prevention of political polarisation and the reinstallation of stability coincided perfectly with the need to contain oppositional forces likely to arise due to severe social dislocations, to be created by neoliberal policies (Coşar & Yeğenoğlu, 2009; Öniş, 1997; See Yalman's contribution to this volume).

The structural adjustment of the Turkish economy led to the shrinking of the public sector and the revision of the social security system and labour laws according to the exigencies of an export-oriented free market economy. Moreover, the "ongoing processes of transfer of the economic surplus from the wage-labour in particular, and the industrial/real sectors in general, towards the financial sectors" had contributed greatly to the economic marginalisation of lower classes and exacerbation of social inequalities (Balkan & Yeldan, 2001, p.5). In the first phase of the structural adjustment (1981-1988), real wages gradually declined due to the *de facto* exclusion of organised labour from industrial bargaining processes. Then came a brief period in which real wages were

4: Islamist Bourgeoisie and Democracy under the AKP's
Rule: Democratisation or Marketisation of Politics?

109

recovered, underwritten by populist economic policies that only
lasted until the 1994 economic crisis (Balkan & Yeldan, 2001;
Boratav, Yeldan, & Köse, 2000). Increasing unemployment levels
accompanied this negative trend in real wages. The proportion of
the total labour force as a fraction of the working age population
decreased from two-thirds to less than one half from 1978 to 2004
(Cam, 2006). Moreover, informal and precarious employment
forms became so widespread that in 1994, the Turkish informal
economy was employing more people than the formal one and, by
1996, two thirds of all private sector employees worked without
being covered by any kind of public social security scheme
(Boratav *et al.*, 2000). [80] All in all, after two decades of political
repression and structural adjustment, the Turkish bourgeoisie did
not have much to fear from the democratic empowerment of lower
classes, and hence could wholeheartedly endorse democratisation
reforms.

The impact of neoliberal globalisation on the political preferences of Islamic businesses

Islamic businesses today represent one of the most integrated sections of the Turkish economy into global chains of
production, distribution, and consumption. Their economic
fortunes have been closely related to domestic policy changes
and commercial opportunities brought about by neoliberal
globalisation (Öniş, 1997). Consequently, these conservatively-
minded entrepreneurs have a vested interest in the continuation
and deepening of the integration of Turkish economy into the
global economy, which constitutes nothing less than their *raison
d'étre*. Successful economic integration, in turn, is conditional
upon the acceptance of democratic norms and values presently
prevailing in the global community that certainly do not include
an authoritarian Islamic regime into its list of legitimate forms
of government. As succinctly stated by Öniş (2005, p.76),

> [f]or the political and business elites in emerging
> democracies, the costs involved in failure to
> conform to global norms are considerable. Failure to
> conform means isolation, insecurity and inability to
> capitalize on economic benefits such as large-scale
> investment on the part of transnational capital and
> membership of supra-national organisations such
> as the European Union (p.176).

Regarding state-society relations, neoliberal forces have
helped to discredit authoritarian state practices, which had
been tolerated previously within the framework of Cold War
politics. Authoritarian regimes are now considered by the core
countries of the global economic liabilities rather than assets
due to their unstable and unpredictable nature (Drake, 1998).
On the cultural plane, they have lent increased legitimacy
to identity-based politics, including those based on religion,
by turning recognition of difference and the development of
civil society into key parameters of democratic performance
(Öniş, 1997). Consequently, they have played a key role in
the transformation of the official state secularism towards a
more Islam-friendly and less authoritarian direction, which is
a major historical factor in the rise of the Muslim bourgeoisie.

Narrow Boundaries of the Islamic Bourgeoisie's Democratic Sensibilities

A closer inspection of the MÜSİAD's democratisation agenda
reveals that the Association, to date, has largely displayed a
minimalist approach to democracy concentrated mostly on
meeting the formal institutional requirements of democracy as
opposed to a substantial one that regards citizen participation
and social equality as essential features of a democratic order.
To put it more precisely, the Association has adopted a very

4: Islamist Bourgeoisie and Democracy under the AKP's
Rule: Democratisation or Marketisation of Politics?

111

vocal stance on the necessity to remove military influence over civilian politics, to ensure the rule of law, to improve government accountability and transparency, and to better protect civil and political rights with special emphasis on economic freedoms and the freedoms of thought and belief as they are the ones "most worthy of protection" (MÜSİAD, 2008, p.12).

In contrast to its assertiveness regarding a rather self-serving set of democratic reforms, the Association has largely remained silent on the democratic inadequacy of the Turkish social, economic, and minority rights regime except for occasional references to the desirability of increasing popular participation in political processes (MÜSİAD, 2000, 2008).

In the case of social and economic rights, MÜSİAD preferred to ignore the issue altogether in its first major intervention in the democratisation debate, *Constitutional Reform and Democratisation of Government* report published in 2000. Its 2008 report, instead, first highlights the material costs associated with the implementation of socio-economic provisions of the constitution arguing that the state can use its discretion when it comes to these rights; then, proposes a small number of cosmetic changes in their wording and classification (MÜSİAD, 2008, p.14). It should also be noted that, unlike other basic social needs, the right to education is frequently mentioned in these reports, yet not within the framework of the state's social obligations towards its citizens but as a matter of removing the existing legal restrictions on religious education, and allowing veiled students to enter higher education institutions. Labour rights, too, are conspicuously missing from the Association's democratisation agenda, which has generally displayed an anti-labour attitude in major policy debates regarding social security and labour market flexibility arrangements.[81]

MÜSİAD's approach to minority rights, on the other hand, has been infused with a high dose of Sunni-Turkish nation-

alism reflecting in part the continuing grip of the *Millî Görüş*
(National Outlook) tradition on the political imagination of
the Association. In this respect, even though the Association, in the last decade, has become part of the broad-based
social coalition supporting Turkey's EU membership bid after
parting ways with the Islamist movement, it has continued to
criticise the Union, first and foremost, for overemphasising
the problems of religious and ethnic minorities including the
Kurds, Alevis, and non-Muslims at the expense of the Muslim
majority on the grounds that reforms directed at improving
their status might damage Turkey's national interests and
unity ("AB elbisesi", 2005).[82] Even in the case of freedom of
conscience and belief, a democratic right vocally endorsed
by the Association since its inception, MÜSAID's position
has been characterised by severe inconsistencies. Crucial, in
this respect, is the fact that the Association objects both to the
abolition of compulsory religious classes and to the dissolution of the *Diyanet İşleri Başkanlığı* (Presidency of Religious
Affairs) even though these have been the main institutional
bearers of the Republican establishment's desire to keep
the religious realm under its strict control (MÜSİAD, 2000,
2008). Arguably, this objection results from another ideological function performed by these institutions, the reproduction
of the cultural hegemony of a predominantly Sunni interpretation of Islam, that seems to belittle their anti-pluralist thrust
in the eyes of the Islamic bourgeoisie.

As noted previously, democratisation has become the
centerpiece of the political discourses of not only conservative small and medium enterprises represented by
MÜSİAD, but also secular big businesses represented by
TÜSİAD in the late 1990s. Nevertheless, TÜSİAD differs
significantly from MÜSİAD in terms of the scope and depth
of the democratisation reforms it calls for. The differences
are particularly striking in the fields of social and cultural

4: Islamist Bourgeoisie and Democracy under the AKP's
Rule: Democratisation or Marketisation of Politics?

113

rights in that TÜSİAD has been a firm defender of granting
Kurds and other ethnic and religious minorities cultural
rights in addition to adopting a generally favourable
approach towards the participation of labour in industrial
relations despite its overall commitment to a stability-
oriented, technocratic vision of democracy, informed by
neoliberal premises (Buğra, 1998; Öniş, 2005).

Both TÜSİAD and MÜSİAD are voluntary associations
established by the business sector to further their economic
and political interests in the civil societal realm. Yet, in addition to interest representation in a strict sense, the activities of
these associations have always had the broader aim of influencing the direction of social change at the macro level on the
basis of two different cultural models. More precisely,

> against the economic, political, and social charac-
> teristics of the European model that can be said to
> define TÜSİAD's general outlook, MÜSİAD largely
> draws on the East Asian model in a rival strategy in
> which a certain interpretation of Islam is used as a
> resource to bind the businessmen whom it represents
> into a coherent community and to represent their
> economic interests as an integral component of an
> ideological mission (Buğra, 1998, p.522).

Arguably, it is these differences in cultural outlook
that explain the reason why the secular and Islamic sub-
sections of the Turkish bourgeoisie uphold different
notions of democracy beyond their agreement on the necessity of reshaping state-business relations in favour of the
latter. In the case of minority rights, most of MÜSİAD's
reservations appear to result from the incompatibility of
its religio-nationalistic outlook with the pluralist thrust in
the EU accession criteria as evident in their being hailed

as "narrow dresses constraining the lifestyles of people carrying a Muslim identity" by the Association ("AB elbisesi", 2005).

In the case of labour rights, MÜSİAD has success-fully instrumentalised its Muslim identity to legitimise the oppressive labour practices prevalent in member enterprises in a manner that arrests the development of a rights-based approach to the management of industrial conflicts. As noted by Buğra (1998, 2002a), MÜSİAD-affiliated employers characteristically emphasise the Islamic values of harmony and brotherhood in industrial relations to paper over real and potential conflicts. The Islamic perspective on labour relations depicts the model Muslim entrepreneur as one who manages to reconcile his profit-maximisation drive with the Islamic principles of fairness and social responsibility (Buğra, 1998). To recip-rocate the goodwill of the employer, Muslim workers are expected to be hard-working and docile. Then, from this perspective, "'Islamic' labour markets ... do not really need a formal labour code, or, especially, labour unions" (Buğra, 1998, p.533). In fact, according to an expert in Islamic labour relations, MÜSİAD tolerates trade unions only as "voluntarily appointed representatives of workers" while it considers strikes completely illegitimate (Balcı as cited in Buğra, 1998, p.533).[83]

In sum, MÜSİAD's political identity, despite its conversion to the cause of democracy promotion in the late 1990s, still bears the marks of its Islamist past as evident in the restricted nature of democratisation reforms it has been promoting since then. These ideological marks are particularly visible in the generally negative attitude of the Association towards minority and labour rights where restrictions are generally justified on the basis of their incompatibility with the Asso-ciation's religio-nationalistic worldwiew.

Conclusion

In his introduction to the edited volume *The Emergence of a New Turkey: Democracy and the AK Party*, Yavuz (2006a) described Islamic entrepreneurs as "those pious individuals who identify Islam as their identity and formulate their everyday cognitive map by using Islamic ideas and history to vernacularise (Islamicise) modern economic relations that promote the market forces and cherish neoliberal projects" (p.4). Thus, its capacity to mix and mesh religious devotion with a commitment to free-market capitalism constitutes the main defining characteristic of the newly emerging Muslim bourgeoisie of Turkey.[84] This chapter attempted to explore the implications of this mixture for democracy, and thereby reassess the Islamic bourgeoisie's potential as an agent of democratisation. The theoretical framework that informs the analysis is a rich line of historical-comparative research that has challenged the mainstream assumptions regarding the bourgeoisie-democracy nexus by demonstrating the historically contingent nature of the propertied classes' support for democracy. This perspective, thus, considers democracy promotion just one of the political strategies available to business actors trying to further their interests at the intersection of a complex web of power relations involving the state, other social classes, and international economic and geopolitical dynamics.

Accordingly, the first section of the chapter examined the three key elements of the historical conjuncture that enabled the transformation of the Muslim bourgeoisie's political outlook in the late 1990s away from religious integralism and towards liberal democracy. In this regard, it first pointed to the Muslim bourgeoisie's desire to erode the power of the secular Republican establishment both on the political and economic terrains. Second, it underlined the considerable reduction in the threat perception of upper classes after two decades of neoliberal economic restructuring and parallel suppression of labour activism. Finally, it highlighted the impact of the global pressures for political liberalisation and democratisation on the ideological landscape of entrepreneurial classes.

The second section investigated more closely the democratisation agenda of MÜSİAD, and found that a minimalist approach to democracy permeates the main policy statements of the Association. In addition, it attempted to account for this state of affairs by focusing on the restraining influence of the Association's Islamic identity with nationalistic undertones on the formulation of its democratic stance. This was done first by highlighting the particular way in which these businesses instrumentalise Islamic values to depoliticise labour relations, which they do by relegating them to the realm of religious morality instead of democratic rights and freedoms. Second, it stressed the anti-pluralist repercussions of Islamic businesses' religiously-oriented worldview by showing the Muslim bias in the fundamental rights and freedoms promoted by the MÜSİAD. Overall, in the case of Islamic entrepreneurs, their religious identity appears to be compatible with only certain forms of democracy, which are procedural in form and limited in content.

4: Islamist Bourgeoisie and Democracy under the AKP's
Rule: Democratisation or Marketisation of Politics?

117

REFERENCES

AB elbisesi müslümana dar. (2005). *Hürriyet (Turkish daily)*, April 7. Retrieved from http://www.hurriyet.com.tr

Akdoğan, Y. (2006). The meaning of conservative democratic political identity. In H. Yavuz (Ed.), *Secularism and Muslim Democracy in Turkey* (pp. 49-65). New York: Cambridge University Press.

AKP'nin ampulünü biz yaktık (2004, April 4). *Milliyet Business Supplement*, 6-7.

Balkan, E., & Yeldan, E. (2001). *Peripheral Development under Financial Liberalization: The Turkish Experience* (Hamilton College Economics Department Working Paper 01/01). Retrieved July 10, 2010, from http://academics.hamilton.edu/economics/home/Workpap/01_01.pdf

Bellin, E. (2000). Contingent democrats: Industrialists, labor and democratisation in late-developing countries. *World Politics, 52* (2), 175-205.

Berberoğlu, E. (2006, October 3). TÜSİAD mı büyük yoksa MÜSİAD mı? *Hürriyet*. Retrieved from http://www.hurriyet.com.tr

Birtek, F., & Toprak, B. (1993). The conflictual agendas of neo-liberal reconstruction and the rise of Islamic politics in Turkey: The hazards of rewriting modernity. *Praxis International, 13* (2), 192-212.

Bollen, K. (1979). Political democracy and the timing of development. *American Sociological Review, 44* (4), 572-587.

Boratav, K., Yeldan, A. E., & Köse, A. H. (2000, February). *Globalization, distribution and social policy: Turkey, 1980-1998* (Center for Economic Policy Analysis-New School University Working Paper 20). Retrieved July 10, 2010, from http://www.newschool.edu/scepa/publications/workingpapers/archive/cepa0120.pdf

Buğra, A. (1998). Class, culture and state: An analysis of interest representation by two Turkish business associations. *International Journal of Middle East Studies, 30* (4), 521-539.

Buğra, A. (2002a). Labor, capital, and religion: Harmony and conflict among the constituency of political Islam in Turkey. *Middle Eastern Studies, 38* (2), 187-204.

Buğra, A. (2002b). Political Islam in Turkey in historical context: Strengths and weaknesses. In N. Balkan, & S. Savran (Eds.), *The politics of permanent crisis: Class, ideology and state in Turkey* (pp.107-144). New York: Nova Science Publishers.

Buğra, A. (2003). The place of the economy in Turkish society. *South Atlantic Quarterly, 102* (2/3), 453-470.

Buğra, A. (2004). *State and Business in Modern Turkey: A Comparative Study.* Albany, N.Y.: State University of New York Press.

Cam, S. (2006). *Institutional oppression and neo-liberalism in Turkey* (Cardiff School of Social Sciences Working Paper 81). Retrieved July 5, 2010, from http://www.cf.ac.uk/socsi/resources/wrkgpaper-81.pdf

Çakır, R. (2004). Millî Görüş Hareketi. In *Modern Türkiye'de siyasi düşünce, Vol. 6* (pp. 544-575). İstanbul: İletişim.

Çınar, M. (2006). Turkey's transformation under the AKP rule. *The Muslim World, 96,* 469-486.

Cizre, Ü. (Ed.). (2007). *Secular and Islamic Politics in Turkey: The Making of the Justice and Development Party.* London: Routledge.

Cizre-Sakallıoğlu, Ü., & Çınar, M. (2003). Turkey 2002: Kemalism, Islamism, and politics in the light of the February 28 process. *South Atlantic Quarterly, 102* (2/3), 309-332.

Clark, J. A. (2006). The conditions of Islamist moderation: Unpacking cross-ideological cooperation in Jordan. *International Journal of Middle East Studies, 38,* 539-560.

Clark, W. R., Golder, M., & Golder, S. N. (2008). *Principles of comparative politics.* Washington, D.C.: CQ Press.

Coşar, S., & Özman, A. (2004). Centre-right politics in Turkey after the November 2002 general election: Neo-liberalism with a Muslim face. *Contemporary Politics, 10* (1), 57-74.

Coşar, S., & Yeğenoğlu, M. (2009, April). The neoliberal restructuring of Turkey's social security system. *Monthly Review, 60* (11), 34-47.

Dağı, İ. (2005). Transformation of Islamic political identity in Turkey: Rethinking the West and Westernization. *Turkish Studies, 6* (1), 21-37.

Dağı, İ. (2006). The Justice and Development Party: Identity, politics, and discourse of human rights in the search for security and legitimacy. In H. Yavuz (Ed.), *The Emergence of a New Turkey: Democracy and the AK Parti* (pp. 88-106). Salt Lake City: Utah University Press.

Demiralp, S. (2009). The rise of Islamic capital and the decline of Islamic radicalism in Turkey. *Comparative Politics, 41* (3), 315-335.

Drake, P.W. (1998). The international causes of democratization, 1974–1990. In P. W. Drake, & M. D. McCubbins (Eds.), *The Origins of Liberty: Political and Economic Liberalization in the Modern World* (pp. 70-91). Princeton, NJ: Princeton University Press.

Erol Yarar: Gerçek burjuva sınıfı biziz. (2009, July 20). *Star.* Retrieved from http://www.stargundem .com.

Gümüşçü, Ş. (2010). Class, status and party: The changing face of political Islam in Turkey and Egypt. *Comparative Political Studies, 43* (7), 835-861.

Harris, N. (1987). *Newly emergent bourgeoisies?* Hong Kong: University of Hong Kong.

Helliwell, J. F. (1994). Empirical linkages between democracy and economic growth. *British Journal of Political Science, 24,* 225-248.

Heper, M. (Ed.). (1991). *Strong state and economic interest groups.* Berlin and New York: Walter de Gruyter.

Heper, M., & Toktaş, Ş. (2003). Islam, modernity and democracy in contemporary Turkey: The case of Recep Tayyip Erdoğan. *The Muslim World, 93* (2), 157-185.

Huber, E., & Stephens, J. D. (1997, April). *The bourgeoisie and democracy: Historical and contemporary perspectives from Europe and Latin America.* Paper presented at the Annual Meeting of the Latin American Studies Association, Guadalajara, Mexico. Retrieved February 23, 2010, from http://lasa.international.pitt.edu/LASA97/huberstephens.pdf

Huber, E., Rueschemeyer, D., & Stephens, J. D. (1993). The impact of economic development on democracy. *Journal of Economic Perspectives, 7* (3), 71-85.

Huber, E., Rueschemeyer, D., & Stephens, J. D. (1997). The paradoxes of contemporary democracy: Formal, participatory, and social dimensions. *Comparative Politics, 29* (3), 323-342.

İnsel, A. (2003). The AKP and normalizing democracy in Turkey. *South Atlantic Quarterly, 102* (2-3), 293-308.

İş dünyasında iktidar modası. (1999, October 16). *Milliyet (Turkish daily),* p.11.

İş güvencesi isyanı. (2002, August 5). *Milliyet.* Retrieved from http://www.milliyet.com.tr

Keyder, Ç. (1987). *State and class in Turkey.* London and New York: Verso.

Landman, T. (1999). Economic development and democracy: The view from Latin America. *Political Studies, 47* (4), 607-626.

Landman, T. (2003). *Issues and methods in comparative politics: An introduction.* London and New York: Routledge. 2nd Ed.

Lipset, S. M. (1959). Some social requisites for democracy: Economic development and political legitimacy. *The American Political Science Review, 53* (1), 69-105.

Lipset, S. M. (1994). The social requisites of democracy revisited: 1993 presidential address. *American Sociological Review, 59* (1), 1-22.

Mecham, R. Q. (2004). From the ashes of Virtue, a promise of light: The transformation of political Islam in Turkey. *Third World Quarterly, 25* (2), 339-358.

Moore, B. (1966). *The social origins of dictatorship and democracy: Lord and peasant in the making of the modern world.* Boston, MA: Beacon Press.

MÜSİAD. (1995, July). *The Turkish Economy 1995* (MÜSİAD Research Report No.12). Retrieved June 25, 2010, from http://www.musiad. org.tr/img/arastirmalaryayin/pdf/arastirma_raporlari_12.pdf

MÜSİAD. (2000, April). *Anayasa reformu ve yönetimin demokratikleşmesi* (MÜSİAD Research Report No.37). Retrieved June 25, 2010, from http://www.musiad.org.tr/img/arastirmalaryayin/pdf/arastirma_raporlari_37.pdf

MÜSİAD. (2008, January). *Yeni bir anayasa için görüş ve öneriler* (MÜSİAD Research Report No.52). Retrieved June 25, 2010, from http://www.musiad.org.tr/img/arastirmalaryayin/pdf/arastirma_raporlari_52.pdf

MÜSİAD Uzakdoğu'da devleti oynadı. (1996, March 13). *Milliyet*, p.9.

MÜSİAD'ı tasfiye operasyonu. (1998, November 7). *Hürriyet*. Retrieved from http://www.hurriyet.com.tr

Nasr, V. (2005). The rise of "Muslim democracy". *Journal of Democracy, 16* (2), 13-27.

O'Donnell, G. (1973). *Economic modernization and bureaucratic authoritarianism.* Berkeley, CA: Institute of International Studies.

Öniş, Z. (1997). The political economy of Islamic resurgence in Turkey. *Third World Quarterly, 18* (4), 743-766.

Öniş, Z. (2001). Political Islam at the crossroads: From hegemony to co-existence. *Contemporary Politics, 7* (4), 281-298.

Öniş, Z. (2005). Entrepreneurs, citizenship and the European Union: The changing nature of state-business relations in Turkey. In E. F. Keyman, & A. İçduygu (Eds.), *Challenges to citizenship in a globalizing world: European questions and Turkish experiences* (pp. 173-195). London: Routledge.

Öniş, Z. (2006). Globalization and party transformation: Turkey's Justice and Development Party in perspective. In P. Burnell (Ed.), *Globalizing democracy: Party politics in emerging democracies* (pp.122-140). London: Routledge, Warwick Studies on Globalization.

Öniş, Z., & Türem, U. (2001). Business, globalization and democracy: A comparative analysis of Turkish business associations. *Turkish Studies, 2* (2), 94-120.

Öniş, Z., & Türem, U. (2002). Entrepreneurs, democracy and citizenship in Turkey. *Comparative Politics, 34* (4), 439-456.

Onlar Refah'ı refahsız istiyor (1996, April 15). *Milliyet*, p.7.

Özbudun, E. (2006a). From political Islam to conservative democracy: The case of the Justice and Development Party in Turkey. *South European Society & Politics, 11* (3-4), 543-557.

Özbudun, E. (2006b). Changes and continuities in the Turkish party system. *Representation, 42* (2), 129-137.

Özdemir, S. (2004). MÜSİAD ve Hak-İş'i birlikte anlamak. In *Modern Türkiye'de Siyasi Düşünce 6* (pp. 837-869). İstanbul: İletişim.

Perthes, V. (1994). The private sector, economic liberalization, and the prospects of democratisation: The case of Syria and some other Arab countries. In G. Salamé (Ed.), *Democracy without democrats? The renewal of politics in the Muslim world* (pp.243-269). London and New York: I. B. Tauris.

Przeworski, A., & Limongi, F. (1997). Modernization: Theories and facts. *World Politics, 59*, 155-183.

Przeworski, A., Alvarez, M. E., Cheibub, J. A., & Limongi, F. (2000). *Democracy and development: political institutions and well-being in the world, 1950-1990*. Cambridge: Cambridge University Press.

Refah için söz yargıda. (1997, October 6). *Hürriyet*. Retrieved from http://www.hurriyet.com.tr

Robins, P. (2007). Turkish foreign policy since 2002: Between a 'post-Islamist' government and a Kemalist state. *International Affairs, 83* (1), 289-304.

Rueschemeyer, D., Stephens, E. H., & Stephens, J. D. (1992). *Capitalist development and democracy*. Cambridge: Polity Press.

Somer, M. (2004, March). *Muslim democrats in the making? Explaining Turkey's AKP*. Paper presented at the Annual Convention of the International Studies Association, Montreal, Canada. Retrieved January 15, 2010, from http://home.ku.edu.tr/~musomer/research_files/ISA%20paper5.pdf

Tanıyıcı, S. (2003). Transformation of political Islam in Turkey: Islamist Welfare Party's pro-EU turn. *Party Politics, 9* (4), 463-483.

Toprak, B. (1990). Religion as state ideology in a secular setting: The Turkish-Islamic synthesis. In M. Wagstaff (Ed.), *Aspects of religion in secular Turkey* (pp.10-15). UK: University of Durham, Centre for Middle Eastern and Islamic Studies, Occasional Paper Series, No 40.

Therborn, G. (1977, May-June). The rule of capital and the rise of democracy. *New Left Review 1* (103), 3-41.

Valenzuela, J. S., & Valenzuela, A. (1978). Modernization and dependency: Alternative perspectives in the study of Latin American underdevelopment. *Comparative Politics, 10* (4), 535-557.

Wickham, C. R. (2004). The path to moderation: Strategy and learning in the formation of Egypt's *Wasat* party. *Comparative Politics, 36* (2), 205-228.

Wickham, C. R. (2006, May). *Democratization and Islamists - Auto-reform.* Paper presented at the Center for the Study of Islam and Democracy Annual Conference, Washington, DC.

Yavuz, H. (2000). Cleansing Islam from the public sphere. *Journal of International Affairs, 54* (1), 21-42.

Yavuz, H. (2006a). Introduction: The role of the new bourgeoisie in the transformation of the Turkish Islamic movement. In H. Yavuz (Ed.), *Secularism and Muslim democracy in Turkey* (pp. 1-19). New York: Cambridge University Press.

Yavuz, H. (Ed.). (2006b). *Secularism and Muslim democracy in Turkey.* New York: Cambridge University Press.

Yavuz, H. (2009). *Secularism and Muslim democracy in Turkey.* New York: Cambridge University Press.

Yıldırım, E. (2006). Labor pains or Achilles' heel: JDP and labor. In H. Yavuz (Ed.), *Secularism and Muslim democracy in Turkey* (pp. 235-257). New York: Cambridge University Press.

PART II:
SOCIAL POLICY,
CITIZENSHIP
AND GENDER

5

THE SOCIAL POLICY REGIME IN THE AKP YEARS: THE EMPEROR'S NEW CLOTHES

Gamze Yücesan-Özdemir

All the people standing by and at the windows cheered and cried,
"Oh, how splendid are the Emperor's new clothes.
What a magnificent train! How well the clothes fit!"
No one dared to admit that he couldn't see anything,
But among the crowds a little child suddenly gasped out,
"But he hasn't got anything on."
                    H. C. Anderson, "The Emperor's New Clothes"

Introduction

This chapter evaluates the social policy regime in Turkey under the rule of the AKP governments. It discusses the recent developments, describes the current scheme, and reveals the neoliberal and Islamic-conservative guises dominant in Turkish social policy and in the discoveries of policy makers. The underlying argument is that Turkey is currently on the road to adopting a social policy regime that is deeply influenced by neoliberalism, Islam, and conservatism.

The social policy regime that has developed under the AKP governments bears the imprints of neoliberalism. Like a hurricane, neoliberalism swept across the political landscape, laying all before it to waste. Furthermore, neoliberal theory, based on a very particular set of assumptions about human behavior and institutions, has played an important role in the sustained attack upon institutionalised welfare provision and the interventionist state. Of these said assumptions, the most important are methodological individualism, rationality, and the supremacy of the free market. Similarly, the key individual components of the whole neoliberal intellectual system are rationality, the supremacy of the market as an allocative mechanism, public choice theory, the public burden theory of welfare, government overload, and the superior morality of individual responsibility and self-reliance over the "culture of dependency."

Although this is a tendency that can be observed in the entire *developing* world that *sustains* its development by way of applying neoliberal economic policies, the Turkish case is unique in that this change has been realised under an Islamist political orientation. Hence, a conservative-neoliberal tendency has emerged, whereby Islamic notions of charity successfully complement attempts to downsize the state through strict controls over social spending. Yet, the AKP's social policy regime does not exist only in theory.

It is also important to explore the experience of living under the AKP's social policy regime. Thus far, the two main results of the social policy regime have been the rise in precarious work and in the need for social assistance. In other words, Turkish society is faced with informal work, with the lack of social security and with de-unionisation, which results in endemic insecurity. Hence, the society as a whole is rendered dependent upon social assistance. Therefore, an examination of the living conditions under the social policy regime is important not only in the assessment of the nature of the social policy regime, but also in looking at the sources and limits of resistance, consent, and compliance. The question is one of whether, against the rise of the precarious work and the rise of social assistance, it is possible to find someone like the little child in Anderson's deathless tale *"The Emperor's New Clothes,"* gasping out, "But things are getting worse!"

This chapter, firstly, illustrates the spirit of the social policy regime during the AKP's rule: one reflecting element of neoliberalism, conservatism, and Islam. Secondly, it focuses on the effects of the social policy regime that has come out of the AKP's rule at the individual level. These experiences are discussed under two separate headings: the endemic insecurity of precarious work and reliance on social assistance.

The Spirit of the Social Policy Regime during the AKP's Rule: Neoliberalism, Conservatism, and Islam

The AKP has described itself as a moderate Islamic political organisation. Fittingly then, the reform plans in the social policies initiated by the Party by their arrival to the government was an amalgam of Islamic conservatism and neoliberalism (see Yeğenoğlu's & Coşar's contribution to this volume). Such a program might further be described as one in opposition with the basic premises of rights-based approaches to social policy. Firstly, the social policy regime of the AKP targets a process of transition from community-based ideals to those of individualism. The focus here is on individual responsibility and it is stressed that there are no rights without duties. So, in neoliberal social policy, as MacGregor notes, "rather than risks being shared and collective responsibility accepted, the focus is on a balance of rights and obligations at the level of the individual" (Mac Gregor, 1999, p.108). Put differently, rather than depending on the state for healthcare, education, and care for the elderly, the individual has to accept more responsibility for him/herself in accessing to healthcare, education and care in old age. Hence, personal consumption is presented as the key to a good life and low taxation on income becomes essential (George & Miller, 2000).

Specifically, the private pension system is a good example of this stress on individualism during the AKP's rule. The Turkish Private Pension Law was drafted in 1999 and approved by parliament in October 2001. However, the overall legal and institutional framework of the Turkish Private Pension System was not completed until 2002. In its approach, the finished bill (No. 4447) resembled the route proposed by the World Bank and supported by the *Türkiye Sanayici ve İşadamları Birliği* (Association of Turkish Industrialists and Businessmen, TÜSİAD). In essence, the World Bank proposed a three-tier system of benefits. According to this system, the first pillar consists of a minimum package of publicly-provided benefits. This mandatory first pillar covers a minimum range of risks. The second pillar is also mandatory, but the services provided therein would generally be provided by the private sector and managed privately. Finally, the third pillar is voluntary. The services included in this third stage aim to provide a 'high life quality' in return for high contributions.

Secondly, the social policy regime of the AKP emphasises the market and its role in the reproduction of society. The party has led the process of market colonisation or rather, the penetration of market norms into non-market spheres. In other words, under the AKP's rule, life itself, with its social, academic and cultural dimensions, has become a marketplace. Both in the classical political economy and in neoliberal theory, the market is often defended as a sphere of freedom, of voluntary, uncoerced contracts between free and independent agents. Hence, it is assumed that in the marketplace, free men are able to simultaneously maximise the general interests and pursue their own interests by freely exchanging goods and services, without intervention from the state. Hayek, whose ideas have very much influenced neoliberal writings, displayed a profound distaste for the whole concept of an interventionist state and argued that any and every attempt to replace the market with a system of politically-administered decision-making was bound to end in tyranny and disaster (Hayek, 1994).

The social security reform, which was started before the AKP came to power but was finalised under the party, is a good example of the subjection of health and social security systems to the disciplines of the market. The prime motive of the AKP-initiated reform was the unsustainability of what had been the existing social security system. Essentially, it was the rise in costs that had become the prominent source of legitimacy for the reform programs in social security (Ağartan, 2005). The transfers made from the state budget to cover the social security system deficit amounted to 6 percent of Turkey's GDP in 2003 (Koray, 2005). This 6 percent has become a real obstacle in the face of an economic policy aiming to build market confidence and to decrease the risk margins for international finance capital. Meanwhile, the IMF announced that it would release a substantial loan to Turkey if the country enacted the necessary legislation to initiate the social security reform. With their looming financial concerns, the AKP set out to reform the system.

The social security reform was based on a view of the marketplace as the main mode of coordination in the production of services that are financed and provided by the social security system, such as pensions and healthcare. However, the campaign launched for the legitimisation of the reform was based first on the equalitarian aspects of social security measures that operate independently of employment status, and secondly, on the expansion of the total coverage of the social security system. The market-based *egalitarianism* of the new reforms required different employment statutes to be calculated for even the worst positions. Market-based *egalitarianism* is achieved by way of contribution fees and by way of 'clean' registration proving that the premiums of the service consumer is paid regularly. Such an *egalitarianism* served to deny the mentality behind the collective character of social rights and fostered the freedom of contract.

Under the emerging social conflicts provided by the newly unfolding urban poverty, the social security measures that were designed to operate independently of employment status and the expansion in the coverage of social security instruments had a certain level of charm, for both the ruling power bloc and for the poor dealing with unregistered work and activities. Yet, the organised labour force, including many trade unions and strong interest groups, opposed the so-called reform.[85]

Thirdly, the AKP's neoliberal agenda is in line with the so-called "structural reforms" introduced in conjunction with the IMF and the World Bank. Since the 1980s, the IMF and the World Bank have functioned as a surveillance mechanism over Turkey, just as they have in other countries where they have providing funding. One of the main requirements and/ or reforms, which both the IMF and World Bank have established as stipulations for providing funds, is the restructuring of the social policy in line with neoliberal ideas. One important example in this respect is the parallelism between the structure and application of social assistance in Turkey and the strategies envisaged by the World Bank to reduce poverty. The World Bank's "Social Risk Mitigation Project" (SRMP), which was started on September 11, 2001 and commenced in 2006, is a direct reflection of the bank's approach to reducing poverty. For this project, in which the *Sosyal Yardımlaşma ve Dayanışmayı Teşvik Fonu* (Fund for the Encouragement of Social Assistance and Solidarity, SYDTF) acted as the implementer, the World Bank extended $500 million over a five-year grace period and on the condition that it would be repaid in fifteen years. According to Ajay Chibber, the incumbent World Bank representative in Turkey, the aim of the SRMP was to decrease the effect of the 2001 economic crisis on poor families (Zabcı, 2009, p. 99; see also Zabcı's contribution to this volume).[86]

Fourthly, the AKP's social policy regime is based on Islamic references. Indeed, in the pursuit of its reform program, the AKP referred to a Turkish culture in which Islam is situated and influences its social policy. More briefly, Islam is the point of reference for some of the most delicate issues that Turkish society needs to face: how to treat the poor, promote charity, and establish fair relations among communities and within families.[87] Essential to all religions, charity is also a central organising principle in Islam, which the AKP refers to rather often. According to Coşar and Yeğenoğlu (2009, p.37), the version of Islam that the AKP has been promoting is Islam as a cultural phenomenon, rather than political Islam:

> This state of affairs works to the advantage of the party in three respects. First, appealing to Islam on a socio-cultural basis helps the party to fend off the claims of the hawkish secularists that the AKP is a pro-Islamist political party. Second, it works to convince the Western allies of Turkey that the AKP is the best possible example of a moderate Islamic standpoint—one which neither denies Western values nor Muslimhood as the most comprehensive cultural trait of the Turkish population. Third, it is also functional in terms of reproducing the already established connection between Muslimhood and Turkishness, thus giving the party a centrist appearance. The AKP's version of nationalism, however, can be considered a "banal nationalism."

The Islamic elements in the ideological orientation of the ruling party also appear to be very useful in motivating and mobilising civil initiatives towards providing social assistance. An important example of the purpose of orienting Islamic elements is the rise of Islamic NGOs in the realm of social assistance. Of these, the *Deniz Feneri Derneği* (Lighthouse Association) is the most prominent. The *Deniz Feneri* was registered in 1998 as an association and then became a corporate structure in 2002, under the framework of the association with the same name.[88] It provides food, health services, shelter, guest houses, public kitchens, clothing education, occupational courses, and in-cash benefits to its beneficiaries. Ultimately, its approach represents a combination of the liberal-conservative attitude towards poverty on the one hand, and Islamist charity on the other.[89] However, while the *Deniz Feneri* is indeed the leading NGO of its kind, it is not the only one within the Islamist power bloc. In the same vein, the issue of Turkish social assistance, including those benefits allocated by municipalities and by the government, is not simply a matter of assistance to the poor. It is rather a strategy, which is used in the construction of the political and ideological bonds/links that keep the AKP in the power.

Living under the Social Policy Regime during the AKP's Rule: The Endemic Anxiety of Precarious Work

As previously mentioned, beginning in 2002 with the AKP's election to power, the party's social policy regime has led to the rise in precarious work. Today, paid employment is becoming increasingly precarious, and as the foundations of Turkey's quasi-social welfare state continue to collapse, old-age poverty and even new forms of poverty now seem inevitable. In fact, those who have the benefit of a full-time wage or salary have come to represent a minority of the economically-active population. Conversely, the majority earn their living under more precarious conditions. Growing numbers of people are traveling vendors, small retailers, or craftspeople. Many are forced to either offer a variety of services or to alternate between different fields of work, ranging from agricultural to home-based labour. This nomadic multi-activity is not a pre-modern relic but a rapidly spreading variant in contemporary Turkey. As a result of this increased deregulation and flexibility of work, the labour market has been transformed into a risk society incalculable in terms of individual lives. In answer to this crisis, state intervention has taken on the form of a legal/ economic policy of regime transition. Yet, the destination of this transition is unclear. Nonetheless, under these conditions, one trend is clear: a majority of the Turkish people, including the middle classes, will continue to live in endemic insecurity.

As one might guess, precarious work has become a political mantra. Incompliance with the nomadic multi-activity occurred throughout the world and consequently the available jobs became short-term and easily terminable. The European Union's (EU) labour politics, various treaties, and the discursive set consisted of structural adjustment programs (SAP) for greater flexibility, together with domestic demands for the stabilisation of the workforce and costs, had a profound impact on the *discoveries* of regulatory devices. The orthodox defense strategies were relegated to a position in which they had to be defended. Moreover, the redistribution of risks away from the state and the bourgeoisie, and towards the individual, was achieved under the banner of flexibility. Subsequently, precarious work became highly heterogeneous, encompassing various production units and a wide range of economic activities, as well as people working or producing under many different employment relations and production arrangements.

Yet, in spite of the heterogeneity of precarious work, and its multiple dimensions, conceptual and statistical definitions of *this* market are not as clear-cut as one might expect.

Firstly, precarious work is a result of the increasing proletarianism in Turkey (Table 1). In the 2000s, for instance, wage and salary earners accounted for around 60 percent of the total workforce, while unpaid family workers and the self-employed represented almost 35 percent (Table 5.1). According to Hart, a British economist who was the first to coin the term 'informal sector,' the main component of a formal sector is wage and salary earners, whereas the main component of an informal sector is the self-employed (Hart quoted in Selçuk, 2002, p. 5). Self-employed workers,[90] most of whom are own-account, and unpaid family workers represent an important part of the total labour force and are considered the bulk of the rural and urban informal sector in Turkey.

Table 5.1. Status in Employment in Turkey (percent)

	Wage and Salary Earners	Employers	Self-employed	Unpaid Family Workers	Total (%)
1990	39.0	4.5	26.4	30.1	100
1995	41.9	5.6	24.9	27.6	100
2000	49.6	5.3	24.5	24.5	100
2006	56.5	5.4	23.5	14.7	100
2008	61.0	5.6	24.6	11.2	100

Source: *Türkiye İstatistik Kurumu* (State Institute of Statistics, TÜİK) Household Labour Force Survey Results

Secondly, precarious work is the result of an informal workforce (Table 2). One example of this is the severe lack of social security provision for a considerable number of workers in Turkey. In 2008, for instance, 51.5 percent of the civilian employment worked without any social security (Table 2). This present situation can be seen as a continuance of that of the 1980s, when the marketisation of public goods like education, healthcare, and social security had increased. However, from 1994 onwards, entrepreneurs started to move into these sectors and the share of the private sector in total education and healthcare investments reached 50 percent by 1997 (Boratav *et al.*, 2000, p. 34). This privatisation of education and health services led to an expensive, modern, and luxurious system of private healthcare and education for the upper classes. As a result, the lower classes, or those covered by social security schemes, are currently dependent on an overextended public health system.

Table 5.2. Informal Employment in Turkey (percent)

	Informal Employment in Wage and Salary Earners	Informal Employment in Total Employment
1990	26.9	43.7
1998	26.2	36.7
2002	30.3	52.1
2006	29.8	50.1
2008	27.3	51.5

Source: *Türkiye İstatistik Kurumu* (State Institute of Statistics, TÜİK) Household Labour Force Survey Results

Thirdly, precarious work seems to flourish especially in the growing service sector. This is largely due to the fact that the AKP's structural reforms have rather poor records in job creation in industry,[91] meaning that services and agriculture continue to offer the majority of employment opportunities. To better demonstrate this, employment in industry was around 17 percent in the 2000s, whereas the corresponding ratio for agriculture and services was around 34 percent and 49 percent respectively (Table 3). It is also important to note that due to the decrease in agricultural employment in the post-1980 period in Turkey, a relatively significant part of the labour force was employed in the service sector throughout the 2000s.

Table 5.3. Sectoral Distribution of Employment in Turkey (percent)

	Agriculture	Industry	Service
1980	55.0	14.1	30.9
1985	50.9	15.3	33.8
1995	48.1	15.0	36.9
2000	34.5	17.2	48.3
2006	27.3	19.7	53.0
2008	23.7	20.6	55.7

Source: *Türkiye İstatistik Kurumu* (State Institute of Statistics, TÜİK) Household Labour Force Survey Results

Table 5.4. Unemployment and Underemployment Rates in Turkey (percent)

	1989	1990	1995	1998	2000	2002	2009
Unemployment Rate (%)	8.9	8.2	6.9	7.3	6.6	10.6	14.8
Underemployment Rate (%)	5.8	6.4	6.9	6.9	6.9	5.4	7.3
Rate of unemployment + Labour Force Idle because of Underemployment	14.7	14.6	13.8	14.2	13.5	16	22.1

Source: *Türkiye İstatistik Kurumu* (State Institute of Statistics, TÜİK) Household Labour Force Survey Results

The expansion of precarious work had negative impacts on wages and affected all areas of productive activity. Additionally, import substitution[92] as a hegemonic project disappeared, but as a social reality it continued to be decisive in the reproduction of capitalist relations in production.[93] New institutionalism in the workplace, together with the refusal to deepen import substitution, caused a drop in the number of skilled workers in the overall workforce. Given that trade unions weakened significantly in the post-1980 period, the informal sector expanded and the pressure from the reserve army on the labour power intensified. As a result, the limited rigidity paradigm of the 1970s lost its meaning. Since production is orientated predominantly towards the internal market, the decline of wages had a decisive impact on overall growth. Furthermore, mainly after 1989, with trade liberalisation, the limited domestic market became subject to competition. Throughout these years, the industrial capital, as the fraction of capital and of the ruling class, lost some of its significance in the face of the rising power of financial capital. This state of affairs has unfolded into a situation whereby since 1994, the main dynamics of growth have become the ongoing deterioration of wages, and thus, of conditions of reproduction of the collective labour power, rather than successful management of the economy over domestic implementers of the IMF-designed programs.

Last but not the least, precarious work is a result of the decline in unionisation (Table 5). In the 1980s, as a result of Turkey's conformity with the global decline in unionisation (Hyman, 2000; Munck, 2002; Munck & Waterman, 1999) and with the excessive usage of repressive means of domination in domestic politics,[94] trade unions weakened. Chiefly, workers' rights to organise and to collectively bargain were limited severely. Even the white-collar workers in the public and private sectors were precluded from joining a union, presumably, due to their role as "petty bourgeoisie" in the "making of the working class"(Işıklı, 2003). Furthermore, the role of anti-democratic regulations in unionisation was decisive in the first half of the 1980s.

Unions are the organisational forms implemented throughout competitive and monopolistic modes of regulation, yet their function has been in ongoing transformation (Hyman, 2000; Munck & Waterman, 1999). Yalman (1997, p. 231) notes that parallel to the reign of certain authoritarian regimes in the Third World (Pinochet's Chile being the prime example), the new labour containment strategy in Turkey after the 1980s recognised the market as a mechanism to control and weaken the unions to the extent that they would not have the potential to become the arenas for counter-hegemonic strategies. What was offered/imposed was an export-oriented trade and development strategy based on the legitimisation provided by the neoclassical principle of comparative advantages. However this time, it was closely paired with the aim of reaching a more market-directed system of resource allocation within the framework of the re-organisation of existing structural forms, within which working class representation has been almost non-existent, and in which the bourgeoisie's political signifi-cance was preserved–as it had been in the pre-1980 period. [95]

The root causes of the current crisis in trade unionism in Turkey can be divided into four major areas and these areas are the four main subjects of inquiry that run through this chapter. Firstly, union bureaucracy and union structure have been shaped in accordance with traditional core membership. Thus, they are rather rigid and inflexible in terms of reaching a labour force, which has become increasingly comprised of part-time and temporary workers, and flexible working arrange-ments. Secondly, given that the representation of workers as the bearers of class relations *vis-à-vis* the bourgeoisie in the post-1980s had been implicitly denied, and that neoliberal rhetoric had to be backed up with the slogan *"putting an end to class-based politics"* - itself a class strategy *par excellence* (Yalman, 2002) - unions are rather weak in their negotiations with the state. Thirdly, the level of international solidarity is insufficient. Turkish unions do not have healthy relationships with inter-national union organisations. Although most of the unions are members of international federations, and all the confederations are members of the international confederations, trade unionism in Turkey does not benefit greatly from international strategies and/or contacts with unions around the world. Fourthly, union politics and culture suffer from a lack of knowledge, awareness, and strategy to confront economic, political, and ideological development. Thus in order to attract members and to win the support of the broader public, unions should redefine their organ-isations, their members, and their politics.

Tablo 5.5. Unionisation Rates in Turkey (percent)

	Wage and Salary Earners*	Statistics of Ministry of Labour and Social Security		Statistics of Social Insurance Institution		
		Unioni-sation	Wage and Salary Earners Covered by Collective Bargain-ings/ Wage and Salary Earners	Unioni-sation	Public	Private
1980				47.6	89.2	24.2
1990	3.563.527	56.1	36.9	42.5	93.3	22.7
1995	3.905.118	68.3	25.4	24.5	79.3	10.3
2000	4.521.081	54.6	22.9	16.0	55.4	6.4
2005	5.022.584	58.6	11.7	14.9	50.2	6.0
2008	5.414.423	58.72	10.8	8.19	50.1	6.0

Source: *Çalışma ve Sosyal Güvenlik Bakanlığı (*Ministry of Labour and Social Security) and *Sosyal Sigortalar Kurumu* (Social Insurance Institution, SSK)
* These are formal wage and salary earners. Both institutions use these numbers.

All in all, the AKP's rule has led Turkey to erratic rates of real growth and investment, a worsened income distribution and social equity, a paralysed fiscal apparatus and an ever-growing amount of precarious work.[96]

Living under the Social Policy Regime during the AKP's Rule: At the Mercy of Social Assistance

These erratic rates of growth, worsened income distribution and social equity, paralyzed fiscal apparatus and growing amount of precarious work lead to the rise in systematic measures of poverty alleviation and social assistance. [97] In general, these measures taken to alleviate poverty generally fall under the rubric of World Bank-type policies.

First, social assistance in post-1980 Turkey should be considered in connection with the increase in poverty and the following means and mechanisms that have been put into force for its alleviation. [98] In Turkey, policies for addressing poverty in some ways parallel the transformation in the economic program and the accumulation regime. In this respect, the paradigm that offered grounds for the strategies of reducing poverty was initiated by the January 24, 1980 decisions. The process thenceforth has evolved through "the liberalisation of domestic financial markets, commodity market, foreign trade regime and exchange rate regime" (Ansal *et al.*, 2000, p. 69), and through the policies directed toward the privatisation and reduction of labour costs. In the meantime, public employment has been gradually eliminated through these policies, which were devised and implemented for Turkey's articulation into the capitalist world order as a depository of a cheap and harmonious labour force. Furthermore, the establishment of the SYDTF in 1986 and the initiation of the Green Card service in 1992 can be considered within this framework,[99] and certainly as a product of the *populist concerns* for addressing liberal policies (Sallan-Gül, 2002, p. 117).

The SYDTF was transformed into the *Sosyal Yardımlaşma ve Dayanışma Genel Müdürlüğü* (Social Assistance and Solidarity General Directorate, SYDGM) by Law No. 5263, which was put into force on December 1, 2004. The social assistance activities are now run through a total of 973 *Sosyal Yardımlaşma ve Dayanışma Vakıfları* (Social Assistance and Solidarity Foundations, SYDV) under the authority of governors in 81 provinces and of the district administrators in 892 districts. Within this scope, 948 foundations were established and as of 2009, 25 foundations were in the process of being launched (Yazıcı, 2009). The composition of the SYDVs and the way in which the benefits[100] are distributed, paired with the testing requirement and the Green Card program, have become sources of controversy, especially after the 2001 crisis. SYDVs are chaired by governors or district governors, and the rest of their managerial boards include the mayor, the provincial director of social services, the provincial head of finance, a health official, a representative of the directorate of the regional affairs at the local level, and three prominent members of the local population. The beneficiaries are tested by SYDVs being independent in the decision-making process. Hence, SYDVs are entwined by patronage networks.

Second, in post-1980 Turkey one cannot conclude that the simultaneous "rise of local governments and the transition from national scale to local scale in the economic growth strategies followed by the state" (Avcuoğlu, 2009, p. 33) on the one hand, and the reliance on local institutions and dynamics in the struggle against poverty on the other hand, was a coincidence. The transferring of authority from national governments to local administrations was realised, and resources allocated to the municipalities were increased. Another aspect of this tendency towards localisation is the development of market mechanisms (Avcuoğlu, 2009, p. 33). At this point, the connection between such practices as integrating the poor into the market and increasing human capital on the one hand, and "local economic strategies for having a share in the financial capital flows, international trade and global production chains" (Avcuoğlu, 2009: 34) on the other,

should not be ignored. In effect, the tendency to divert capital
to the localities as an important aspect of Turkey's neoliberal
economic transformation can be regarded among the factors
that form the strategies for combating poverty (Avcuoğlu,
2009, p.38).

Since 2002, the central government's share in funds
spent on social assistance to the poor has declined (Elveren,
2008). On the other hand, the social assistance provided by
municipalities has increased significantly. The in-kind assistance provided by municipalities including food, coal, and
clothing are financed mostly by charities. Therefore, it is
nearly impossible to investigate the amount and the management of these funds, as they are largely the donations of rich
individuals. Consequently, there is no adequate information
on the amount of funds used for different social assistance
schemes of the municipalities (Government of Turkey, 2004).
The magnitude of these charities is in clear contrast with the
failure of the SYDTF to attract private funds. It is clear that
municipalities are channeling the donations made by promi-
nent/rich people who are not willing to donate to the SYDTF,
but only to municipalities. The reason behind this *choice*
might be something other than charity, and in fact, it is. It has
been said that, under the AKP's rule, Turkey has witnessed
semi-official negotiations between municipalities and people
seeking urban rents. In addition, municipal plans are organised and reorganised for the purpose of creating capital for
the supporters of the AKP government. Further, it is possible
to argue that municipalities collect donations in return for
organising/reorganising municipal plans, for agreeing not to
take legal action against illegal activities, and/or for using the
power of the state in other ways that contribute to the individual capitalists supporting the AKP government in public
bids and in the privatisation of publicly-owned companies.
This situation, if true, may best be described as a specific

kind of bribery disguised as charity. The bribery in this case is specific because it is carried out for the purpose of raising electoral support, in addition to appealing to individual benefits (Buğra & Keyder, 2006).

In post-1980 Turkey, the increase in the social assistance expenditure and in the "assistance of the local administrations toward the urban poor" has been intertwined with the weakening of the social state (Özbek, 2002, pp. 24-25). One should also consider the political dimensions of these practices. Actually, the dominant policy in contemporary Turkey is pauperisation and then beggarisation—a product of populist policies:

> (…) one should note that the social policy preferences of the dominant neoliberal discourse–whilst the social state is eliminated–tend to involve paternalism, clientelism and conservatism. It is no secret that in Turkey, too, the assistance funds are determined by the existing governments, and are used to support political groups that opt for conservative and neoliberal policies (Özdemir & Yücesan-Özdemir, 2009, p. 331).

Third, it should be noted that social assistance programs have seriously damaged the perception of social policy as a symbol of a rights-based regime in terms of citizenship rights (for a similar argument with respect to citizenship see Soyarık-Şentürk's contribution to this volume). Social aids have been one of the most important ingredients of social policy practices within the scope of the social state. In Turkey, where there is no tradition of a welfare state, and thus the lack of a social security system, reducing poverty is done mainly through social assistance. More briefly, especially for those sections that are excluded from the social security system, reducing poverty necessitated the prioritisation of in-kind and monetary assistance, like the Green Card and various income transfers. The SYDGM has turned out to be the most prominent actor in such policies. "The World Bank has selected" the General Directorate "as the unit that would implement the resource allocation for alleviating the effects of poverty" (Yalman, 2007, p. 655), with the aim of minimising the "political and social costs" of structural adjustment programs. As a result, "there emerges an opportunity to realise a resource transfer for the poor" (Yalman, 2007, p. 657) without resorting to taxation–one of the fundamental means of a social state (Güler, 2006).

The Conditional Cash Transfer (CCT) is one of the main significant ingredient in social assistance practices in Turkey. It is understood that the CCTs "are the most important means" of alleviating poverty within the scope of SRMP, which began in the aftermath of the 2001 economic crisis (T.C. Başbakanlık, 2007, p. 659). There is a common agreement in the literature on the alleviation of poverty that in those countries where unequal income distribution is high, the CCTs have little effect in eliminating such inequality (Lomeli, 2008). Yet, it is also argued that these transfers are significant for those who receive them, partially improving their life standards. In the official document on the project in Turkey, the CCT is considered "a part of the recent development programs that enable the accumulation of human capital, which is one of the most effective methods to break the chain of poverty among generations" (T.C. Başbakanlık, 2007, p. 58). The rationale behind the implementation of this means of social assistance is stated as follows: "One of the fundamental reasons behind poverty is the pretty low levels of access to education and health services among poor families. Therefore, programs aiming at alleviating poverty should first enable the access of poor families to education and health services."[101]

Fourth, it should immediately be noted that though a paternalist approach involves "a societal feature and aspect," it does not foresee a social state (Koray, 2000, p. 111). The representation of a policy not in terms of rights but in terms of charity–grace and the reproduction of state involvement in the labour market on neoliberal lines - result in what the Ankara Metropolitan Municipality calls "Life Support" (Büyükşehir Ankara, 2006, p. 3). The reference to this term is not a coincidence; actually, it is telling about the state of affairs in the neoliberal dislocation of the social from the state-citizenship vocabulary: it underlines the fine line between death and life, the fact that the people addressed by these policies live on the edge of starvation. However, in the new paradigm, the reasons behind starvation are excluded from the agenda, as is the case with those behind poverty.

Fifth, it can be argued that in Turkey, such policies center on family and religious organisations (Avcuoğlu, 2009, p. 35), which are stronger than public protection organisations and the market institutions, and that through these institutions "traditional religious community-based solidarity patterns" are reproduced, thus reinforcing a "communitarian-conservative" liberal welfare regime (Erder, 2004, p. 39). Here, it should be noted that "forms of social solidarity, based on family-neighborhood-religious community" have had a continuous role in Turkey's welfare regime (Özbek, 2002, p. 11). Under the AKP, Turkey's notion of the family as a unit of labour reproduction has had a specific place in terms of the conjunction of neoliberalism and Islamic conservatism. In this respect, Mingione's (2008, p.281) arguments might also apply for Turkey:

(…) in places where there is excessive familialism the weak state becomes parsimonious; finds it hard to implement reforms and institutional changes nation-wide and to develop services for social welfare and orientation to employment.

Sixth, in this welfare regime, the policies are implemented not on the axis of social citizenship and universal principles, but in regard to charity. Moreover, the state itself refrains from defining these policies in terms of rights. In the Workshop Report (2008) of the SYDGM, it is overtly stated that "if the social assistance extended by the state is recognised as a right it is possible that social assistance might cause an expectation on the part of the beneficiaries, which might ultimately result in the citizens' adjustment to freeloading" (SYDGM, 2008, p. 56). It is apt to argue that this contention is based on a liberal understanding, which accuses the owners of the rights of laziness, and at the same time eschews the possibility that the prioritisation of the rights-based discourse might lead to demand-struggle aspect. Here, Talas' (1997, p.55) arguments are relevant for delineating the difference between rights and assistance from the contemporary social policy perspective:

> Assistance does not qualify as a right. (...) The state's interventions are oriented toward individual poverty and toward individuals. On contrariety, contemporary social policy involves distinct features in a couple of respects. First, it considers not the individual [in solitude] but her/his class. In other words, the measures that it foresees are oriented toward the general, to the working class. Besides, the interventions and regulations that the state realises through legislation have the capacity to create rights. Relying on these rights individuals can make claims from the state and employers.

As a matter of fact, in Turkey the state has been attempting to regulate the space of social assistance within the existing system through the family (see Yeğenoğlu & Coşar's contribution to this volume), and it has been considering the issue of poverty on the basis of charity. The containment of social assistance within the family-charity nexus brings forth the role of the "domestic sphere-familial sphere" in the transformation of the Turkish welfare regime.

Conclusion

During the AKP's rule, the plan to construct a social policy regime encompassing the essences of neoliberalism, conservatism, and Islam has widened the chasm between the rich and the poor by way of promoting the interest of the capitalist class over the interest of the public as a whole. It is certain that this combination of neoliberalism, conservatism, and Islam will not provide acceptable solutions to many vulnerable sectors of the population. Indeed, it seems that the existing social policy regime will result in the diminished welfare of the majority of the population. The regime is expected to expose individuals to the threat of fluctuations more than ever before, in the peripheral capitalist economy of Turkey.

In the 2000s, the AKP's rule has exemplified the restructuring of the labour market towards the wisdom of *precarious work* by informalizing the market through increased sub-contracting opportunities, contractual and temporary workers, and by minimising the privileges of the industrial wage workers in the formal sector by restricting their wages and their rights. To conclude, it is clear that labour regulations, democratic organisations, and workers' rights and quality of life are not compatible with the coercive imperatives of the AKP's social policy regime.

Actually, this so-called social policy regime is built on the prioritisation of the free market *vis-á-vis* the society. To put it differently, in line with neoliberal requisites the free market is not only offered as the best model for social organisation but more than so it is defended in the face of society. This state of affairs leads to the marketisation of social policy spheres.

The ones who fail to compete with the market rationality are re-invited into the market *via* charity-cum-social assistance programmes. This structure presupposes and calls for the negation of labour-human-rights axis from the social policy sphere, replacing it by individual as consumer in a communitarian structure.

All in all, Turkey's entire society faces the unregulated and uncushioned effects of the AKP's social policy regime. Living in endemic insecurity separates the workforce from a kind of identity and autonomy that would be capable of building new strategies for resisting class conflict and alienation, social exclusion, political indifference, and individualised survival strategies, which are likely to be realities for the majority of the population.

REFERENCES

Ağartan, T. (2005). "Health sector reform in Turkey: Old policies new politics" Retrieved June 15, 2009 from ESPANET Young Researchers website: http://www.cevipof.msh-paris.fr/rencontres/jours/200509-ante/palier/clegg/YR_papers/Agartan.pdf

Ansal, H., Küçükçifçi, S., Onaran, Ö. & Orbay, B. Z. (2000). *Türkiye emek piyasasının yapısı ve işsizlik*. İstanbul: Türkiye Ekonomik ve Toplumsal Tarih Vakfı.

Avcuoğlu, Ö. (2009). Belediyeler ve sosyal yardımlar üzerine. *Birikim*, 241, 21-24.

Buğra, A. & Keyder, Ç. (2006). The Turkish welfare regime in transformation. *Journal of European Social Policy, 16* (3), 211-228.

Büyükşehir Ankara (2009). Büyükşehir'den 265 bin aileye yaşam desteği. Ankara: Ankara Büyükşehir Belediyesi Yayını.

Coşar, S. & Yeğenoğlu, M. (2009). The Neoliberal restructuring of Turkey's social security system. *Monthly Review 60* (11), 34-47.

Elveren, A.Y. (2008). Social security reform in Turkey: A critical perspective. *Review of Radical Political Economics, 40* (2), 212-232.

Erder, S. (2004). Geçiş toplumları nereye?' 'yeni' yoksulluk ve 'yeni' modeller. *Kızılcık*, 42, 32-37.

George, V. & Miller, S, (1994). *Social Policy Towards 2000*. London: Routledge.

Government of Turkey (2004). *Hükümetin sosyal politikaya yaklaşımı ve yoksulluğu azaltmaya yönelik uygulamalar*. Ankara.

Güler, B. A. (2006). Sosyal devlet ve yerelleşme. *Memleket Siyaset Yönetim* (2), 14-35.

Hayek, F. (1994). *The Road to Serfdom: The Fiftieth Anniversary Edition*, New York: NY First Editions, Rare & Signed Books.

Heyneman, S. (2004). *Islam and Social Policy*. Nashville: Vanderbilt University Press.

Hyman, R. (2004). "An emerging agenda for trade unions." Retrieved August 16, 2008 from International Labor Organization website: www.ilo.org/public/english/bureau/inst/research/network/hyman.html

Işıklı, A. (2003). *Gerçek örgütlenme: sendikacılık*. Ankara, İmge.

Kepenek, Y. & Yentürk, N. (2011) *Türkiye ekonomisi*, İstanbul: Remzi Kitabevi.

Koray, M. (2000). *Sosyal politika*. Bursa: Ezgi Kitabevi Yayınları.

Lomeli, E. V. (2008). Conditional cash transfers as social policy in Latin America: An assessment of their contributions and limitations. *Annual Review of Sociology 34*, 475–99.

MacGregor, S. (1999). Welfare, neo-liberalism and new paternalism: three ways for social policy in late capitalist societies. *Capital and Class* (67), 91-118.

Mingione, E. (2008). Güney Avrupa refah modeli ve yoksulluk ve sosyal dışlanmaya karşı mücadele. In A. Buğra & Ç. Keyder (Eds.), *Sosyal politika yazıları* (pp. 218-245). Ankara: İletişim.

Munck, R. (2002). *Globalisation and labour: The new great transformation.* London: Zed Books.

Munck, R. & Waterman, P. (Eds.). (1999). *Labor Wordwide in the Era of Globalisation: Alternative Union Models in the New World Order.* London: MacMillan.

Özbek, N. (2002). Osmanlı'dan günümüze Türkiye'de sosyal devlet. *Toplum ve Bilim* (92), 113-125.

Özdemir, A. M. & Yücesan Özdemir, G. (2009). 21. yüzyıl için sosyal politika: mevcut söylemlerin eleştirisi. In P. Esin, İ. Savcı, Ş. Gökbayrak, M. Kart & F. Yıldırım (Eds.), *Sosyal politikada güncel sorunlar* (pp.323-359). Ankara: Ankara Üniversitesi Siyasal Bilgiler Fakültesi Sosyal Politika Araştırma ve Uygulama Merkezi.

Özkan, Ö. (2004). Dünya Bankası Türkiye'de yoksulluğu araştırıyor. *Toplum ve Hekim, 19* (1), 25-32.

Sallan Gül, S. (2002). Türkiye'de yoksulluk ve yoksullukla mücadelenin sosyolojik boyutları: göreliden mutlak yoksulluğa. In Y. Özdek (Ed.), *Yoksulluk, şiddet ve insan hakları* (pp. 109-118). Ankara: TODAİE.

Selçuk, F. Ü. (2002). *Örgütsüzlerin örgütlenmesi: Enformal sektörde işçi örgütleri.* Ankara: Atölye Yayınları.

Sethuraman, S.V. (Ed.). (1984). *The urban informal sector in developing countries.* Geneva: ILO.

Sosyal Yardımlaşma ve Genel Müdürlüğü (SYDGM). (2008). *Faaliyet raporu.* Ankara: T.C. Başbakanlık Sosyal Yardımlaşma ve Dayanışma Genel Müdürlüğü.

SYDGM. (2007). *Sosyal riski azaltma projesi.* Ankara: T.C. Başbakanlık Sosyal Yardımlaşma ve Dayanışma Genel Müdürlüğü.

Türkiye İstatistik Kurumu. (2010). *Hanehalkı işgücü istatistikleri.* Retrieved July 18, 2011 from State Institute of Statistics website:http://www.die. gov.tr/TURKISH/SONIST/ISGUCU/isgucu.html

Türkiye İstatistik Kurumu (2009). *Gelir ve Yaşam Koşulları Araştırması,* Retrieved July 18, 2011 from State Institute of Statistics, website: www.die.gov.tr

Türkiye İstatistik Kurumu. (2002). *Hanehalkı işgücü istatistikleri.* Retrieved July 18, 2011 from State Institute of Statistics website: www.die.gov.tr/english/SONIST/ISGUCU/270502.html

Talas, C. (1997). *Toplumsal politika.* Ankara: İmge.

Tugal, C. (2008). The greening of Istanbul. *New Left Review 51,* 64-80.

World Health Organization (2006). Turkey: Country cooperation strategy at a glance. Retrieved June 10, 2009 from World Health Organization website: http:// www.who.int/countryfocus/resources/ ccsbrief_turkey_tur_06_en.pdf

Yalman, G. (2002). The Turkish state and bourgeoisie in historical perspective: A relativist paradigm or a panoply of hegemonic strategies. In N. Balkan & S. Sarvan (Eds.), *The politics of permanent crisis: Class, ideology and state in Turkey* (pp. 21-54). New York, Nova Science Publishers.

Yalman, G. (2007). Sosyal politika: Refah devletinden sosyal risk yönetimine. In B. Ataman (Ed.), *Cahit Talas anısına, güncel sosyal politika tartışmaları* (pp.655-670). Ankara: Ankara Üniversitesi Siyasal Bilgiler Fakültesi Sosyal Politika Araştırma ve Uygulama Merkezi.

Yazıcı, H. (2009). 2009 mali yılı bütçe sunuş konuşması. Retrieved from SYDGM website: http://www.sydgm.gov.tr/tr/html/65/2009+mali+yi li+bitce+sunus+konusmasi+-+Hayati+YAZICI

Yeldan, E. and Ercan, H. (2011) *Growth, Employment Policies and Economic Linkages: Turkey,* Employment Working Paper no. 84, Geneva: ILO.

Yeldan, E. (2003). Neoliberalizmin ideolojik bir söylemi olarak küreselleşme. In A. H. Köse, F. Şenses & E. Yeldan (Eds.), *İktisat Üzerine Yazılar I: Küresel Düzen: Birikim, Devlet ve Sınıflar* (pp. 427-453). İstanbul: İletişim.

Yücesan-Özdemir, G. and Özdemir, A. M. (2007) Turkey. In C. Phelan (Ed.), *Trade union revitalisation: Trends and prospects in 38 nations* (pp. 461-475). Oxford: Peter Lang.

Zabcı, F. (2009). *Dünya Bankası: Yanılsama ve gerçekler.* İstanbul: Yordam Kitap.

6

THE AKP'S CITIZENISATION PROJECT: WHERE TO?

Nalan Soyarık-Şentürk

Introduction

In May 2009, Turkey's forty-year old citizenship law was changed and a revised citizenship law was proclaimed. In its second term in power (2007-), the AKP saw the change in the citizenship legislation as part of Turkey's attempts to fine tune its legal structure to conform to the European standards. Indeed, the issue of citizenship has mostly been related to the modernisation and westernisation efforts in Turkey, almost since the eighteenth century - during the reform period of the Ottoman Empire (Kahraman, 2005).[102] However, the proclamation of the Republic in 1923 marked a turning point in this reform process. Briefly, it signified the culmination of the Ottoman reforms in respect to citizenship (Soyarık-Şentürk, 2010). At the same time, it also brought about a decisive discontinuity since all the reforms that ensued thereafter would be realised within a republican, and not an imperial setting. In this respect, the history of citizenship in the Ottoman-Turkish context is full of continuities and discontinuities: first, it contained continuities since the whole citizenisation process came out of the attempts at modernisation and westernisation. Second, the republican understanding involved a new understanding of state-society relations, fit for the modern nation-state that would ensure the making up

of a new citizenry in respect of the labour force required for
the world capitalist order. Such an endeavour also contained a
citizenisation process that would dislocate Islam as the moral
basis of social relations, and replace it with the secular capitalist spirit. Yet, the prevalent understanding of citizenship
throughout the republican history has, in itself, contained
contradictions. Briefly, it is possible to observe divergences from the mainstream understanding especially in the
instances of constitutional amendments regarding citizenship
(Soyarık-Şentürk, 2005). In this respect, the AKP's terms in
government are especially illustrative in understanding both
the inner contradictions of republican citizenship in Turkey
and the AKP's understanding that challenges it.

The aim of this chapter is to focus on the AKP governments since the party's induction in 2002, and to analyse
whether they have so far presented an understanding of
citizenship, distinct from the mainstream understanding. In
so doing, the findings are related to the broader context of
neoliberal globalisation process on the one hand, and to the
lingering Turkish-Islamic synthesis on the other. The chapter
is composed of four sections. In the first section, the outlines
of the mainstream understanding of citizenship in Turkey—
i.e., the republican understanding—are briefly discussed.
Then, in the second section, the legal reform process, which
has been presented as an *opening* in relation to the mainstream
understanding, is analysed in order to lay the grounds for
understanding the divergences and continuities in the AKP's
approach to the issue of citizenship. In the third section, the
party's discourse on citizenship is elaborated with a nod to
identity issues. Lastly, in the fourth and concluding section,
the main argument of the chapter in terms of the ambiguity
of the party's approach to citizenship is located within the
neoliberal frame. The underlying question is how so? In other
words, do AKP's discourse and policies related to citizenship

represent an essential departure from the established republican version or not?

The Dominant Understanding of Citizenship in the Turkish Republican Frame

A thorough understanding of the AKP's discursive practices
on the issue of citizenship requires an analysis related to the
neoliberal structuration in Turkey, which had been first implemented during the military interim regime (1980-1983) and
involved a blend of socio-cultural conservatism with pro-free
market economic policies (see Yalman's and Coşar's contributions to this volume). The reflection of this merger in the
understanding of citizenship would come to the governmental
agenda in the late 1990s, especially within the context of
Turkey's accession to the European Union (EU). The AKP's
two terms in government have been significant in the sense
that they can be considered both the final stage of the neoliberal structuration process in Turkey, and the materialisation
of the contradictions in this process. In this respect, the AKP
governments' discursive practices related to citizenship are
exemplary. First, the exclusion of the social aspect from
the official definition of citizenship and its relegation to the
private sphere through the discourse on charity forms attests to
the consolidation of neoliberal structuration in socio-cultural
terms (See Yücesan-Özdemir's contribution to this volume).
Second, the contradictions that are inherent to neoliberal
capitalism can be observed in the reaction of the AKP governments to social opposition in general, and opposition from the
labour movement in particular. Arguing for pluralism as an
asset of its proclaimed (neo)liberal identity the AKP has so
far envisaged the "plural political space" in terms of capital
owning groups, thus excluding, for example, the labour-based
political claims. More briefly, the party has been consistent in

denying the right to oppose through a discourse of citizenisation, based on the otherisation of opposition (Coşar & Özman,
forthcoming). Thus, AKP's citizenisation project challenged
the established republican citizenship understanding. Yet, this
challenge has been, in essence, in line with the requisites of
the neoliberal phase of capitalism in the Turkish context.

To begin with, the AKP's approach and policy implementations regarding citizenship status and practice can be
considered a projection of the debates on the dominant understanding and practice of the Republican regime, which have
occupied the political and academic agenda since the early
1990s. In brief, the Republican regime has been associated
with the Kemalist establishment, which offered the founding
principles for defining the construction of the nation-state
in the early twentieth century. The discussions that ensued,
especially by the 1990s, and that put their mark on the assessments of the AKP's political identity in the past decade,
have been mainstreamed on the basis of a binary opposition
between republicanism and liberalism. Having originated
from within the Islamist political tradition, the AKP has
maneuvered from within the identity politics that marked the
post-1980 period in Turkey. Briefly, the neoliberal structuration process in the Turkish context has worked through the
rise of identity politics, which provided the grounds for the
surfacing of identity issues of the nation-state construction
that had long been suppressed through republican practices.
In this respect, the Kurdish ethnic resurgence, the LGBT and
women's movement, and the Islamist movement have found
the space for re-articulating political claims based on identity issues. The 1990s were marked with the intensification
of violence in both Kurdish ethnic resurgence and the policies offered to come to terms with this resurgence, with the
institutionalisation in LGBT and women's movement and the
transfer of Islamist movement from the civil societal sphere

to political power circles. It is at this point that the cultural clash between republican and liberal approaches to citizenship is revealed. The AKP has so far leaned on this clash by its neoliberal agenda, and through manevouring with recourse to liberal principles. In this respect, Islamist origins of the party has offered available grounds for its discursive practices that favoured the *victim*—victim of suppressive republican policies. However, the AKP's political practices and especially the party's record in terms of citizenship have so far attested to the futility of starting from this binary opposition. Yet, it is apt to note the differences between the republican version of citizenship and the AKP's approach, which might be tentatively named neoliberal.

The foundation period of modern Turkey (1923-1945) was marked with the typical emphasis on the sovereignty of the people during the nation-state construction. With the aim to break the historical ties with the then collapsed Ottoman Empire, the founding fathers of the Republic sought to revitalise the essence of Turkishness as the basis of the individual and collective political identity. Accordingly, Turkishness was defined in terms of the land and the will to national unity (Soyarık, 2000, p.77). This process was accompanied by the steps taken to define a citizen of the Republic, which were directly enmeshed in the efforts to revitalise Turkish national identity. Thus, the construction of citizenship in the early-republican era was an integral endeavor within the construction of the dominant national identity. In this dual process, a modal citizen identity was envisaged, first, in terms of "civilised" and "patriotic" features. While the term "civilised" basically meant one's distance from religion in their political stance and the adoption of a certain life style as a means to counter the Ottoman past, "patriotic" corresponded to the prioritisation of the common good and national interest (Soyarık, 2000, pp.87-88). The founding fathers of the Republic aimed at constructing a new identity for the individual-citizen-as-Turk that involved not only the public sphere with reference to rights and responsibilities—the latter being translated into duties—but also the private sphere—a certain mode of conduct and manners (Soyarık, 2000, p.95).[103] The latter signified the modernizing mission embedded in the republican construction in Turkey, which intended to discipline the people physically and intellectually. One such practice concerned physical education, which was considered an essential part of the education of all citizens. While physical education was made obligatory by the law of physical education (1938), playing sports was also defined as an obligation until the age of 45 (Akın, 2004).

This disciplining process was also related to the corresponding phase of the world capitalist order, which the new Republic was attempting to articulate with. Though capitalism was not new on Ottoman-Turkish lands, the twentieth-century integration process certainly differed from the Ottoman times in terms of its centralised economy of the nation-state, which crosscut the nationalist policies of the republican governments. Side by side with the citizenisation *via* Turkificiation of the people, which fit into the implementation of the nation-state, the disciplinary practices for the construction of the modal citizen identity also involved a capitalist spirit—Taylorism (Arat, 2005, p.18). In this early phase of the Republic, in the official state discourse, class differentiation was denied through a constant call for loyalty to national values and unity, and "work[ing] in solidarity ... towards the same aim and target" (Mesut, [1927]1992, p. 477). Yet, class hierarchy actually worked through the mechanisms of altruism, compassion, complacency, and moderation. Actually, the civilised and patriotic requisites of citizenship were accompanied by a directly societal factor: the citizen was also expected to fit into the middle-class value set. As Kancı (2008, pp.169-170) elaborates, both the physical and emotional criteria required for being "good citizens" involved the imposition of "a puritan work ethic, with emphasis on work and duty ... [while asking for the co-existence of] competitiveness and altruism and benevolence toward the poor." In terms of the phases of the early-Republican articulation into the world capitalist economy–namely, the "reconstruction under the conditions of open economy," (1923-1929) and the "protective statist industrialisation" (1930-1939) (Boratav, 1995, p. 305), the ideal citizen identity stayed constant. Thus, the hardworking and compassionate citizen was the cultural asset for both the policy preferences within the context of "national economy," where the main aim was the creation of national bourgeoisie and also for the policy preferences for building national industry. This necessitated the denial of classes to preempt the strengthening of the labour and the citizenisation policies were functional in this respect. In so doing, the republican cadres relied on corporatism. This preferential frame continued throughout the following decades. The statement by the General Secretary of the CHP, Recep Peker, illustrates the rejections of class politics, vividly: "The Labour Code will sweep away clouds, which enable the birth and survival of class consciousness" (Peker, 1936).[104]

While this early-republican understanding was maintained all throughout the decades until the 1980s, the contours of the citizenisation were extended by the 1960s through the recognition of civil and social rights as natural assets for citizenship. The 1960s witnessed the adoption of import substitution industrialisation policies accompanying an increase in the strength of the labour movement. Yet, this extension in citizenship rights did not last long. The 1971 coup by memorandum and the following 1980 military *coup d'état* curtailed first the civil dimension and then the social dimension of rights. Post-1980 period is especially important in this respect since it marked the beginning of a new period in Turkey's articulation into the world economic order. The neoliberal phase of capitalism that ensued in the Turkish context in the post-1980 period opened the door to a more substantial change compared to that of previous periods, for it asked for the restructuration of the nation-state (see Yalman's and Özdemir's contributions to this volume).

Hindess (2002) argues that the citizenship regime of a country is very much related to what is going on in the international arena, more so than the hypothetical domestic contractual relationship between the state and the citizens. Turkey does not offer an exceptional example in this respect. By the early 1990s, Turkish citizenship fell under scrutiny. Many studies were conducted on the emergence of Turkish citizenship, with the aim of trying to shed light on contemporary debates.[105] Those studies depicted the prevalence of a strong republican understanding of citizenship in the Turkish context. That republican understanding was also identified as the source of various problems regarding the status, rights, and identity dimensions of citizenship (Soyarık, 2000). Various recommendations and suggestions were made, generally emphasising an inclination towards a more liberal, rights-oriented version, or a more Habermasian form of constitutional citizenship (Keyman & İçduygu, 2005; Soyarık-Şentürk, 2005).

The AKP's Challenge to the Republican Citizenship through Neoliberal Identity Politics

At the turn of the twenty-first century, the AKP emerged as a brand new party with a call for change, transformation, and with the claim to determinant leadership. This call also has implications for citizenship matters. The party symbolised a political turn in the sense that it emerged from within an Islamist movement—the *Millî Görüş* (National Outlook movement)—and as such it represented the first political party in Republican history with Islamist roots which could succeed in assuming political power on its own. Additionally, the party also symbolised a turn in the mainstream Islamist political stance with respect to its approach to the "West," which overlapped more with the secularist Kemalist stance rather than the established stance of Islamists. On the other hand, it proposed an effective leadership led by its devotion to democracy by being a majoritarian government.[106] As might be guessed, the status aspect of citizenship has undergone many changes during the past seven years of AKP government. These were mostly the result of the need to conform to the standards set forth by the EU, which can be regarded as the bedrock of the criteria for a liberal understanding of citizenship. This section elaborates on the subject with a view to three dimensions of citizenship, that is, status, rights, and identity aspects. In doing so, I follow the argument set forth by Joppke (2007, pp.37-38), who points to the contemporary changes in citizenship issues by stressing the need to elaborate on all three aspects of citizenship together in order to grasp the issue comprehensively. In this frame, Joppke argues that the status dimension is being liberalised, and that subsequently, naturalisation for immigrants is becoming easier. With respect to the rights dimension, it is noted that while social rights are becoming increasingly undermined, minority rights and non-discrimination principles are moving to the fore. In terms of the identity dimension, Joppke (2007, p.37) argues that "citizenship identities today are universalistic, which limits states' attempts to counter the centrifugal dynamics of ethnically diversifying societies with unity and integration campaigns," and therefore states pursue new ways of generating or sustaining unity and integration. Actually, all three aspects point at the reorganisation of the understanding of citizenship and the related policies within the neoliberal context. More briefly, neoliberal politics hosts the segmentation of citizenship identity into three seemingly separate spheres. This, it does so, through the elimination of the social dimension from the context of the citizenship rights and the relegation of the former to the private sphere. The privatisation of the rights of the citizens is, in turn, managed by an emphasis on the identity aspect. I argue that a similar line of development can also be observed in the Turkish context under the AKP governments. What marks the AKP's case is the peripheral status of the country in the world capitalist system: AKP's citizenisation process takes its share of neoliberal globalisation in the transfer of welfare concerns to the privacy of the individuals—i.e. charity networks—in the form of flexible production and employment strategies in line with foreign capital interests and the liquidification of social security systems with recourse to the calls for minimal state—minimal in public services as an extension of citizenship rights.

The AKP first came to office after the November 2002 elections after getting 34.28 percent of the total votes and winning 368 seats in the Parliament. The party was a relatively young party, established on August 14, 2001 by the so-called "reformist wing" of the *Fazilet Partisi* (Virtue Party, FP) after its imposed closure by the Constitutional Court in 2000. Its political stance at that time had been a debated one. As most of the party members came from the tradition of the *Millî Görüş* or were former members of the banned *Refah Partisi* (1983-1998) (Welfare Party, RP)–FP lineage, the party was and is usually viewed as an Islamist Party, especially among the secularist circles. Although the forerunners of the party repeatedly tried to express that the AKP is "not a religious party," it was accused of disguising its real religious (and/or fundamentalist) aspirations. According to Coşar and Özman (2004), the party might be considered conservative-democratic when its stance on democracy and political and

economic policies are analysed. Also, by aspiring to a position at the center-right, the party defines itself as democratic,
conservative, reformist, and modern.

This mix of adjectives in the party's self-definition can be
explicated in terms of its policies related to the international
sphere, and specifically to Turkey's EU membership process.
Yet, understanding the AKP's pro-EU stance necessitates
connecting it to its neoliberal preferences. According to the
party program, one of the major goals of the party is Turkey's
integration into the EU, which is in fact common to most
of the contemporary political party programs (Öniş, 2000).
Therefore, in line with their conceptualisation of democracy
as "a vision of Turkey where differences are perceived not
as a source of conflict but as richness," they stressed that
the Copenhagen Criteria would be pursued for "the fulfillment of the freedom of thought and expression, lifting the
obstacles which limit freedom of enterprise, transparency in
government, and strengthening of local government" (The
Programme of AKP, 2002; and AKP's Election Manifesto,
2002). This being the de-economised statement of the party's
pro-EU policies, the fact that the EU credentials also ask for
the neoliberal recipe for the free market turns the Europeanisation process into a process of neoliberal citizenisation (for
further elaboration on the EU's neoliberal track see Yeşilyurt-
Gündüz's contribution to this volume).

The AKP has further expressed its intention in terms
of setting the institutional framework "that guaranteed
human rights, secured rule of law, participatory democracy,
secularism, and freedoms of faith and conscience at the
international standards" in the National Program (2003) for
Turkey's accession to the EU. In party discourse, the most
significant project that would ensure reaching those goals is
considered full membership to the EU; therefore Turkey's
desire for integration is interpreted as a social transforma-

tion project. Since the formation of their first government, the AKP has devised five subsequent reform packages, in January 2003, February 2003, July 2003, August 2003, and May 2004, and a constitutional amendment in the hopes of carrying out this project. Those reforms have touched upon issues ranging from the protection of human rights to the financial control of military expenditures. Also, the freedoms of expression, of meeting and demonstration, of association, of cultural rights, and of civilian control over the military have recently been the issues of concern.

In this frame, the permission for community foundations of the non-Muslim minorities to obtain real estates was among the legal amendments of the fourth legislative package, which was the first package of the AKP, issued in January 2003. Also the right to petition was clarified by this package, which was a significant step for the institutionalisation of the principle of accountability. The fifth legislative package was related to the extended possibility of retrial due to the decisions of the European Court of Human Rights, issued on February 2003. Concerning the names given to children, the sixth reform package issued in June 2003 stated that only those names which are not proper to moral codes and which are offensive to the public cannot be given, which signified a major change in the attitude towards Kurdish names (6th Adaptation Laws no. 4978, 15.7.2003). Previously, Kurdish names were banned by article 16 of the Population Law, which was amended in 1972/ 1587, and especially during the 1980s and early 1990s, when the use of the Kurdish language in general was banned (Yeğen, 2006, pp. 67, 68). However, a new limitation on names with this reform package was the requirement to be in conformity with the Turkish alphabet, which in fact covertly aimed at deferring Kurdish names and which displays the limits to the *recognition* of native language rights. On another note, the reference to *mosques* in the Law of Construction was changed to "places of worship" by this package, which was meant to include the churches, synagogues, and the *cemevi* –the places of worship for the Alevi population.[107] The permission to broadcast in languages and dialects other than Turkish was also granted with the change in the Press Law. According to this law, all nationwide radio and TV channels (state/ private) could broadcast in different languages and dialects after being granted permission from the *Radyo ve Televizyon Üst Kurulu* (Higher Board of Radio and Television, RTÜK). Such programs, however, were not to exceed forty five minutes in length per day and four hours weekly on news, music, and traditional culture with Turkish subtitles.

The seventh reform package was issued in July 2003. Its main areas of reform were concerning the status and role of the *Millî Güvenlik Kurulu* (National Security Council, MGK),[108] and the extension of the freedoms of thought, forming associations, and broadcasting. With this law, the MGK was transformed into an advisory body and would be chaired by a civilian secretary general. Also, any public expressions of criticism, which do not aim to insult, deride, or curse would not be sentenced with the new amendment to the Anti-Terror Law and other related laws (see Coşar's contribution for the insufficient nature of the change in the Law on Struggle against Terror). Therefore, the cases of those who were persecuted for their expressions of criticism were thereby either released or acquitted. From there, the eighth package concerned the limitation of the President's powers, closure of the *Devlet Güvenlik Mahkemeleri* (State Security Courts, DGMs) and the elimination of the member of the military from the *Yüksek Öğretim Kurulu* (Board of Higher Education, YÖK). Finally, with another amendment in May 2004, the DGMs were replaced by *Özel Yetkili Mahkemeler* (Regional Serious Felony Courts), and the executive powers of the President were further limited.

The inconsistencies and problems aside, the legal reforms in one sphere led to the need for reforms in other laws as well. For instance, amendments to the Constitution, such as Article 66 clarifying citizenship and safeguarding the equality of genders in terms of law, by eliminating the distinction between mother and father in acquiring citizenship, and reforms and changes in the Civil Code and the like, have aggravated the need for a restructuration of the Citizenship Law. This need has also from time to time been expressed and emphasised by some scholars of law (see Sargın, 2004; Aybar, 2006). Consequently, a bill was introduced to the *Türkiye Büyük Millet Meclisi* (Turkish Grand National Assembly, TBMM) in February 2006, and the resulting law was passed in May 2009, bringing about some profound changes, new adjustments, and even some continuations of the state's understanding of citizenship.

The former Turkish Citizenship Law (Law No. 403/1964) was prepared to meet the standards of the international law on citizenship and in order to clarify who would be considered a "Turkish citizen" (Soyarık, 2000, pp.153-165). Over time, however, the Law No. 403 had been subject to significant changes. The most fundamental of those changes were carried out after the military coup of 1980. We can argue that changes were made in two crucial aspects. One was related to the question of "who deserves membership?" and subsequent legislation introduced a serious denaturalisation of those who were regarded as violating or threatening the internal, external, economic, or financial security of the country (Article 25(g)).This change has caused a denaturalisation process especially effecting the dissidents or leftist groups who had fled the country during the military intervention (fearing the elimination of potential opposition to the September 12 regime in Turkey, which mainly targeted the Left (see Coşar's contribution to this volume). The second aspect reflected an adaptation to the changing circumstances in the international arena. Essentially, the state tried to adjust its legislation in response to the problems encountered by Turkish migrants living abroad. With the amendments made in the early 1980s, Turkish migrants living abroad acquired an opportunity to apply for citizenship in their host countries. It was assumed that naturalisation in host countries would only alter the status of Turkish migrants, meaning that they would still be proponents of the Turkish Republic in their host countries and would thus serve the interests of Turkey. In other words, the Turkish state was more adaptive to the changes in legislation for dual or even multiple citizenship (İçduygu, et al., 1999).

The major reason for the recent preparation of a new law was first and foremost the deterioration of the uniformity of Law No. 403. In addition, changes at the international level became binding over Turkish domestic legislation. In this respect, the European Convention on Nationality provided the basis for the new law. Although Turkey was not one of the signatory countries of the Convention, it was noted that it would occupy the agenda in the near future as part of its accession to the EU. Thus, the principle of non-discrimination for naturalisation, adopting the status of multiple citizenship in legal documents, and the clarification of the naturalisation process with clear-cut procedures were the emphasised premises, which in fact reflect the core of the Convention. In Turkey, the new legislation was viewed mostly as an attempt to solve the problems of Turkish migrants residing abroad and their process of naturalisation in their host countries. As mentioned above, this was a two-decades long process. However, during the parliamentary discussions, the status of the Turkish migrants was the most stressed aspect (Parliamentary Debates, May 28, 2009). In relation to this aspect, the military service question was also hoped to be solved in the new legislation, again in conformity with the Convention.

Therefore, the new law would no longer make people lose their citizenship on the grounds of compulsory military service. More briefly, the requirement to fulfill military service before applying for another country's citizenship or to do so in order to hold Turkish citizenship with another country's citizenship was removed.[109]

Another significant development occurred during the parliamentary discussions, which in fact departed from the rationale of the bill. The bill called for the annulment of Article 3, Article 4 (Ç) and article 6 of the Settlement Law (No. 2510/1934). These articles were devised to make the migration and naturalisation of people of Turkish descent or close to Turkish culture easier. Accordingly, those who are deemed to be anarchists, spies, or who did not adhere to Turkish culture as well as those who were deported would not be admitted as migrants by article 4. The annulment of those articles symbolised a significant departure from the discriminatory practices in the process of naturalisation, and the bill stated that those people of Turkish descent or close to Turkish culture would be treated the same as other foreigners in the naturalisation process by the end of 2010. That is, they would be subject to the same criteria and same residence requirement of five years.

Interestingly, the Settlement Law (Law No. 2510/1934) had already been annulled in 2006 and was then replaced by another Settlement Law (Law No. 5543/2006). The citizenship bill referred to the Settlement Law of 1934 since it had been prepared before the passing of the new law in 2006, which led to problems of clarity. After a swift suggestion of the members of the AKP, the controversial statement that referred to the Settlement Law of 1934 was omitted from the bill. This brings us to an ironical development. On the one hand, the rationale of the new citizenship law was to conform to the principles stated in the Convention and not to discriminate against one group or the other in citizenship matters. Therefore, the reference to the Settlement Law and the annulment of its related articles had a significant meaning. However, with a quick vote on the removal of the statement without any discussion, we again ended up with the Settlement Law 5543/2006, which identifies only those people of "Turkish descent, and/or close to Turkish culture as immigrant" (article3 (d)), and makes naturalisation easier for them (article 8(4)). In this respect and despite the AKP's discourse to the contrary, the new legislation was passed with largely the same discriminatory content.

Yet, the reforms and changes at the legal sphere reflect a turn in the citizenship understanding, though a slight one. As noted above, the main motive behind these particular amendments had been to conform to the standards set forth by the European Commission. This development, on the one hand, reflects the significance of the international context for citizenship issues, in which human rights and neoliberal understanding came to the fore. On the other hand, continuity in the official understanding can be depicted, in which the Turkish state seems very adaptive to the global trends within a certain boundary (see İçduygu et al., 1999). This means that the AKP was adaptive in terms of legal structure to the global trend in citizenship, which, in fact, was the outcome of the developments in migrant-receiving countries.

However, when the amendments are analysed in terms of citizens' rights, one is tempted to focus on the neoliberal frame. Turkey under the AKP governments is not immune to the erosion of social rights, which according to Marshall (1965), was the product of the developments of the twentieth century. However, since the last quarter of the twentieth century the neoliberal capitalist model diminished the extent of social rights all around the globe. The lust for a minimal and effective state stripped the citizens of the safety nets that had been provided by social welfare policies. Yücesan-Özdemir elaborates on this topic in her chapter. Yet, I would like to point to the transformation in the rights dimension towards minority rights and non-discrimination with reference to Joppke's conceptual framework.

The problems and questions over minority issues started to be voiced in a stronger manner in the previous decade. As mentioned above, the legal reforms within the scope of Turkey's accession to the EU referred to safeguarding minority rights. Taken together with the obligations of the Turkish state towards the officially acknowledged minorities in the Lausanne Treaty, which had previously been ignored to some extent, the AKP found itself in the midst of identity claims, which have already been on the rise since the 1990s. It espoused to handle these claims in various ways.

This endeavour has also proven representative of Turkey's commitment to the Copenhagen criteria, which affected especially the series of reforms in the early 2000s. As one of the criteria was related to "respect for and protection of minorities," significant and coherent steps had to be taken on the part of the Turkish governments. For that purpose, the reform packages included new legislation regarding the situation of minorities. However, it should also be noted that the official definition of minorities is limited to the non-Muslim population in a specified manner, or in other words, that Jews, orthodox Greeks, and Armenians are officially recognised as minorities. Other non-Muslims such as the Assyrians, or ethnic minorities with Muslim affiliation, such as Kurds, are not recognised as minorities. On the part of the non-Muslim minorities, it is argued that the AKP government has departed from the security-oriented approach towards a more human rights-oriented one (Soner, 2010). This argument is based on the reform packages, which involved articles related with the inclusion of synagogues and churches, in addition to mosques, as "places of worship." The problems related with the property rights of the community foundations or the questions over the educational rights, or the organisations of the community structures, which have not thoroughly been solved, will not be elaborated in detail in this chapter (for a detailed listing of the reforms concerned see Soner, 2010).

Overall, there are two intertwined developments regarding non-Muslim minorities in Turkey. On the one hand, there is a more human rights-oriented approach at the governmental level. On the other hand, public awareness about minority issues has increased. This is to do especially with the assassination of the Armenian journalist Hrant Dink (2007), who became the spokesperson for the solution of the "Armenian problem" through first the recognition of the problem and then mutual dialogue. On the eve of his assassination, Dink was tried on the accusation of "insulting Turkishness." Thousands mourned and asked for justice in his funeral. In the meantime, the government fell short of reforming its legislation. This is a reflection of the hesitancy on the part of the AKP governments in terms of setting the necessary legal grounds for the implementation and realisation of minority rights. In other words, and in parallel to trends throughout the world in terms of human rights and the recognition of identity claims, the government made promises, and made some profound legal changes. However, in terms of practice, not much has been achieved. In this respect, the positive outcomes of the past decade might be due to the slight emphasis on the recognition of difference at the governmental level, yet the approach towards difference is not so different from the legacy of the Ottoman Empire, which divided the population along religious lines. For the time being, the AKP governments can be thought of as walking on a tightrope between their prioritisation of Turkish-Muslim identity as the basis of their national appeal, on the one hand, and their self-proclaimed allegiance

to universal human rights standards as a proof of their democratic stance, on the other hand.

One other issue related to identity claims is the Kurdish
question. Seemingly in response to this issue, the government
introduced a "Democratic Opening" process in 2010, giving
rise to hopes for the end of the armed struggles between the
Turkish Armed Forces and the *Partiya Karkerên Kurdistan*
[Kurdistan Workers' Party] - PKK). The *Demokratik Açılım
Kitabı* (The Book of Democratic Opening, January 2010)
released by the AKP might aptly be considered the main
source for understanding this process. According to the party,
the Democratic Opening stood for furthering democracy and
economic improvement, not only for the Kurdish people,
but also for minorities in general and Alevites in particular.
The aspiration that underlined the process was relatively
extensive in that the government expressed its aim for "total
development," which they hoped would also resolve many
socio-economic problems. Apart from this aspiration, the
AKP's views expressed in the book actually recall the early-
republican will to institute and maintain a sense of belonging
to the nation as a decisive feature of the ideal citizen: "common
history, culture, civilisation, … , flag, fate, and ideals making
us brothers" (p.3). In this respect, "socio-economic development" is articulated into the project of the "acknowledgment
of the natural rights of our citizens" (p. 70), through the
citizenship law, which the AKP names as the "brotherhood
law" (p. 62). Here, one should instantly note the emphasis on
national unity and the organicised reading of national ties, not
only in relation to the dominant understanding and practice
of citizenship in the early-republican era, but also in relation
to the Turkish-Islamic synthesis as one definitive feature of
the socio-political space in post-1980 Turkey (see Coşar's
contribution to this volume). Besides, the party's discourse,
which at times involves the prioritisation of the unifying

function of Islam among the Turks and the Kurds as attested to in Erdoğan's statement stressing "the same prayer... and the same religious community" (Demokratik Açılım Kitabı, p.77) points more to the direction of a religious-conservative approach in identity issues when the Kurdish issue is at stake, rather than a democratic approach based on identity rights. The Democratic Opening process was launched with an extensive announcement, and is still referred to when relevant issues come to the agenda. However, the content of the process is quite vague and the rhetoric does not differentiate the present from the early republican documents by referring to common history, culture, and ideals.[110] Also, the reference to the indivisibility of the unitary state through recurrent emphasis on "one state, one nation, one homeland, one flag" (p.16) is similar. This emphasis can also be read as the AKP's fragile balance between its appeals to the international community with a liberal-democratic discourse and its interactions with the majority of its electoral base, which is defined, certainly, on the basis of conservative-national values. This balance should be analysed in parallel to the AKP's claim to distance itself from the traditionalised official approach to the Kurdish issue in particular, and identity issues in general, merely on the basis of state security concerns, and also to the party's inability and/or reluctance to clarify the distinctiveness of its approach.

In this respect, it is Joppke's approach to the identity dimension as the third dimension of citizenship that guides research to the current developments concerning citizenship. According to Joppke (2007, p.46), the state tries to cope with identity problems "... with centripetal campaigns for unity and integration, which, however, have to be conducted in a universalistic idiom." The Democratic Opening Process seems like a vain effort to address the identity claims. It is an effort in vain in the sense that the process does not contain

the substantial steps to be taken, but rather aspires to intro-
duce a universalistic rhetoric, with Turkish citizenship as an
umbrella notion for the diverse identities across the population in Turkey.

Conclusion

The AKP's rise to power in 2002 raised hopes among diverse
social segments for a new citizenship understanding, moving
beyond the republican version of citizenship. This chapter has
tried to highlight those developments within a broader framework of the consolidation of the neoliberal capitalist model.
As argued above, the current trends at the international level
also find room for themselves in the domestic context. The
status aspect of citizenship in Turkey is being liberalised in
the new millenium, largely due to its articulation within the
frame of Turkey's accession to the EU. Therefore, rights and
freedoms in the liberal sense are being granted from above
once again. As far as the human rights aspect of citizenship
is concerned, while social rights are increasingly becoming a
neglected area, the minority rights –either in terms of recognition or claims- have grown more visible. However, this does
not mean that the AKP is eager to *recognise* the reality of
distinct ethnic or religious minorities. Rather, it is again part
of the neoliberal process, in which those claims have acquired
a universal character. Therefore, suppressing or undermining
those claims would no longer represent an acceptable attitude. Yet, the neoliberal ordering of things also provide the
grounds for the segmentation of different aspects of citizenship claims, thus absorbing the claims themselves into the
dominant discourse. In this respect, the party's approach to
the "Kurdish issue", outlined above is an example as far as
the identity-based rights claims are concerned. Likewise,
the AKP's dealing with the claims for social righs through

suppressive and/or otherising mechanisms, as attested in its reaction to the opposition to the flow of privatisation process also symbolises the neoliberal pre-emption of any possible systemic opposition. Thus, the reluctance of the AKP towards a significant solution is evident in its projects and suggestions, which remain flawed and unfounded. Yet, this is the *global way to do things* and in its aspirations of integration into the global world, the AKP has in truth, few choices, since it stands as the peripheral carrier of the neoliberal dictate over the economies. Finally, we can argue that what the AKP has done so far in terms of citizenship fits quite well into the neoliberal framework, yet it is also in limbo by trying to strike a balance between the requirements of this neoliberal framework and satisfying its religious-conservative yet nationalist electoral basis, which it tries to stall through the liberal legitimation of the capitalist order.

REFERENCES

Adalet ve Kalkınma Partisi programı (2002). Ankara: AKP.

AK Parti seçim beyannamesi. (2002). Ankara: AKP.

Akın, Y. (2004). *"Gürbüz ve yavuz evlatlar": Erken cumhuriyet'te beden terbiyesi ve spor.* İstanbul: İletişim.

Berkes, N. (1964). *The Development of Secularism in Turkey.* Montreal: McGill University.

Coşar, S. & Özman, A. (forthcoming). Neoliberal Politics, state and privatization in Turkey: The case of TEKEL. In J. Paulson, C. Fanelli, C. Lefebvre and G. Özcan (Eds.), *Capitalism and confrontation: Critical perspectives.* Ottawa: Red Quill Books.

Coşar, S. & Özman, A. (2004). Centre-right politics in Turkey after November 2002 general elections: Neo-Liberalism with a Muslim face. *Contemporary Politics, 10* (1), 57-74.

Davison, R.H. (1963). *Reform in the Ottoman Empire 1856-1876.* Princeton, New Jersy: Princeton University Press.

Demokratik açılım kitabı. (2010). Retrieved June 10, 2011 from http://www.demokratikacilimkitabi.com

Habermas, J.(1994). Struggles for recognition in the democratic constitutional state. In A. Gutmann (Ed.), *Multiculturalism: Examining the Politics of Recognition* (pp. 107-148). Princeton: Princeton University Press.

Heper, M. (2006). *Türkiye sözlüğü: Siyaset, toplum ve kültür* (Z. Mertoğlu, Trans.) Ankara: Doğu Batı.

Hindess, B. (2002). Neoliberal citizenship. *Citizenship Studies, 6* (2), 127-143.

İçduygu, Ahmet, (1996). Türkiye'de vatandaşlık kavramı üzerine tartışmaların arka planı. *Diyalog, 1* (1), 134-147.

İçduygu, A., Çolak, Y., & Soyarık N. (1999). What is the matter with citizenship? – A Turkish debate. *Middle Eastern Studies, 35* (4), 187-208.

İçduygu, A., & Keyman, E. F. (2000). Globalization, security and migration: the case of Turkey. *Global Governance, 6* (3), 383-398.

Joppke, C. (2007). Transformation of citizenship: status, rights, identity. *Citizenship Studies, 11* (1), 37-48.

Kahraman, H. B. (2005). The cultural and historical foundation of Turkish citizenship: modernity and Westernization. In E.F. Keyman, & A. İçduygu (Eds.), *Citizenship in a Global World: European Questions and Turkish Experiences* (pp. 70-86). London and New York: Routledge.

Keyman, E.F. and İçduygu, A. (2005). Introduction: Citizenship, identity, and the question of democracy in Turkey. In E.F. Keyman, & A. İçduygu (Eds.), *Citizenship in a Global world: European Questions and Turkish Experiences* (pp. 1-27). London and New York: Routledge.

Marshall, T.H. (1965). *Class, Citizenship and Social Development.* Garden City, New York: Anchor Books, Doubleday and Company.

Nermi, M. (1928, June 8). Yaşar'a mektuplar. *Hayat* IV(80), 24 reprint in M. Kaplan, E. Enginün, N. Birinci, & Z. Kemran (Eds.) (1992). *Atatürk devri fikir hayatı 2* (pp.487-491). Ankara: Kültür Bakanlığı Yayınları.

Ortaylı, İ. (1995). *İmparatorluğun en uzun yüzyılı.* İstanbul: Hil.

Öniş, Z. (2000). Neoliberal globalization and democracy paradox. *Journal of International Affairs, 54* (1), 283-306.

Parliamentary debates, speech of Beşir Atalay, Minister of Interior Affairs, 23rd Period, May 28, 2009 Retrieved June 11, 2010 from http://www.tbmm.gov.tr/develop/owa/tutanak_g_sd.birlesim

Peker, R. (1936). Cited in Toprak, Z. (1998). *Bir yurttaş yaratmak: muasır bir medeniyet için seferberlik bilgileri 1923-1950.* İstanbul: Yapı Kredi Kültür Sanat Yayıncılık.

Sargın, F. (2004). Türk vatandaşlığı kanununda değişiklik yapan 2003 tarihli ve 4866 sayılı kanun kapsamında bir değerlendirme. *AUHF, 53* (1), 27-63.

Soner, B. A. (2010). The Justice and Development Party's policies towards non-Muslim minorities in Turkey. *Journal of Balkan and Near Eastern Studies. 12* (1), 23-40.

Soyarık, N. (2000). *The citizen of the State and the State of the Citizen: an Analysis of the Citizenization Process in Turkey.* (Unpublished Ph.D. Thesis). Bilkent University, Turkey.

Soyarık-Şentürk, N. (2005). Legal and constitutional foundations of Turkish citizenship: changes and continuities. In E.F. Keyman, & A. İçduygu (Eds.), *Citizenship in a Global world: European Questions and Turkish Experiences* (pp.124-143). London and New York: Routledge.

Soyarık-Şentürk, N. (2010). Vatandaşlığın imparatorluk kökleri: Osmanlı'ya bakmak. *Doğu Batı* (54), 121-137.

Üstel, F. (2004)."*Makbul vatandaş*"*ın peşinde: II. Meşrutiyet'ten bugüne vatandaşlık eğitimi.* İstanbul: İletişim.

Yeğen, M. (2006). *Müstakbel Türk'ten sözde vatandaşa: Cumhuriyet ve Kürtler.* İstanbul: İletişim.

7

THE AKP AND THE GENDER ISSUE: SHUTTLING BETWEEN NEOLIBERALISM AND PATRIARCHY

An earlier version of this study was published in the May 2011 i*First edition of the South European Society & Politics*(May 2011). The study was published in print form of the journal's December 2011 issue [*16* (4)] (December 2011).

Metin Yeğenoğlu & Simten Coşar

Introduction

As the AKP's third term in government has started in Summer 2011 the discussions that basically center on the party's political identity continue. As explicated in the contributions to this volume, actually, there is one constant theme for defining the party that is beyond discussion: "neoliberalism with a Muslim face" (Coşar & Özman, 2004). It is the aim of this chapter to elaborate on the reflections of this thematic continuity in the AKP's a decade long governmental experience on the established pattern of gendered politics in republican Turkey. In this respect, the chapter first takes issue with the developments regarding women's rights under the AKP governments. In so doing, we also touch upon the significance of women's rights/ feminist activism for the developments concerned. In the second part, we outline the historical background to the current political position of the women's movement in Turkey. In the third part, we locate the AKP's approach to the women's issues into the patriarchal pattern that has characterised republican Turkey. In the fourth and concluding part, we offer a brief account of the new version of patriarchy that characterises the AKP's gendered policies.

The chapter starts from the argument that the AKP's three terms in government (2002-7; 2007-2011; 2011-) have witnessed increasing conservatisation in social, cultural and political spheres. The party's approach to the women's issues can be considered a testament to this process. However, this conservatisation in terms of women's issues shall not be identified with the pro-Islamist origins of the party. Rather, it should be considered as a neoliberal version of the patriarchal structure that permeates almost all political tendencies in Turkey. In this version, national and religious political priorities are synthesised in a neoliberal frame. As Coşar in her contribution to this volume outlines, Turkey's neoliberalisation process has so far depended on a fine synthesis among nationalist and religious motifs on the socio-cultural plane—i.e., the Turkish-Islamic synthesis. In line with this synthesis, it is not only the AKP but all the governments in the post-1980 period adopted an economically liberal, yet culturally conservative discourse, characteristic of neoliberal times worldwide. Briefly, the liberal-conservative discourse involved both an emphasis on individual rights and liberties and a call for preserving the cultural characteristics of Turkishness. In this respect, the AKP represents the last phase of the consolidation of the fine-tuning between individualism in the market place and preservation of communal traits of the Turkish society. Apart from this consolidation, what makes the AKP an interesting case in point is its Islamist origins. As for the women's issues, the party's policies represent both an ambivalent pattern as well as a well-established disposition that reproduces women's subordination. The ambivalence arises out of the party's initial tendency to get into dialogue with civil society organisations in general and women's rights organisations in particular while at the same time preserving and at times deepening its conservative approach to gender. It can also be observed in the party's rather irregular and arbitrary adjustment to the demands of women's rights organisations during a series of amendments within the scope of Turkey's accession to the European Union (EU).

Between the Rhetoric of "Women-friendliness" and Anti-feminist Discourse

The results of the 2011 general elections not only reinforced the AKP's power at the ballot box but also it gave rise to the highest percentage of women in the parliament throughout Republican history (1923 -). Women got 78 seats in the parliament, thus increasing their parliamentary share to 14.18 percent for the first time. Likewise, the AKP's first and second terms in office (2002-2007; 2007-2011) also witnessed a series of legal amendments in favor of women's rights. The reforms were made within the scope of Turkey's accession to the EU, through which the women's rights/feminist organisations have had active lobbying and pressure opportunities for gender-sensitive legal amendments.[111]

Examples in this respect are the amendments to the Turkish Penal Code (2004), the regulation that obliges the municipalities with more than 50,000 inhabitants to open women's shelters, the formation of the *TBMM Kadın Erkek Fırsat Eşitliği Komisyonu* (Parliamentary Commission for the Equality of Opportunity for Women and Men). As far as the Turkish Penal Code is concerned, sexual crimes were recognised as the 'crimes against individuals/crimes against the inviolability of sexual integrity' (WWHR 2005, p. 14); the provisions enabling the rapists to escape from legal punishment in case they marry to the victim were lifted up; and new provisions to preempt discrimination against unmarried-yet-non-virgin women were included into the body of the Code. In dealing with violence against women the AKP government issued a decree signifying the recognition of opening women's shelters as part of public service. Though recognised at the status of decree this development is important in that it points at the recognition of domestic violence as a political issue—long sought by the women's movement. Lastly, though contested by the feminist organisations due to the inclusion of the phrase, "equality of opportunity" into its title, the formation of a parliamentary body for ensuring gender equality also provides grounds for the institutionalisation of gender issues.

These acts might convey one to assume that the AKP has so far presented a "women-friendly" profile. Obviously, these are not sufficient to name the AKP as a pro-women's rights political party. This is especially so when one considers the party's response to feminist demands coming from within the women's movement in Turkey. Exemplary in this respect is the government's reluctance to include affirmative action as a constitutional provision as well as to amend the Electoral Law and Law on Political Parties both in the way of decreasing the electoral threshold (10 percent) and making it compulsory to include gender quota in party statutes.[112] These deficiencies aside, the positive developments regarding women's rights, especially in the legal sphere attest a discontinuity in respect to the approach to gender relations within the frame of political Islam insofar as the AKP has emerged out of the *Millî Görüş* movement. At the same time, they point at a discontinuity in respect to the established version of the patriarchal structure in republican Turkey. In other words, looked through the feminist lenses one can note the shifts in the mode of the patriarchy that marked the republican history rather than a major transformation.

To start with, as also acknowledged by the majority of women's rights organisations in Turkey, though the new Penal Code embodies provisions that represent important corrections in terms of gender discrimination, it still falls short of involving a substantial interference to gender-based inequality.

For example, the demands coming from the women's movement, which address "the definition of honor crimes ... as aggravated homicide; the penalisation of discrimination based on sexual orientation; the criminalisation of virginity testing under all circumstances; and the extension of the legal abortion period from 10 to 12 weeks," have so far been ignored (WWHR 2005, p. 15). Similarly, although the amendment to the Law on Municipalities, which made the opening of shelters for women who are subjected to domestic violence obligatory for the metropolitan municipalities and municipalities with more than 50.000 inhabitants, was enacted on July 2005, as of October 2009, the total number of women's shelters was recorded 54 (see Coşar & Yeğenoğlu, 2011). When the fact that as of 2009, the number of municipalities whose population exceeds 50.000 was 244 and that of the shelters operated by the municipalities was just 19, one cannot conclude that the positive developments regarding women's issues hint at a substantial pro-gender equality stance (Coşar & Yeğenoğlu, 2011). Lastly, the insistence of the AKP government to name the parliamentary commission on gender equality along a pro-"equality of opportunity" perspective further gives clues about the party's approach to the women's issues. The name of the commission was adopted despite the rejections from the feminist organisations, which have long demanded the formation of a Parliamentary Commission on Gender Equality, thus restricting the sphere of commission to a concern with equality of opportunity. At a time, when the equality of opportunity principle has long been questioned and when extensions have been proposed to the notion of equality—as in the case of the claim to "parity democracy" (Stratigaki, 2005)—in feminist literature and activism (see for example, Eisenstein 1982; Elliott 1984) this insistence recalls the tendency to control the shift in patriarchal boundaries. It can also be considered in terms of the new rightist feature of the AKP's identity.

It is possible to relate the AKP's gender policies to new
right politics, certainly, with overwhelmingly Islamic motifs.
The AKP's approach to the women's issues differs from
the *Millî Görüş* movement. This is especially so in terms
of the party's enthusiasm for women's public visibility and
its discursive preferences for dialogue with civil society
in general and women's rights organisations in particular.
Though women's political activism is not new to the Turkish
context, what marks the AKP as a case in point is the nature
of this activism. In the *Millî Görüş* tradition Islamist women's
political visibility was mostly restricted to electoral politics—in the *kitchen* of electoral politics and/or in reaching
to conservative women voters (Çakır, 2000, pp. 14-18). In
the case of the AKP the women found the grounds for more
visibility in regular local and parliamentary politics (Ayata
& Tütüncü 2008, pp. 382; Çıtak & Tür 2008, pp. 455-469).
This shift in the religious-conservative gender politics can be
understood both in terms of the "post-Islamist" identity of the
party (Dağı, 2007, p.107) and also in terms of the hegemonic
new rightist preferences that have marked the politics in post-
1980 Turkey (Tünay, 1993; see also Yalman's and Coşar's
contributions to this volume). In parallel to the moment
that it signified for Turkey's experience with neoliberalism
the AKP's coming to power also accompanied a moment in
the history of women's movement in Turkey. Briefly, by the
2000s one can note the consolidation of neoliberal hegemony
in the country that started with the 1980s, the increase in civil
societal activism starting with the 1990s, in which feminist
activism has occupied a significant place, and the speeding up
of the process of Turkey's accession to the EU, starting with
the late 1990s. From a feminist perspective these juxtapositions involved clashes among alternative modes of patriarchy,
namely, republican patriarchy, liberal patriarchy, and neoliberal-conservative patriarchy.

The republican patriarchy hegemonised the discourse on women's emancipation until the late 1980s. The underlying claim was that republican politics emancipated the Turkish women from the clutches of tradition–connoting Ottoman Empire and Islamic way of life–and made them equal citizens of the Republic (Berktay, 2001, pp. 348-361). This mode of patriarchy worked through the then state ideology; Kemalism. Through the gender related reforms, enacted within the Kemalist frame, women got the economic and political rights they had been demanding since the late Ottoman period (Çakır, 1994). Likewise, they got the opportunity for more public visibility, compared to the pre-republican context. It is in this respect that gendered policies pursued with a Kemalist stance have been perceived in terms of "state feminism" (Tekeli, 1986, p. 193; White, 2003). Naturally, the experience with state feminism did not amount to a break with patriarchy. Rather, it signified a transformation within patriarchal limits "from the absolute sovereignty of the father to the republic of brothers" (Berktay, 2001, p. 356). In this respect, in the attainment and use of the rights they got in the republican context, the women had to "bargain with patriarchy" (Kandiyoti, 1988) through loyalty to the republican morals, which first and foremost placed them as (potential) wives and/or mothers. The motherhood was not restricted to the actual state of mothering but also, and more importantly, it has worked symbolically. The metaphor of "national motherhood" (Coşar, 2007; Sirman, 2005, p. 163) is explanatory in this respect: Having children or not have been assumed as part and parcel of the same category–i.e. women have been perceived as mothers either of their genetic or of symbolic children–i.e., the nation–or both.

The second mode of patriarchy—liberal patriarchy—has permeated the women's movement in Turkey starting with the 1990s. In this version, the wifehood and motherhood roles—

as the essentials of womanhood in republican patriarchal imagination—are seemingly disconnected from the public sphere. In other words, in the liberal mode these roles are restricted to the sphere of private issues. In this respect, it is assumed that the *essential roles*, supposed to be ingrained in the womanhood, would not disrupt women's public partici-pation. This assumption though bringing in new opportunity spaces for women to get their claims in the political and social spheres also carried the potential to marginalise the hardships that only women experience by turning a blind eye to the connections between the public and the private.[113] Briefly, for the liberal approach, the recognition of women as equal individuals with men would be sufficient in chal-lenging the republican hindrance to women's liberation. This contention bears the risk of overlooking the reproduction of patriarchal modes in different styles. For example, from a liberal perspective, women's liberation is not understood in terms of the elimination of the motherhood role from the defi-nition of womanhood. Rather, the integration of the principle of choice into the discourse on motherhood is accredited as the liberating force, which also gets the women out of the box of national motherhood. In contemporary Turkey, it is possible to note the conflation of this version of patriarchy with the other two versions so long as it carves a distinct space for itself mainly in the market place, and aims, first and foremost, at getting women into the free market. Thus, it flirts with the other two versions by arguing for women as equal individuals, and ignoring the masculinist mark in the category of the individual as well as in the concept and practice of choice itself.

The third mode of patriarchy, which can tentatively be named as neoliberal-conservative patriarchy as it took hold in the Turkish context, we argue, characterises the AKP's period in government, and explains the ambiguity in the party's

gendered politics. It is widely accepted that neoliberal times
have brought in a gradual backlash for the feminist movement
worldwide. In the hegemonic discourse that characterised the
neoliberal political space since the mid-1970s backlash was
forged through a consistent attack on the feminists as the
main *instigators* for moral corruption. The divergences along
the women's rights/feminist movements also had the side
effect of reinforcing this attack. Briefly, feminists have been
accused of reinforcing the dissolution of the then traditionalised nuclear family and thus deepening moral degeneration
in the society. For the neoconservative approach, which does
not have a major problem with the neoliberal political order,
the progress in women's rights that carved out a relatively
independent socio-economic space for women was considered to be one of the main reasons behind the dissolution
of the family. In other words, the feminists were accused
of playing against the nature, playing against the morals of
the society, disrupting the natural order of the family. In this
stance, the neoconservatives also manipulated the neoliberal
zeal to eliminate the social welfare state policies. The rise in
the number of single-parent households, unmarried women,
and in divorce rates has been manipulated by the rightist
governments of neoliberal times in their justification of the
neoliberal economic policies. Thus, the anti-feminist argument was articulated into the attack on the social/welfare
state. Hence, both the feminist claims and the rights-based
policies of the social state were read as means for the *castra-
tion* of the male head of the household (Eisenstein, 1982, pp.
567-588; Mitchell and Goody, 1997; Heath, 1997).

   The new moment of capitalism that was characterised by neoliberalism invited a new moment of patriarchal
configuration, certainly with a considerable dose of conservative morals, built on the sanctity of the tradition, faith and
family values (Mitchell&Goody, 1997; Romito, 1997). In

this respect, the neoliberal-neoconservative alliance, though seemingly contradictory, functioned harmoniously in countering the socio-political setting of the welfare state. Briefly, the neoliberal order involved the dissolution of the social rights, embraced in welfare state practices. In so doing, it first and foremost leaned on the sanctity of property rights. The neoconservatives, on the other hand, though criticizing the libertarian cultural stance of the neoliberals (Wolfson, 2004, pp. 213-231; Wilson and Kelling, 2004, pp. 149-166) shared the emphasis on private property, as one of the building blocks of the family, and the family as the moral pillar of society. Thus, in this alliance the neoliberal prioritisation of individual as *homo oeconomicus* was smoothly merged with the neoconservative re-moralisation of private property *via* the emphasis on the sanctity of the family.

The implications of this seemingly contradictory alliance for women's public participation are revealed by a closer look at the new mode of capitalist patriarchy. It is certain that neoliberal-conservative patriarchy can act as a medium for women's increased participation in the economic sphere. Yet, this effect does not necessarily mean to serve for gender equality since in this alliance one cannot talk about a tendency to eliminate women's subordination. On the contrary, women are vulnerable to further subordination through labour policies that dismiss social rights (Coşar & Yeğenoğlu, 2009). Within the frame of this new mode of patriarchy the women might simultaneously be required to participate in labour force and to stay at home. In other words, they are called for adjusting to the flexible market conditions, while at the same time keeping track of their normalised wifehood and motherhood roles. Since the working of the neoliberal order involves the prioritisation of workfare over welfare—actually, individualizing the latter and making it dependent on the former—the female labour force is considered to be the most practical means to resort to in the running of the flexible market space. Put differently, because women are traditionally underprivileged in worklife and they experience double poverty compared to the male labour force they are more easily *forced into* the labour market in return of almost no social rights. Thus, it has been less cumbersome for the neoliberal policy makers to manipulate and/or to overlook the rights-based demands of the women labour force (Bergeron, 2001). First, because of their double disadvantage—due to gender and class-based exploitation—women turn out to be the most available employees for the neoliberal policy makers in that they can be easily employed in low wage jobs with minimum or no benefits, and equally easily dismissed. Second, since partici-pation of women into the flexible market does not eliminate the prioritisation of familial responsibilities, the justification for their dismissal from the labour market finds comfortable grounds in the reference to the significance of the family for the society. In this sense, the exploitation of women through exclusion from the labour market is transformed into exploi-tation through partial/flexible inclusion without almost any security concern (Toksöz, 2002, p.198).[114]

The AKP's neoliberal patriarchy is in line with the neoliberal-conservative alliance. Certainly, its structure, working and strategies shall be elaborated on the basis of the contextual dynamics that accompanied Turkey's articula-tion into the neoliberal world order. Such an elaboration asks for including two factors into the analysis: the increase in the public effectivity of Islamist politics and the rise of the women's movement within the course of the rising tide of civil societalism. In this respect, the harmonious co-existence of certain attributes, which seem to be mutually exclusive, in the AKP's discursive practices, can be understood. More briefly, including the current state of Islamist politics within the scope of the AKP's *non-shariah*, and "post-Islamist" but

yet pro-religion performance, and tracing the (dis)connec-
tions between the mainstream discourse on civil societalism
and women's movement might help one to relocate the fine
synthesis between neoliberalism and Islam in the Turkish
context. At first sight, a pro-religion government, which
has emphasised conservative family values, conceding to
take a positive stance *vis-à-vis* the liberalisation in terms of
women's rights might sound contradictory. However, when
considered with reference to these factors one might reach a
less ambiguous picture that would avoid to readily identify
the AKP governments either in terms of *a* liberal tendency for
dialogue on women's issues or as essential challengers to the
achievements and the demands of the women's movement in
Turkey.

Articulation into and/or Challenging the Neoliberal Aura?: Women's Movement in Turkey's Neoliberal Times

It is not possible to define the AKP's approach to the women
issue exclusively in Islamist, republican, and/or liberal terms
even though it incorporates all of these currents to differing
extents. Thus, one should take into consideration the structural juxtaposition of Islamist, republican and liberal terms
under neoliberal conditions. Doing so necessitates an account
of the intertwining of neoliberal politics with conservative
socio-cultural policies. In this respect, one has to involve in
a multi-dimensional analysis of not only the AKP's political
preferences but also how the women's issues have been articulated into the post-1980 political space in Turkey.

Following the radical reforms during the early-republican era (1923-1945) the women's issues long laid dormant
in Turkish political history. This was partly due to the
established contention among the ruling modernizing (over-

whelmingly) male elite that the reforms had more than satisfied the requisites for women's emancipation from the clutches of traditional, religious patriarchy. Also effective in this was the rather repressive attitude of the early-republican establishment toward any possibility of an independent feminist organisation (Zihnioğlu, 2003). It is certain that in this period women got many of their rights that they had been demanding since the first instances of women's activism in the late-Ottoman period. However, despite the improvements the patriarchal bounds on women continued, though in a different mode (Arat, 1989; 2005).

The foundation period of the Turkish Republic was overwhelmingly characterised by modernisation, secularisation, and the articulation of the socio-political structure to capitalist world economy. In this process, women's voices were not heard yet. Rather, they have been contained within the still developing ideological formations, which would mark the following decades of Turkish political history: Kemalism, Leftism and Islamism (Tekeli, 1986, pp. 192-195; Kadıoğlu, 1998). It was only after the 1980 military intervention that women—mainly from the leftist organisations of the 1970s—would start to voice their demands from an independent feminist perspective. This seems paradoxical since politics was a fiercely authoritarian one, and the military's dominance of the first three years of the 1980s was still in place.

A brief look at the decade helps one to understand the context in which an independent feminist organising emerged. 1980 military *coup d'état*, the most brutal one among the four military interventions in Turkish political history (1960, 1971, 1980, 1997), and one, after which the longest military regime was established, can be considered to mark a critical juncture (Coşar & Özman, 2007). The critical juncture refers to a structural change, backed by the shift in the value system (Scully, 1992, pp. 11-16). The structural change that had already been underway in the political turmoil of the late 1970s was meant to be the transformation from a statist economic and political system to a neoliberal one. The three years long military rule was functional in two respects. First, it ensured the narrowing down of the political space so as to eliminate any possible opposition. In the meantime, it legitimised authoritarian measures on the basis of a concern for stability. Second, it set the appropriate grounds for the transformation from state-centric economic sphere to a neoliberal one. As for the change in the value system, a version of Turkish nationalism, known with reference to the Turkish-Islamic synthesis, was both espoused by the rulers of the interim regime and also adopted by the ensuing centre-right governments after the transition to civilian rule. Actually, the synthesis that had the largest share in the content of the value system, which would dominate the post-1980 period in Turkey, was not a new formula. It was devised and claimed by a group of nationalist intellectuals with organic ties to the extreme nationalist *Milliyetçi Hareket Partisi* (Nationalist Action Party, MHP) of the 1970s (Poulton, 1999, pp. 220ff). The synthesis involved an argument for a historically constructed organic connection between Turkish-ness and Muslimhood. The military's preference on the side of the synthesis can be read as an attempt to forge societal consent. The preference on the part of the ensuing civilian governments of the mid- and late 1980s, on the other hand, can be related to their patchwork identities whose main parts were made up of cultural conservatism and economic liber-alism (see Coşar's contribution to this volume).

The feminists who initiated the first steps of feminist organising did so in times of such a critical juncture. They were keen on dressing in an apolitical style due to the ongoing restrictions on political rights (Tekeli in Özman, 2008). In parallel, both at that time and afterwards, when the bans on political activity were gradually lifted up, the governments for a while did not consider them seriously, which led to relative independence in the gathering of the activists, and subsequently, in the maturing of the feminist movement in Turkey. Thus, the decade, following the military *coup d'état,* hosted two rather contradictory developments in the socio-political space: Increasing conservatisation in the social sphere and institutionalisation of women's activism. These two contradictory developments can be understood with reference to the pragmatic politics as an integral part of neoliberal agenda. As noted above, the military *coup d'état* and the following restructuration of the political space through repressive measures buried the political activism of the 1970s. In a parallel vein, civil societal activism along free market lines was promoted as one of the requisites of global neoliberal agenda. As in the case of other components of neoliberal structure, civil societalism also signified the inner contradictions of this new structure. First, there was the apparent contradiction between a culturally conservative social formation, built on the Turkish-Islamic synthesis, and the discourse on civil societalism. Second, there was the underlying contradiction within civil societalism in neoliberal times: The discourse on civil societalism emphasised individual liberties. The practice classified activism first in terms of access to the market, and then in terms of identity issues, which is by no means problematic at first sight. Still, the restriction of opposition into the civil societal boundaries, and to identity issues preempted the emergence of a persistent network of opposition to neoliberal hegemony (On an elaboration of the restriction of political opportunity spaces to identity issues with a view to citizenship under the AKP's neoliberal rule see Soyarık-Şentürk's contribution to this volume).

Women's movement in Turkey, with a significant degree of institutionalisation that it achieved throughout the 1990s could take advantage of the post-1980 (inter)national dynamics in

struggling for the improvement of women's rights. Yet it
has also experienced the neoliberal bottlenecks to women's
emancipation. The women's rights/feminist organisations
have been strategic in maneuvering through the rising tide
of identity-based politics, through the pro-EU stance at the
governmental level,[115] and most importantly through the dominance of neoliberal politics, which required a less controlling
state—certainly in the market, considered to be the bedrock
of individual liberty. Yet, at the same, and especially in the
course of accessing the spaces for directly affecting the
running of politics—in lobbying at the governmental level—
the women's movement also encountered the risk of division
on two planes. First, the movement has been forced into an
internal classification along specific issue areas. Second, apart
from issue-based division, and hence the risk of incapacita-
tion in terms of initiating structural opposition, one other
and more acute risk has been the reproduction of divergence
on the long-established ideological affinities that once had
hampered the rise of autonomous feminist organising (Coşar
& Gençoğlu-Onbaşı, 2008). Paralleling these planes of division, the hegemonisation of identity politics brought in the
risk of overlooking the intertwined working of the neoliberal
exploitation system through class, gender and ethnic lines.

In this respect, the risk of articulation into the mainstream,
and thus, *malestream* politics under neoliberal hegemony can
be outlined in terms of three factors: First, the modeling of
the hegemonic civil societal discourse on the free market
instills competition. As for the women's civil societal
activism this might cause hardship in sustaining cooperation
and solidarity. Second, activism along issue-based concerns
might signify endurance of ideological cleavages, which
might hamper the possibilities for common feminist platform
(Coşar & Gençoğlu-Onbaşı, 2008), that would forge different
facets of exploitation and oppression into a systemic oppo-

sitionary bloc. And third, the conceptualisation of liberty
in free market frame, which defines autonomy on the basis
of financial independence—i.e., no state support—might
cause the organisations grapple with the problem of survival
through project-based activism, which in turn might result in
a trade-off between activism and professionalism. Actually,
the seemingly contradictory state of women's civil societal
activism in contemporary Turkey, in terms of demands and
achievements at the governmental level, points at the materialisation of these problems.

The Good Old Patriarchy Works
through the AKP's Policies

The AKP's first victory at the ballot box in 2002 general election was set against the critical juncture that we outlined above.
Partly due to its efforts to fend off the hawkish suspicions
regarding its pro-Islamist origins, the party readily adopted
the neoliberal agenda of the late 1990s and early 2000s. But
more than that, the party emerged from within the neoliberal
political space. In other words, both its *raison d'être* and
its existential basis are forged in the neoliberal politics (see
Coşar's contribution to this volume). Thus, it turned a liberal
face to the international sphere (see Yeşilyurt-Gündüz's and
Demirtaş's contributions to this volume), while in domestic
politics its discourse has developed through a combination
of religious conservatism, nationalism and civil societal
activism. Each one of these ingredients has had a certain role
in the party's relation with the republican establishment and
society, and thus in its gendered practices. A brief look at the
party discourse and the party's policy preferences regarding
feminism, gender equality and family structure on these three
axes sheds light on the patriarchal route that the AKP has
been following.

To start with, in the party's practices regarding the women's issues, civil societalism has turned out to be the weakest factor. This is so, though the party started its political life span with an emphasis on cooperation with civil societal organisations. Thus, during the first phase of the AKP's term in power (2002-2007) the women's rights/feminist organisations got the opportunity to push for gender-sensitive amendments in subsequent legal reforms. As noted above, this process proved to be relatively successful—in the case of the amendments to the Penal Code (Ayata & Tütüncü, 2008, p. 381)—and this success depended to a large extent on the experience of the women's movement in lobbying for gender-sensitive amendments to the new Civil Code, during the previous coalition government (1999-2001). Yet, the party's enthusiasm for cooperation and/or dialogue with the women's rights organisations has been dubious since throughout its experience at the governmental level the AKP's preference for cooperation with civil society increasingly meant cooperation with the market forces.

In this respect, the party's lack of interest in women's demands concerning gender equality can first be observed in its already existing but increasingly materialising distance to interaction with women's rights/feminist organisations. Actually, its stance gradually evolved from expressed willingness for cooperation with the women's rights organisations to disinterest, and frequently, hostility toward feminist demands. One example of disinterest can be observed in the party's response to the demands that call for making gender quota legally binding for the political parties (Ayata & Tütüncü, 2008, pp. 375-378):[116]

> It is unjust to privilege women by means of [gender] quota. Women are powerful enough to achieve representation at any level of politics without the need for privilege. We want that the percentage of

our women candidates exceed 50 percent by the
application of many women [for candidacy in local
elections]. (Erdoğan, quoted in Yeni Dünya için
Çağrı 2004).

In line with this indifference, the party's relations with
certain women's rights organisation have always been fragile.
It is possible to note periodic clashes between the leading party
members and/or party spokespersons and women's rights
organisations. One such instance was the conflict between the
incumbent Minister responsible for the Family and Women in
the 59th AKP government (2003-2007)[117] and feminist organisations (Armutçu, 2006; Durukan, 2006). Accompanying the
clash were the statements by prominent party members in
which one can observe a heavy dose of anti-feminism:

The AKP has a significantly different outlook
toward women. We do not support the conflict that
is created by feminist thought between women
and men. The women of the *Adalet ve Kalkınma
Partisi* have not been and will never be enslaved to
feminist ideology (Fırat, quoted in NTVMSNBC
2008).

Yet, the most conspicuous example of the hostility toward
feminism can be derived from the Prime Minister's reaction
to the feminists who protested the party's attempts to crimi-
nalise adultery in 2004. In that instance the feminists were
considered to be "a bunch of marginal women… who do not
comply with Turkish morality" (Mutlu, 2004). This personal
statement aside, the anti-feminist stance has also infiltrated
the policy set of the government. For instance the declaration
by the Presidency of Religious Affairs explicitly put forth the
government's aversion to feminism:

[F]eminism leads to grave consequences in moral and social respects. Above all, the woman who falls into the feminist movement, [by acting] through the principle of unconditional freedom ignores many of the rules and values, which are indispensible for the family (cited in Gürsözlü-Süslü, 2008).

And finally, the decisions by *Aile ve Sosyal Araştırmalar Genel Müdürlüğü* (General Directorate of Family and Social Research, ASAGEM), established to deal with family matters and affiliated to the Prime Ministry, present a similar distaste with feminism. In this respect, Article 17 of the decisions taken in the Consultative Meeting with Civil Society Organisations in Family Services, held on 29 February–2 March 2008, organised by the General Directorate is telling about the discomfort of the AKP governments in the face of feminist demands. Briefly, Article 17 is reserved to the necessity "to change feminist terminology in mass media in matters of custom killings ..." (Gürsoy, 2009).

Thus, it is possible to consider the AKP's gender policies as the prime site of neoliberal–conservative alliance in the Turkish context.[118] They offer the grounds that help the party to come to terms with the basics of the neoliberal settings, which host seemingly contradictory phenomenon simultaneously (Duggan, 2003, p. 70). Thus, while the party has leaned on liberal discourse in the steps that it took toward the pro-EU reforms, and especially in terms of civilian-military balance in the political sphere, the same discourse has not been that prominent in the party's consideration of women's rights. Though one might put a reservation on this assessment with reference to the party's manipulation of the issue of headscarf ban in public buildings in terms of the individual right to choice it should be noted that the AKP has so far also successfully managed the infiltration of *this* individual right by conservative motifs. More briefly, the party's attempts toward the solution of the problem—exclusion of women wearing headscarves mainly from higher educational institutions unless they give up wearing headscarves—has almost totally excluded the possibility of cooperation with the women's rights/feminist organisations. More significantly, through time it slipped into conservative lands in its attempts to define the style of and limits to the appropriate veiling (Coşar, 2008). Actually, the reference to individual right to choice is ironically replaced by the prioritisation of social order and the emphasis on the significant role of the family in the maintenance of social order when women's rights in general are concerned (Ayata & Tütüncü, 2008, pp. 378-379). The party's policy documents starting with the *Acil Eylem Plânı* (Urgent Action Plan) (2003) and extending to the Decisions of the Fifth Family Council (2008), organised by the ASAGEM evince this state of affairs.

The emphasis on the family lies in the dominant understanding that runs through the party. The family, in this respect, is considered to be the prime unit for women's existence. It follows that when the concern is with women's rights then the proper site for their consideration is not the women's worlds but the family world. Underlying this identification is the contention with the women's essential role of "upbringing of next generations and ensuring happiness in the family" (AKP, 2002). Unsurprisingly, in the party's family politics women's rights are marginalised. Thus, for example, in the projects that were accepted to be realised within the scope of the ASAGEM's activities in 2006, it is not possible to trace an involvement with gender equality within the family. Certainly, there are exceptions, like one project among whose aims raising consciousness about human rights through media— and not about *women's* human rights—is also included. A similar exception is a project that is directly related with the family counseling system, and which includes an item on the elimination of domestic violence. (http://www.aile.gov.tr/images/strateji/BTYKPROJELERİ.pdf)

In understanding the marginalisation of women's rights in family politics one has to consider the ideal model of family, which the party builds on its culturalist approach to the society. The Decisions of the Fourth and Fifth Councils (2004; 2008), organised by the ASAGEM, are illustrative in this respect. The concluding documents of both councils emphasise the importance of the family *vis-à-vis* the individuals in general and women in particular. Likewise, in both, the single mother households are barely mentioned—just in the case of widowers (ASAGEM, 2004; 2008). More significantly, especially in the Decisions of the Fifth Council, one can immediately discern the dominance of an essentialist reading of Turkish family structure. Unsurprisingly, this family is first and foremost the heterosexual family with children. Besides, identifying the family in Turkish society as a "social security institution" the decisions portray social solidarity as an essential feature of the Turkish family (ASAGEM, 2008, p. 8).

The emphasis on the essential features of the Turkish family and identification of traditional support mechanisms with social solidarity offer the grounds for the juxtaposition of conservatism, nationalism and neoliberal requisites in the AKP's policies. This juxtaposition is substantiated by the policies that the AKP governments have so far pursued in the sphere of national education. An analysis of the textbooks taught at all levels of education up to the university education connotes an essentialist approach to the Turkish history and Turkish identity (Tarih Vakfı, 2009). In this respect, the "holiness" of the Turkish family tradition is naturalised and alternative versions of family formation—on ethnic and gender grounds—are totally disregarded (Güvenli & Uğur-Tanrıöver, 2009, pp. 109-110). More briefly, the patriarchal division of labour is maintained, while the positioning of the working women is defined first and foremost in compliance with their wifehood and motherhood *duties*.

This state of affairs also attests the intertwining between conservative and neoliberal priorities. In the very same textbooks the maintenance of the "traditional roles" of women are re-read to comply with the requisites of the neoliberal lifeworlds. In other words, working women's daily plans are delineated so as to run in accordance with the requisites of the flexible labour market, while at the same time the precautions are taken to prevent their work lives from disrupting their familial duties. Thus, women are required to be programmed for the seamless running of home affairs in the workdays, which eventually increases the time span of a workday beyond fifteen hours (Uğur-Tanrıover, 2003, p. 117). In this time schedule, the working women are expected to wake up and clean the house in 10 minutes (06:00-06:10), to do "personal cleanup" and "to rest" in 30 minutes after the work (18:30-19:00), to manage that the dinner finishes in 15 minutes (19:30-19:45), to prepare the dinner for the next evening in an hour (20:15-21:15), and to tidy the rooms in 15 minutes. Only after then, they were given the time for personal work and resting (Uğur-Tanrıöver 2003, p. 117).

Actually, the designing of the familial sphere as the primary locus for the women is in parallel to the militaristic discourse, imbued with the call for a constant state of alertness against "enemies," "the willingness to die for the country," and the *warrior identity* as the essential features of Turkishness, which automatically excludes the attributes deemed feminine (Bora, 2003; 2009) from the public identity of the *Turk*. The style of conservatism that echoes in all these aspects of the identity of Turkish family is certainly built on the Sunni Islamic basis. In this respect, the instruction in the course on religion and morals forges Islamic assets into the Turkish national features, both reinforcing the holiness of Turkishness and instituting Islam as a historically fixed natural ingredient of being a Turk (Gözaydın, 2009, pp. 167-193). Though the assessment by Güvenli and Uğur-Tanrıöver (2009, p. 113) points that among the textbooks the lowest level of gender discrimination can be observed in those on religion and morals, the portrayal of the morals exclusively within the frame of religion hints at the limits to an optimistic appraisal for the elimination of gender inequality in the running of national education. In other words, once the context of morals is restricted to the Sunni Islamic frame it is hard to argue for an alternative and/or counter ethical stance that might challenge the Sunni Islamic interpretation. In fact, when one considers the recent comments and research results by scholars of Turkish politics, which note an ongoing "Islamisation" (Kahraman, 2007, p. 153; Sümer & Yaşlı, 2010) or "conservatisation" in society (Toprak, Bozan, Morgül & Şener, 2009; Çarkoğlu & Toprak, 2006) it can aptly be argued that this assumption is all the more valid.

The AKP's period in government has been a testament to the placement of moralistic/nationalistic political outlook into the neoliberal setting. Both in the statements by the leading AKP members and in the policy proposals prepared for the alleviation of poverty it is possible to observe the emphasis on social solidarity as part of the traits of Turkish culture. Social solidarity in this respect is presented as an evidence for the Turks' moral goodness. Or, one can note the emphasis on "protecting the integrity of the family" by arranging the working conditions for married women who have children on the basis of "flexible," "part-time," and "home-based" work (ASAGEM, 2004)—hence revealing the systemic nature of the neoliberal-conservative patriarchy under the AKP's rule that eliminates any possibility of a coincidence so far as the parallelism between national education and labour policies is concerned. This connection is clarified especially when one

considers the new Labour Law (2003) and the *Sosyal Güvenlik
ve Genel Sağlık Sigortası Yasası* (Law on Social Security and
General Health Insurance, SSGSS) (2008). While the Labour
Law instituted the replacement of welfare by workfare (see
Özdemir's contribution to this volume)—i.e., calling the
women to the labour market in return of no security—the
SSGSS further deepened the subordination of women by
leaving them with two polar options: either conceding to
work under insecure conditions or staying at home as wives
and mothers (Coşar & Yeğenoğlu, 2009).

The consistent reactions from different representatives
of the AKP and/or from institutions affiliated to the government against feminism should be considered within this
socio-political frame. It is not surprising that the attempts to
discipline the body and the time-space management of the
ideal women in such a setting evoke a hostile stance toward
feminist discourse and activism, especially when the latter
asks for social justice on the basis of gender equality. At this
point, it would be apt to say that what marks the AKP's political identity in general and its approach to women's issues
in particular is a new—but not unfamiliar—version of patriarchy of which disciplining power is embedded in modernity,
and fed by nationalism and an updated version of religious
conservatism.

Concluding Remarks

The gendered pattern that can be discerned in the discursive
practices of the AKP governments since 2002 connotes the
consolidation of a new form of patriarchy in the Turkish
socio-political space. This new form of patriarchy has certain
common features with the republican patriarchy that has
characterised modern Turkey since the foundation of the
Republic. One of the most conspicious common points is the

definition of the familial sphere as the natural locus of women. This definition does not ban women from public involvement in political, economic and cultural terms. Rather, it puts the fulfillment of familial responsibilities as the prime requisite for women's public participation. This conditionality also hints at the reasons behind and the style of the distaste that the party has so far displayed towards women's independent activism along feminist lines. It can also be related to the decline in women's employment in recent years (İzdeş, 2010, pp.175-177).

The difference of the new form of patriarchy that has so far been crystallised in the AKP's discursive practices can be found in that it hosts seemingly contradictory features in its body. Briefly, in this version of patriarchy the tendency of the maleist power network to get into dialogue with the women's rights organisations is stylistic and rhetorical in terms of responsiveness to their demands. Likewise, one can observe the gradual retreat of women from the labour market simultaneously with the increasing conservatisation of the discourse on women's rights and distaste of feminist demands. This form of patriarchy is above all informed by neoliberal ideology. In the AKP's case, neoliberalism opens up the opportunity spaces for the party where it can make adjustments between religious conservatism with nationalism.

To conclude, Turkey's experience with the AKP has involved both transformation and consolidation in the patriarchal socio-political structure that has marked the history of modern Turkey. The transformation aspect concerns the new version of modern patriarchy, in which one can trace the coexistence of modern and traditional versions in a continuously (re-)shaped network. This new patriarchy does not necessarily and directly tell the women to keep their hands off the public and social spheres. Rather, it invites them, with a warning about the perils of their involvement in these spheres, especially when they do so from a feminist perspective. It does so by implying that this involvement may risk the children's well-being, integrity of the family, and eventually, social integrity–thus, setting the boundaries of women's primary sphere. The consolidation concerns the neoliberal structuring of the socio-economic sphere, which has been underway since the 1980s. The neoliberal times in Turkey thus contribute to the deepening of patriarchal clutches on women's emancipation with the hand of conservative-nationalist policies.

REFERENCES

Adalet ve Kalkınma Partisi seçim beyannamesi (2002). Ankara: AKP.

Aldıkaçtı-Marshall, G. (2009). Authenticating gender policies through sustained pressure: The strategy behind the success of Turkish feminists. Social *Politics: International Studies in Gender, State and Society, 16* (3) 358-378.

Arat, Y. (2005). *Rethinking Islam and Liberal Democracy, Islamist Women in Turkish Politics.* NY: State University of New York Press.

Arat, Y. (1989). *The Patriarchal Paradox: Women Politicians in Turkey.* Cranbury, NJ: Associated University Presses.

ASAGEM. (2008). *Beşinci Aile Şurası, Aile Destek Hizmetleri Komisyonu kararları.* Ankara.

ASAGEM. (2004). *Dördüncü Aile Şurası komisyon raporları.* Ankara.

Ayata, A. and Tütüncü, F. (2008). Party politics of the AKP (2002-2007) and the predicaments of women at the intersection of the Westernist, Islamist and feminist discourses in Turkey. *British Journal of Middle Eastern Studies, 35* (3), 363-384.

Bergeron, S. (2001). Political economy discourses of globalization and feminist economy politics. *Signs, 26* (4), 983-1006.

Berktay, F. (2001). Osmanlı'dan Cumhuriyet'e feminizm. In T. Bora, M. Gültekin (Eds.), *Tanzimat ve Meşrutiyet'in Birikimi* (pp. 348-361). İstanbul: İletişim.

Bora, T. (2009). Ders kitaplarında milliyetçilik: "Siz bu ülke için neler yapmayı düşünüyorsunuz?" In G. Tüzün (Ed.), *Ders kitaplarında insan hakları II: Tarama sonuçları* (pp.115-141). İstanbul: Tarih Vakfı. http://www.tarihvakfi.org.tr/dkih/download/tanil_bora.pdf

Bora, T. (2003). Ders kitaplarında milliyetçilik. In B. Çotuksöken, A. Erzan & O. Silier (Eds.), *Ders kitaplarında insan hakları: Tarama sonuçları* (pp. 68-89). İstanbul: Tarih Vakfı.

Coşar, S. & Yeğenoğlu, M. (2011). New Grounds for Patriarchy in Turkey? Gender Policy in the Age of the AKP. *South European Society and Politics, 16* (4), .

Coşar, S. & Yeğenoğlu, M. (2009). The neoliberal restructuring of Turkey's social security system. *Monthly Review, 60* (11), 34-47.

Coşar, S. & Gençoğlu-Onbaşı, F. (2008). Women's movement in Turkey at a Crossroads: From women's rights advocacy to feminism. *South European Society and Politics, 13* (3), 325-344.

Coşar, S. (2008). Başörtüsüne/türbana bakmak: Parçalı siyasete dair feminizmin sözü var! *Birikim, 226,* 58-61.

Coşar, S. (2007). Women in Turkish political thought: Between tradition
and modernity. *Feminist Review* (86), 113-131.

Çakır, R. (2000). *Direniş ve itaat: İki iktidar arasında İslamcı kadın.*
İstanbul: Metis.

Çakır, S. (1994). *Osmanlı kadın hareketi.*İstanbul: Metis.

Çarkoğlu, A. & Toprak, B. (2006). *Değişen Türkiye'de din, toplum ve
siyaset.* İstanbul: TESEV.

Çıtak, Zana & Tür, Ö. (2008). Women between tradition and change: The
Justice and Development Party experience in Turkey. *Middle Eastern
Studies, 44*, (3), 455-469.

Dağı, İ. (2007). Islamic identity and the West: Is conflict inevitable? In
P. Kilpadi (Ed.), *Islam and tolerance in wider Europe* (pp. 103-112).
Hungary: International Policy Fellowships, Open University
Institute. http://www.policy.hu/ipf/policyperspectives/D10-ID-
Identity.pdf

Duggan, L. (2003). *The twilight of equality? Neoliberalism, cultural politics
and the attack on democracy.* Boston: Beacon Press.

Eisenstein, Z. (1982). The sexual politics of the New Right:
Understanding "the crisis of liberalism" for the 1980s. *Signs, 7* (3),
567-588.

Eisenstein, Z. (1981). *The Radical Future of Liberal Feminism.* Boston:
Northeastern University Press.

Elliot, R. (1984). How far have we come? Women's organization in the
unions in the United Kingdom. *Feminist Review, 16* (1), 64-73.

Fildes, S. (1983). The inevitability of theory. *Feminist Review, 14* (1),
62-70.

Filmmor (Producer), & Özman, M. (Director). (2008). *İsyan-ı Nisvan.*
İstanbul: Filmmor.

Gözaydın, İ. (2009). Türkiye'de "Din Kültürü ve Ahlâk Bilgisi ders
kitapları"na insan hakları merceğiyle bakış'. In G. Tüzün (Ed.),
Ders kitaplarında insan hakları II: Tarama sonuçları (pp. 167-193).
İstanbul: Tarih Vakfı. http://www.tarihvakfi.org.tr/dkih/download/
tanil_bora.pdf

Gürsoy, G. (2009, April 25). Medyada feminist dilin gerekliliği. *bianet.*
Retrieved July 10, 2009 from http://www.rightsagenda.org/index.
php?option=com_content&view=article&id=405:takmamedyada-
feminist-dilin gereklilii&catid=57:takmakadınıninsanhaklari&It
emid=80

Gürsözlü-Süslü, S. (2008, March 13). "Feminizm ahlâk dersinden kaldı!"
bianet. Retrieved July 10, 2009 from http://bianet.org/biamag/
bianet/105540-feminizm-ahlak-dersinden-kaldi

Güvenli, G. & Uğur-Tanrıöver, H. (2009). Ders kitaplarında toplumsal cinsiyet. In G. Tüzün (Ed.), *Ders kitaplarında insan hakları II: Tarama sonuçları* (pp.97-114). İstanbul: Tarih Vakfı. http://www.tarihvakfi.org.tr/dkih/download/gulsun_guvenli.pdf

Heath, S. (1997). Thoughts of a latecomer: On being a lesbian in the backlash. In A. Oakley & J. Mitchell (Eds.), *Who's afraid of feminism? Seeing through the backlash* (pp.99-110). New York: The New Press.

İzdeş, Ö. (2010). "Türkiye'nin krizleri önce kadınları vuruyor" miti gerçek mi?: Emek piyasasından yanıtlar. In S. Dedeoğlu & M. Yaman Öztürk (Eds.), *Kapitalizm, ataerkillik ve kadın emeği: Türkiye örneği* (pp. 133-182). İstanbul: SAV.

Kadıoğlu, A. (1998). Cinselliğin inkârı: Büyük toplumsal projelerin nesnesi olarak Türk kadınları. In A. Berktay-Hacımirzaoğlu (Ed.), *Bilanço '98, 75 yılda kadınlar ve erkekler* (pp. 89-100). İstanbul: Tarih Vakfı.

Kahraman, H. B. (2007). *Türk sağı ve AKP.* İstanbul: Agora.

Kandiyoti, D. (1988). Bargaining with patriarchy. *Gender and Society, 2* (3), 274-290.

Mitchell, J. & Goody, J. (1997). Feminism, fatherhood and the family in Britain. In A. Oakley & J. Mitchell (Eds.), *Who's afraid of feminism? Seeing through the* backlash (pp. 200-223). New York: The New Press.

Mutlu, M. (2004, September 27). Bir yanda 'ehlen ve şehlen' diğer yanda öztürkçe ceza yasası! *Vatan (Turkish daily).* Retrieved June 10, 2009 from http://haber.gazetevatan.com/Haber/36883/1/Gundem

NTVMSNBC. (2008, May 5). Fırat: AKP kadınları feminizmin kölesi değil. Retrieved June 10, 2009 from http://arsiv.ntvmsnbc.com/news/445128.asp

Öniş, Z. (2007). Conservative globalists versus defensive nationalists: Political parties and paradoxes of Europeanization in Turkey. *Journal of Southern Europe and the Balkans, 9* (3), 247-261.

Özman, A. & Coşar, S. (2007). Reconceptualizing center politics in Turkey: Transformation or continuity? In E. F. Keyman (Ed.), *Remaking Turkey: Globalization, alternative modernities and democracy* (pp. 201-226). Lanham, Boulder, New York, Oxford: Lexington.

Romito, P. (1997). *'Damned if you do and damned if you don't:' Psyhcological and social constraints on motherhood in contemporary Europe.* In A. Oakley & J. Mitchell (Eds.), *Who's afraid of feminism? Seeing through the backlash* (pp. 162-186). New York: The New Press.

Scully, T. (1992). *Rethinking the center: Party politics in nineteenth- and twentieth-century Chile.* Stanford: Stanford University Press.

Sirman, N. (2005). The making of familial citizenship in Turkey. In
E. F. Keyman & A. İçduygu (Eds.), *Citizenship in a global world,
European questions and Turkish experiences* (pp. 147-172). NY:
Routledge.

Stratigaki, M. (2005). Gender mainstreaming vs positive action: An
ongoing conflict in EU gender equality policy. *European Journal of
Women's Studies, 12* (2), 165-186.

Tekeli, Ş. (1986). Emergence of the feminist movement in Turkey. In D.
Dahlerup (Ed.), *The new women's movement* (pp. 179-199). London:
Sage.

Toksöz, G. (2002). "We are the few": Women in labor unions in Turkey.
In N. Balkan & S. Savran (Eds.), *The ravages of neoliberalism,
economy, society and gender in Turkey* (pp.195-209). New York: Nova
Science Publishers.

Toprak, B., Bozan, İ., Morgül, T. & Şener, N. (2009). *Türkiye'de farklı
olmak: Din ve muhafazakârlık ekseninde ötekileştirilenler.* İstanbul:
Metis.

Tünay, M. (1993). The Turkish new right's attempt at hegemony. In A.
Eralp, M. Tünay, & B. Yeşilada (Eds.), *The political and socioeconomic
transformation of Turkey* (pp.11-30). Westport, Connecticut, London:
Praeger.

Tüzün, G. (Ed.). (2009). *Ders kitaplarında insan hakları II: Tarama
sonuçları.* İstanbul: Tarih Vakfı.

Uğur-Tanrıöver, H. (2003). Ders kitaplarında cinsiyet ayrımcılığı. In B.
Çotuksöken, A. Erzan & O. Silier (Eds.), *Ders kitaplarında insan
hakları: Tarama sonuçları* (pp. 106-121). İstanbul: Tarih Vakfı.

Wilson, J. Q. & Kelling G. L. (2004). Broken windows, the police and
neighborhood safety. In I. Stelzer (Ed.), *The NeoCon reader* (pp.
149-166). New York: Grove Press.

White, J. B. (2003). State feminism, modernization and the Turkish
Republican woman. *NWSA, 15* (3), 145-159.

Wolfson, A. (2004). Conservatives and neoconservatives. In I Stelzer
(Ed.), *The NeoCon reader* (pp. 213-231). New York: Grove Press.

WWHR. (2005) "Turkish civil and penal code reforms from a gender
perspective: The success of two nationwide campaigns." Retrieved
June 20, 2008 from http://www.wwhr.org/yayin_3.php?detay=35

Yeni dünya için çağrı. (2004, January 17). Adaylık verilmez, alınır!
Retrieved February 5, 2006 from http://www.ydicagri.com/
Sayilar/075/75ykd_secimler.html

Zihnioğlu, Y. (2003) *Kadınsız inkılap.* İstanbul: Metis.

PART III: GLOBAL INTERFACES: POLITICS, ECONOMY AND INTERNATIONAL RELATIONS

8

TURKISH FOREIGN POLICY UNDER THE AKP GOVERNMENTS: AN INTERPLAY OF IMPERIAL LEGACY, NEOLIBERAL INTERESTS AND PRAGMATISM

Birgül Demirtaş

Introduction

Since the AKP came to power both its internal and external policies have attracted considerable international attention. The fact that it stemmed from the Islamist *Millî Görüş* (National Outlook Movement) became the cause of some concern, leading the party elite to try to prove their commitment to secularism both domestically and internationally. In addition, the party's rise to power occurred at such a conjuncture that there was curiosity about how they would tackle all the challenges simultaneously. On the one hand, since 2001, Turkey had been suffering from its worst financial crisis in its history. On the other hand, there was an urgent need to find a long-lasting solution to the Kurdish problem after the capture of Abdullah Öcalan (the then head and symbolic leader of the *Partiya Karkerên Kurdistan* [Kurdistan Workers' Party] - PKK) by Turkish security forces in February 1999. On the international scene, the international community was still feeling the aftershocks of the

9/11 terrorist attacks and the neo-conservatives in the United States were formulating plans to reshape the (greater) Middle East region, of which Turkey is also a part.

Under these circumstances the AKP's foreign policy came under tight international scrutiny and each step it took led to different reactions, responses, and comments, culminating in a huge quantity of literature. These reactions seem to be centered upon two main issues: First, is the AKP middle easternising the previously Western-oriented Turkish international affairs? And secondly, does it follow a neo-Ottomanist agenda?

This chapter attempts to analyse the AKP's foreign policy by analysing the writings of the current Foreign Minister, Ahmet Davutoğlu and discourses of the leadership cadre, as well as by evaluating the policy outcomes. The main research questions are as follows: Which priorities does the AKP government have when formulating foreign policy behavior? Do the priorities vary from one region to another? What about the impact of neo-Ottomanism? Does the party's neoliberal agenda affect its foreign policy preferences? How are elements of change and continuity manifested in Turkish foreign policy so far?

To make a rough distinction, there are three different views about the AKP's foreign policy approach in the literature. The first group argues that the AKP brought a radical change to Turkish foreign policy in the form of a transformation from hard power to soft power, from decades-long security- and securitisation-oriented foreign policy to a cooperation-oriented one. They base their arguments on critical assessment of the policies of previous governments (Oğuzlu, 2007; Aktay, 2010; Aras, 2009; Çandar 2010).

The second group, however, claims that the AKP represents continuity with the previous governments, mainly with the Özal era. It is claimed that change in Turkish foreign policy started during the rule of the *Anavatan Partisi* (Motherland

8: Turkish Foreign Policy under the AKP Governments:
An Interplay of Imperial Legacy, Neoliberal Interests and
Pragmatism

215

Party) governments under Turgut Özal and continued afterwards. A neo-functionalist approach toward neighbouring
countries as well as neo-Ottomanist outlook in foreign policy
was initiated under Özal governments and maintained by
successive governments. Özal believed in the idea that neoliberal interests must be the key in the formulation of foreign
policy. Here, one can draw parallels with AKP's approach to
international politics. Therefore, the AKP is argued to represent continuity, as opposed to any kind of radical change (İnat
& Duran, 2006; Kardaş, 2010).

Finally, the third approach, on the other hand, states that
the AKP's foreign policy is rather a populist one. The AKP
aims to attract the attention of domestic constituency and international public opinion. In the post-Cold War era there was
an argument about the weakening of the distinction between
foreign and domestic policies.[119] Hence, the AKP's foreign
policy can be considered an extension of domestic politics
in the international realm. For example, the AKP's developing relations with the Sudanese leader, Omer Al Basheer,
for whom the International Criminal Court (ICC) issued an
arrest warrant due to charges on genocide, war crimes and
crimes against humanity in the region of Darfur, can be attributed to Turkey's economic interests. According to this view,
the AKP's foreign policy is also characterised by twists that
can best be observed in its relations with the US. Before the
US occupation of Iraq the AKP government negotiated with
Washington for months and gave every kind of indication of
its positive stance toward the passage of American soldiers
through Turkish terrirory, but then the end result was the
opposite (Criss, 2010).

In light of these various approaches, the main argument of
this chapter is that the AKP's foreign policy can best be characterised as a mixture of neo-Ottomanism, neoliberalism and
pragmatism. Indeed, during the AKP's eight years in power it

is possible fo find evidence for all the approaches summarised above. One can find instances of both continuity and change as well as pragmatism. Accordingly, this study tries to unveil the main dynamics behind the AKP's foreign policy behavior. The chapter is composed of five parts. In the first part, the AKP's understanding of international politics is analysed mainly by looking at the writings and discourse of Davutoğlu. Then it will shed light on Turkey's positioning in global environment according to the approach of the AKP. The AKP's foreign policy preferences are contextualised on the basis of a commercial approach in the third section. Then, in the fourth part, it will look at the impact of a neo-Ottomanist outlook on the AKP's external behavior, and finally, it will examine the pragmatist attitude. The last section will summarise the main findings of the research.

Understanding International Politics from the AKP's Perspective: The Chessboard, Boxing Ring, and Challenge of Globalisation

It is without a doubt that the main architect of the AKP's foreign policy is Ahmet Davutoğlu, who is a professor of International Relations. He served at various universities as a lecturer before becoming chief foreign policy advisor to the prime minister under the AKP. Although he was only appointed foreign minister on May 1, 2009, he has been responsible for the AKP's foreign policy since 2002. Further, Davutoğlu is a prolific academician who has published extensively on issues of international relations. The most important of all his publi- cations is *Stratejik Derinlik (Strategic Depth)*, which was published first in 2001 and is among the bestselling interna- tional relations books in Turkey.[120] The book focuses on the evaluation of Turkish foreign policy from the establishment of the Republic through the end of the 1990s, with the help of mainstream Western geopolitical theories.

8: Turkish Foreign Policy under the AKP Governments: **217**
An Interplay of Imperial Legacy, Neoliberal Interests and
Pragmatism

The state of global affairs that Davutoğlu describes in his
book is mostly of a Hobbesian nature, rather than a Lockean
or Kantian one. By depicting the heartlands and rimlands of
the world, his focus is determined by political geography
as can be expected from his use of traditional geopolitical
theories. Based on his geopolitical approach, he argues, in
order to have their sphere of influence over the critical territories, great powers of international politics have to struggle
with each other. For example, he elaborates on the clash of
interests between the USA and Europe (mainly Germany) at
the international level on the one hand, and between Britain/
France and Germany/Russia on the other. In order to describe
the state of international and regional politics, the "chess"
metaphor of Zbigniew Brzezinski is quite often used (Brzezinski, 1997). Briefly, international relations is considered
similar to chess where actors perceive each other as rivals
and try to foresee the next step of each other. It was within
this framework that the USA launched the first Gulf War in
order to prove its determining impact on regional and global
balances. As a reaction to the US intervention, the German-
led European forces started the Middle East Peace Process
by initiating the Oslo Process and Madrid Conference and
launching the disintegration process of Yugoslavia in order to
prove their sphere of influence over these regions (Davutoğlu,
2001, p. 293-294).

The chess metaphor was used for Middle Eastern politics as well, in which it is argued that politics in the region
resemble chess in which "merciless plays" of balance of
powers are staged (Davutoğlu, 2001, p. 355). It is even stated
that foreign policy making in the region is like a box match
(Davutoğlu, 2001, p. 364). The general approach of the
book is thus in harmony with the most traditional theory of
international relations, realism, according to which the main
actors are states, the main motives behind the state policies

are survival and power-seeking, states perceive each other as rivals, and there is only the self-help mechanism at work.

Davutoğlu's book is rather a continuation of traditional geopolitical studies in Turkey. The study of geopolitics in Turkey started with the works of the military officers during the Second World War, which were then used to prove Turkey's importance for the western world. Similarly, the central state metaphor for Turkey was for the first time used by the military for internal reasons (Bilgin, 2007). It is interesting to note that Davutoğlu claimed to put forward an alternative approach to Turkish foreign policy, however his work is based on one of the most classical perspectives. He comes up with different conclusions, however, he does not elaborate on the more critical versions of those geopolitical approaches.

Although Davutoğlu's main framework is drawn in line with the realist paradigm, one can also find references to elements of the so-called soft power or normative elements both in *Stratejik Derinlik* and in AKP documents. Moreover, the end of the bipolar world order is considered to have led to the emergence of the free movement of goods, services, people, and capital resulting in economic and political integration (AK Parti Seçim Bildirgesi, 2002). There is also acknowledgement that today's international relations consist not only of states, but also other actors, like corporations, NGOs, and regional and international organisations (Davutoğlu, 2001, p. 25). Among the new factors influencing international politics there is an emphasis on the increasing role of the neoliberal economic system, which is considered an instrument contributing to the improvement of political relations among states and the solving of bilateral problems. For example, both Davutoğlu himself and AKP documents emphasise the role of economic factors in improving Turkey's ties both with Iran and Greece (Davutoğlu, 2001, p. 181; AK Parti Seçim Bildir-

8: Turkish Foreign Policy under the AKP Governments: **219**
An Interplay of Imperial Legacy, Neoliberal Interests and
Pragmatism

gesi 2002). Thus, economic interdependence among countries
is perceived to be vital to improve political ties, leading to
the increasing importance of economic actors in the foreign
policy decision-making process. In the party documents it is
also stated that societal actors should be added to the foreign
policy decision-making process (AK Parti Seçim Bildirgesi
2002). In this frame, the private sector is attributed with a
significant role, as the the driver of Turkish foreign policy and
its strategic vision.[121]

The AKP's Positioning of Turkey
within International Politics: An Extraordinary
State in an Ordinary World

Assigning an important part of his book to the evaluation of
the pre-AKP era in Turkish foreign policy, Davutoğlu has
a quite critical approach to the policy preferences of past
governments. His criticisms can be summarised as follows:
first of all, he argues that the Turkish political elite did not
pay attention to the public in the sense that they did not try
to understand the values, beliefs and identity of the Turkish
people. Therefore, their foreign policy was not based on the
public, which, for him, weakened the effectiveness of previous
foreign policy outcomes. Second, the foreign policy of the
Republic of Turkey was too much based on the Western countries, allowing Turkey only to play the role of a peripheral
country within the international system. Third, the foreign
policy approach was mainly based on the PKK issue. It was
stated that Turkish foreign policy should not concentrate
too much on the PKK problem given the possibility that it
would create a weakness in Turkey's strategic vision. At that
point a distinction was made between assertive and passive
countries. The former, first of all, determines its strategies
and then defines threats accordingly. However, the latter first

makes a definition of threats and only then formulates strategies. According to the understanding of Davutoğlu, countries
with a weak foreign policy approach can be defined as the
ones that remain passive in international politics and they are
thus located only in the periphery of global affairs. The US,
Britain, and the former Ottoman Empire are given as examples of the former group, which did not become dependent
on their internal weaknesses in formulating their long-term
foreign policy strategies. Davutoğlu details his argument by
noting that Celali rebellions took place in the Ottoman Empire
during the 16th century, but the Ottoman strategic vision was
determined independent of them (Davutoğlu, 2001, p. 62-63).
Hence, one should be careful not to let other actors play upon
the internal weaknesses of a country.

Based on the criticisms discussed above, Davutoğlu
develops an alternative approach elaborating on both
geographical and historical determinism. Turkey is stated to
be a country with strategic depth because of its extraordinary
features, geographically and historically. Its geographical
depth is determined both by its belonging to various regions at
once and the existence of the Straits. In addition, Turkey has
historical depth because of the Ottoman legacy. The combination of both constitutes strategic depth, which explains why
Turkey is not an ordinary state whatsoever.

Turkey's geographic depth is considered an important
factor that has the potential to contribute to its formulation of
a multi-dimensional foreign policy. Because of its geographical characteristics, Turkey belongs to both to the East and
West at the same time and to the same degree, making the
question of "whether Turkey is Western or Eastern" totally
irrelevant. The argument of Turkey belonging both to the East
and West is not new in Turkish politics. From the beginning
of the détente period different leaders from Ecevit to Özal,
and from Demirel to İsmail Cem, took note of Turkey's multi-

8: Turkish Foreign Policy under the AKP Governments: **221**
An Interplay of Imperial Legacy, Neoliberal Interests and
Pragmatism

dimensionality and underlined the necessity of improving
relations both with eastern and western countries. However,
Davutoğlu's approach differs from the previous leaders by his
more prominent emphasis on neo-Ottomanism.

In his view, Turkey cannot formulate its external relations
without taking its Ottoman heritage into consideration. As
the inheritor of an empire that reigned over its neighbouring
regions for centuries, Turkey should not depend on the West
or any other external actor in formulating its policies toward
the ex-Ottoman territories. It should have enough self-confi-
dence to formulate its independent policies in line with its
own interests. Furthermore, it should also try to create its
own spheres of interest or "hinterland" in the neighbouring
regions (Davutoğlu, 2001, p. 92-93). In this frame, it can be
argued that in the AKP's foreign policy discourse Turkey is an
extraordinary country because of its geographical and historical depth, within an ordinary international system laden with
a realist approach.

A Commercial Reading of Foreign Policy

Although the main emphasis of Davutoğlu's approach is on
geopolitics, as opposed to economics or geoeconomics, from
time to time the importance of economic factors in foreign
policy is pointed out as well. Economics is believed to play the
key role in the solution of regional problems and disputes.[122]
Herewith, the economic dimension of foreign policy comes
into picture in addition to the security dimension, but in a
secondary role, and as an instrument of foreign policy.
Developments in international political economy are also
considered important in preparing Turkish foreign policy, since
the weight of Asian and African countries in global economy
is foreseen to increase. The beginning of 21st century will be
Asian century, the end of it will be African, states Davutoğlu.

Therefore Turkey's decision-makers should follow the developments and act accordingly (Davutoğlu, 2001, p. 218). It is also interesting that when Davutoğlu refers to the importance of economic factors, he at the same time mentions cultural factors, hence in his approach one can see the linkage between economics and culture. Both economic and cultural integration are seen as vital for the solution of inter-state problems (Davutoğlu, 2001, p. 144, 288). Davutoğlu's understanding of foreign policy is revealed in his recourse to the terms of the market in defining the task of a diplomat. In this respect, one should note the similarity between a clever merchant and a clever diplomat that Davutoğlu refers to. A clever merchant is defined as someone who maintains all of their market alternatives. Likewise a smart diplomat should keep all the options at his hand, without making foreign policy dependent on single factors and/or actors. Davutoğlu in his book states the following:

> Turkey's geopolitical location does not necessitate static polices based on strategic preferences of different actors. It necessitates multidimensional dynamic policies that have the capacity to evaluate all kinds of alternatives. A clever merchant does not limit its alternatives on the market. Likewise a clever diplomat should not reduce foreign policy options at his/her hand (Davutoğlu, 2001, p. 499).[123]

In the current state of the world capitalist economy, the role of economic factors in foreign policy making is more conspiciously decisive than ever before. In the Turkish context, it was during the Özal leadership that economics started to be considered much more in the foreign policy decision making process. According to Özal's functionalist approach, economics would play a key role in solving polit-

8: Turkish Foreign Policy under the AKP Governments: **223**
An Interplay of Imperial Legacy, Neoliberal Interests and
Pragmatism

ical disputes, as seen in his approach to Turkey's relations
with Syria and Greece (Altunışık, 2009). With regard to both
countries he especially favored the improvement of economic
relations, which was expected to have repercussions in the
future political sphere.

In this sense, the AKP's foreign policy making can be
considered a continuation of the Özalite style, since it also
seems to give a special importance to economic factors in
the formulation of foreign policy. As was the case during
the Özal era, AKP politicians also invite business people on
foreign trips in order to encourage the rise of Turkey's foreign
economic activities. The practice of taking business people on
foreign visits was halted after the end of Özal era, however, it
was restarted by the AKP government (Kirişci, 2009, p. 49).
Kirişci argues that Turkey under the AKP government is in
the process of becoming a trading state, since the economics
is taken into consideration to a greater degree in the making
of external relations. (Kirişci, 2009, pp. 29-56) The general
manager of *Türkiye İş Bankası,*[124] Ersin Özince, stated that
both the president and government encourage the expansion
of his bank in Turkey's neighbourhood, mainly in the Balkans
and Middle East. This is a good example of how economics
and foreign policy are interwoven in the current period.[125]
Another example is the appointment of the Undersecretary
of Foreign Trade, Tuncer Kayalar, who is an expert on bilateral and multilateral economic relations, as ambassador to
Nairobi, capital of Kenya.[126] This multidimensional approach,
of course, is not a very usual practice in terms of the traditions
of the Turkish Foreign Ministry.

Yet, in the AKP's foreign policy preferences the degree
of the impact of economic factors vary from one region to
another. In the regions where the Ottoman Empire ruled
before, like Balkans, Middle East, and parts of Africa, one
can see the linkage between the approach of neo-Ottomanism

and geo-economics. This connection is evinced in *Stratejik Derinlik*, where Davutoğlu argues for both geographical and historical determinism[127] on the one hand, as well as changing global economic conditions on the other.

Turkey's Policy toward Darfur: A Test Case for Commercial Reading

Within the perspective explicated above, the AKP puts special emphasis on improving Turkey's relations with the African countries. In the first year of the AKP government (2003), the Undersecretary of Foreign Trade prepared a Strategy to Improve Economic Relations with the African Countries. It was therefore of special importance that 2005 was declared "The Year of Africa" in Turkey, during which Turkey had been accepted as an observer to the African Union. Then in 2008, the first Turkey-Africa Cooperation Summit was organised. Another important initiative of the government was the decision to open fifteen new embassies in Africa. Thus, the number of Turkish embassies in the sub-Saharan African will increase to twenty-seven in the coming few years. In response, *Türk Hava Yolları* (Turkish Airlines, THY) started new flight routes to destinations like Hartum, Addis Ababa, Lagos, Johannesburg, Nairobi, Dakar, Darüsselam, and Entebbe.

Certainly, all these steps are in line with the requirements of the world capitalist economy. With the shrinking market opportunities in the Western markets that became salient in the late 2000s, the AKP government has been tempted to look for new markets for the burgeoning Anatolian industrialists which are considered an important part of the AKP's constituency. According to a report of *Türkiye Ekonomi Politikaları Araştırma Vakfı* (Economic Policy Research Foundation of Turkey, TEPAV) report, the share of the EU member states in Turkish exports decreased from 48 to 46 per cent in 2008-2009.

8: Turkish Foreign Policy under the AKP Governments: **225**
An Interplay of Imperial Legacy, Neoliberal Interests and
Pragmatism

This drop was filled by the rise of Middle Eastern, Asian, and North African countries in Turkey's exports. Accordingly, this development was labelled a "change of axis" in Turkey's trade (Dinççağ & Özkale, 2010). One of the countries with which Turkey's economic relations increased considerably during this time was Sudan. Bilateral trade volume increased from 71.707 USD in 2002 to 243.069 in 2008, representing a rise of about 3.5 fold (http://www.dtm.gov.tr/dtmadmin/upload/ANL/AfrikaDb/Sudan.doc). These flourishing economic ties were also reflected in the political relations, since Turkey under the AKP leadership established close relations with the Sudanese government, led by Al Basheer. This increase in Turkish-Sudanese relations were criticised not only domestically, but also internationally, since Al Basheer has been charged by the ICC as committing genocide in Darfur. He is believed to be responsible for the death of thousands of civilian people. The AKP government did not give support to the ruling of the ICC and adopted a milder tone, closer to the approach of the African Union and Arab League, thus differentiating its policy from the mainstream Western approach which condemns the policies of Al Basheer. In addition, Al Basheer was welcomed in Turkey twice, in January and August 2008. He was going to visit Turkey a third time in November 2009, but due to international reactions he cancelled his trip. Without taking the increasing Turkish-Sudanese economic relations into account, it is impossible to understand Turkey's position on the Darfur issue in particular and its policies toward Sudan in general (Özkan & Akgün, 2010; Kanbolat, 2008). Here, it should be noted that Turkey's Darfur policy reveals the contradictions that inevitably arise out the uneasy mixture of neo-Ottomanist and neoliberal worldviews that frame AKP's foreign policy preferences. This is all the more clear in comparison with the foreign policy stance of the party in the Gaza case, where the rights of the Palestinians living in Gaza under the Israeli blockade are supported.

The argument of the trading state is apparent in the AKP's foreign policy toward the Asian countries such as China, Japan, India, South Korea etc. Concerning the relations with these countries the main emphasis is to improve economic relations. It was not coincidental that 105 business people accompanied President Gül during his visit to China on June 24-29, 2009. Here, there is no intermarriage between neo-Ottomanism and geo-economics, but rather an emphasis on the geo-economic importance of the region for Turkey. Hence, it is possible to argue, that in the ex-Ottoman territories the main aim of the AKP government is to increase Turkey's influence so as to to make it possible for Ankara to play a role in global affairs as well. One of the main instruments required to do so is considered economic relations. However, for the regions where there is no Ottoman legacy, the main emphasis and target become geo-economics, as seen in Turkey's relations with the Asian countries.

Foreign Policy on Air: THY and Turkish Foreign Policy

The relationship between THY flights and Turkish foreign policy can be given as an example of a commercial reading of foreign policy. It should be noted that THY received increasing attention in the foreign policy formulation under the AKP. It has been repetitively noted by the AKP circles that the destinations of THY do not concern only itself, but they are also important in terms of Turkey's external ties to the business world. More explicitly, they are related to where Turkish business people will invest, where they will export, and from where they will import (as an example see Interview with Davutoğlu, *Turkish Time*, 2004).

THY flights are seen essential not only to increase Turkish business people's connections, but also to promote

8: Turkish Foreign Policy under the AKP Governments: **227**
An Interplay of Imperial Legacy, Neoliberal Interests and
Pragmatism

regional dialogue and encourage the creation of relations of confidence. For example, during the visit of Massoud Barzani, the President of Iraqi Kurdistan Region and leader of the Kurdistan Democratic Party, to Ankara on 3-4 June 2010, Davutoğlu elaborated on the importance of THY's flights to Erbil (Yanatma, 2010). It is no secret that Turkey is very concerned about the PKK bases in Northern Iraq and increasing attacks from that region on the Turkish military in the 2010 summer. Hence, Davutoğlu's emphasis on increasing economic relations between Turkey and Northern Iraq and starting new THY flights is important to show the employment of economic factors and THY destinations for foreign policy aims. It is also important to note that the THY's logo was put on the website of the Foreign Ministry under the AKP (http//www.mfa.gov.tr). This is a perfect example to prove the weight of THY on a foreign policy understanding of the AKP.

Neo-Ottomanism and the AKP's Foreign Policy[128]

Besides neoliberalism, neo-Ottomanism also plays an important role in the foreign policy behavior of the AKP. As stated above, in the AKP's policies, especially toward the neighbouring ex-Ottoman territories, one can clearly trace the effects of neo-Ottomanist understanding. In this part, in order to search for that impact, the Middle East and Balkans are chosen as relevant case studies.

From a historical perspective, the preservation of neutrality has been Turkey's priority in its Middle Eastern policy. Since the establishment of the Republic in 1923, Turkey has rigorously sought to keep out of regional conflicts and has attempted to maintain neutrality in dealing with conflicting parties. Though Turkey became closely allied with its Western partners in its Middle Eastern policy with the start of the Cold

War (as exemplified by the Baghdad Pact), it only continued till the mid 1960s. From that point on, Turkish decision makers tried to better relations with their Middle Eastern neighbours and act independently of the country's Western allies as much as possible.

As a result, economic relations between Turkey and Middle Eastern countries increased considerably during the 1980s, mainly due to the fact that Turkey retained its impartiality in the Iran-Iraq war that continued from 1980 to 1988. Another salient factor behind this increase was the economy-based attitude of Turgut Özal toward the region (Altunışık, 2009, p. 179-182). However, the 1980s and 1990s at the same time witnessed the securitisation of Turkish-Middle Eastern relations since the region was perceived as a swamp, threatening Turkey's vital interests and forcing Turkey to take extraordinary measures (Altunışık, 2004).

By the late 1990s, the securitisation tide seemed to slow down due to the transformation of Turkey's perception of the Middle East, thus leading to what Altunışık calls "limited desecuritisation" (Altunışık, 2004, p. 376). This shift can be related to both regional dynamics and the changes in Turkish foreign policy. One important change was the election of the moderate leader Mohammad Khatami to the presidency in Iran, which led to a considerable weakening of suspicion toward Iran in Turkey in particular and in international society in general. The second change was related to Turkey's ties to Syria. Syria provided both shelter and support to the PKK for many years and Turkey used political pressure to finally put an end to it. In 1998, Turkish pressure led to the dismissal of Abdullah Öcalan by the Syrian authorities and the ratification of Adana Memorandum in 1998, which foresaw Turkish-Syrian cooperation in different realms, including security. Improving Turkish-Israeli relations since 1996 seemed to contribute to the changing Turkish policy toward Syria as well.

8: Turkish Foreign Policy under the AKP Governments: **229**
An Interplay of Imperial Legacy, Neoliberal Interests and
Pragmatism

However, there have seemingly been more changes in the foreign policy path since 2006. For instance, during the 2008-2009 Israeli attacks on the Gaza Strip, the Turkish government criticised Israel in an uncharacteristically harsh manner while simultaneously presenting itself as a negotiation partner for Hamas, or the Islamic Resistance Movement. Turkey-Israeli relations were deeply troubled once again when Danny Ayalon, Israeli Vice Foreign Minister, invited Turkish ambassador, Oğuz Çelikkol, to a meeting at the Parliament (*Knesset*) in which he had to sit on a lower chair than the others, the Turkish flag was not put on the table intentionally. Furthermore, Israeli media was invited to record the scene. The third and the greatest crisis occurred when Israel intercepted an aid flotilla which was led by a Turkish non-governmental organisation on the way to Gaza in May of 2010.

In the meantime, why have Turkish decision makers begun dialoguing with Hamas, a group that is classified as a terrorist organisation by European countries and the United States? Is Turkey retiring its traditional pro-West orientation in favor of a more active Middle East policy? Notably, Turkey's recognition as a candidate country to the European Union (EU) was followed by an intense "Europeanisation" phase that saw an array of legislative reforms. In recent years, however, the government's enthusiasm for reform has diminished considerably, for a number of reasons: first, the accession negotiations were temporarily suspended due to disagreements between Turkey and the EU on the issue of Cyprus. Secondly, Turkish politicians were not happy with the EU's ambiguous accession policy, and the lack of enthusiasm for Turkish accession from EU member states, mainly France and Germany. The so-called "privileged partnership"—as opposed to full EU membership—proposed first by German Chancellor Angela Merkel and then embraced by other European conservative leaders held little attraction for Turkey.

Another reason for Turkey's declining enthusiasm for the reform process was the resumption of attacks by the PKK. Turkey's democratisation and the growing influence of Kurdish rebels in Iraq caused the PKK leadership to fear that its resistance movement would be marginalised. As a consequence, in 2004 the PKK ended its five-year cease-fire and resumed attacks on Turkish targets. The PKK rebels' ability to withdraw to their base in northern Iraq following attacks on the Turkish military without encountering US-led resistance led to a deterioration in relations between Turkey and the United States. Hence, Turkey's political priorities increasingly shifted from "more democracy" to "more security."

The change in the AKP's foreign policy priorities has also resulted in a disruption of the previously close relationship between Turkey and Israel. In 1949, Turkey became the first state with a Muslim majority to recognise Israel and establish diplomatic relations. Turkish-Israeli relations then gained a strategic dimension in 1996 when the two states signed military and defense cooperation agreements.[129] The United States welcomed this partnership, while the majority of Arab states sharply criticised it, speaking of a new "axis" between the non-Arab states of the region. Initially, what brought Turkey and Israel together was not just their commonalities as democratic and Western-oriented nations, but similar security threats from organisations such as the PKK, Hezbollah, and Hamas.

Beginning in 2003, however, the spirit of partnership between the two countries was seriously undermined. First, Turkey's relations with neighbouring states such as Syria and Iran improved as a result of assurances that they would cease their support for the PKK. Second, the U.S. invasion of Iraq in 2003 dramatically changed the security situation in the region. From a Turkish perspective, the idea of an independent Kurdish state in northern Iraq was a nightmare, which is why Turkish politicians vigorously defended Iraq's territo-

8: Turkish Foreign Policy under the AKP Governments: **231**
   An Interplay of Imperial Legacy, Neoliberal Interests and
   Pragmatism

rial integrity. Israel, however, set other priorities, especially speaking out against hegemonies in the region. A powerful Iraqi state was not in their interests, and furthermore, the Kurds, as a Muslim, non-Arab people, represented a potentially important strategic partner for Israel (Kibaroğlu, 2005; Erkmen, 2005).

The religious identity of the AKP[130] and its electorate also played an important role in the deterioration of Turkish-Israel relations. As a party with roots in the Islamic milieu, the AKP's electorate was predominately religiously conservative and especially sensitive to the plight of Muslim peoples in the region. When Prime Minister Recep Tayyip Erdoğan accused Israel, in 2005, of pursuing a policy of state terror against the Palestinian population, it became clear that a new era in Turkish-Israeli relations had dawned. In addition, the electoral success of Hamas in January 2006 was welcomed by the Turkish government. While the EU and the United States refused to recognise the election result, AKP politicians declared the elections to have been democratic and therefore legitimate. This was an unfamiliar tone; until then, Turkish politicians had firmly rejected any negotiations with organisations such as Hamas in order not to undermine their own position in the struggle against the PKK.

A few days before the Israeli offensive in Gaza, Israeli Prime Minister Ehud Olmert and Erdoğan held talks in Ankara over the Israeli conflict with Syria, which appeared to be successful. On the Turkish side there were hopes that direct negotiations between Israel and Syria would soon commence. Consequently, Israel's three-week assault on Gaza, in which more than 1,300 people were killed, came as a severe shock for Turkey. Erdoğan denounced Israel's actions as reckless, revealing his deep disappointment at the failure of Turkish efforts to bring about a resolution to the Israeli-Syrian conflict.

As Turkish criticism of Israel became increasingly vehement, the AKP government simultaneously began to make overtures to Hamas. Erdoğan's senior foreign policy advisor, Davutoğlu, was in constant contact with Hamas leader, Khaled Meshaal, during the Gaza conflict. Erdoğan even planned to convey Hamas's demands to the United Nations (UN) (Erdoğan: İsrail bir insanlık dramına imza attı, 2009). Shortly after the start of the Israeli attack, Erdoğan personally traveled to Syria, Egypt, Jordan, and Saudi Arabia in an effort to win their support for his two-stage Israeli-Palestinian peace plan. He called for an initial cease-fire, followed by reconciliation between Hamas and the Palestine Liberation Organisation. However, the Turkish initiative failed. The states he visited considered the plan inadequate and the AKP's goal of simultaneously supporting Hamas and acting as neutral mediator in the Middle East appeared irreconcilable. In this respect, Turkey's foreign policy reorientation was foreshadowed in the "neo-Ottoman" discourse of Turkish politicians during the attack on Gaza. Erdoğan spoke repeatedly of the Ottoman legacy and the historical mission of Turkey in the Middle East.[131] While visiting injured Palestinians undergoing treatment in Turkish hospitals, he instructed the interpreter to deliver the following message: "Tell them that they are in a safe country. Tell them that they are in the houses of their brothers and fathers".[132] In sum, Erdoğan's discourse during the Gaza operation was laden with references to Turkey's Ottoman past and its historical responsibilites stemming from it. Both the discourse and policies of Turkish leaders had repercussions on relations with Israel as seen in the case of Davos crisis.

At the World Economic Forum in Davos, Switzerland in January 2009, tension between Ankara and Tel Aviv came to a head when Erdoğan stormed out of a discussion with Israeli President Shimon Peres over the Gaza offensive. On his return to Turkey, he was celebrated by AKP supporters and a sympathetic media as the "hero of Davos." Cengiz Çandar,

8: Turkish Foreign Policy under the AKP Governments: An Interplay of Imperial Legacy, Neoliberal Interests and Pragmatism

233

a prominent Turkish journalist, even described Erdoğan as a "new Nasser" in the Arab world. (Çandar, 2009). In opposition circles however, Erdoğan's unexpected departure was viewed more critically, with some even accusing him of populism (a potentially dangerous affiliation with upcoming local elections). Furthermore, others reproached the government for maintaining close military cooperation with Israel, despite the anti-Israeli rhetoric. Turkish President Abdullah Gül stated that after this event Turkish-Israeli relations could never be same as before. However, surprisingly enough, only several weeks after the attack, without any sign of Turkish preconditions being fulfilled, Davutoğlu met Israeli minister Ben Eliezer in Brussels (Turkish Mfa Confirms Davutoglu's Meeting with Israeli Minister Eliezer, 2010). It was only after the UN Report on the Israeli intervention to aid flotilla "Mavi Marmara" became public in April 2011 that Turkey suspended its military relations with Israel.[133]

As a series of crises were experienced in Turkish-Israeli relations in the first decade of the 21st century, Turkish ties with their Muslim neighbours were booming, as seen especially in relations with Syria and Iran. As explicated above, since the late 1990s Turkish leaders aimed to better ties with the Middle Eastern neighbours and desecuritise these relations. Hence, Turkish rapprochement with the Middle Eastern countries started before the AKP era, but it was certainly intensified after the AKP came to power, mainly following the disappointment in Ankara-Brussels relations over the solution of the Cyprus conflict. In the process of rapprochement, Turkey and Syria lifted visa requirements within the framework of the High Level Strategic Cooperation Council and the AKP government announced that it would seek economic integration with Syria (Dilek, 2009). With regard to Iran, Turkey was opposed to international sanctions over the nuclear question and took all possible initiatives to solve the

nuclear crisis in a diplomatic way. The betterment in Turkish-
Iranian relations started earlier, but it has also increased
during the AKP era. All of these developments point to a new
era in Turkey's Middle Eastern policy, in which the view of
"neo-Ottomanism" plays a strong role. One can perceive the
impact of Davutoğlu doctrine in Turkey's changing relations
with the Middle East.

As explicated above, Davutoğlu criticised Turkey's
Middle Eastern policy during the Cold War, on the grounds
that it was based on an uncritical alliance with the West. As he
sees it, Turkey has to develop an independent Middle Eastern
policy since it has had close connections to its Arab neighbours for centuries. According to Davutoğlu, Turkey should
also recognise the Muslim peoples in its neighbouring regions
as political partners.

Davutoğlu is not the first to emphasise the importance of
neighbouring states in Turkish foreign policy. Many before
him, including former prime ministers Bülent Ecevit and
Turgut Özal, placed importance on good relations with the
Arab world. However, there was also a consensus that the
West held a special significance for Turkey. Davutoğlu is the
first Turkish politician to present a comprehensive foreign
policy doctrine that calls into question Turkey's classic alliance with the West and is keen to develop special relations
with the Middle East.

As a result of AKP's policies discussed above the importance of Turkey within the Middle East has grown in recent
years. This is partly because as a medium-sized regional
power, it is unable to impact politics on a global level. It does,
however, possess sufficient military and economic resources to
influence developments in its neighbouring ex-Ottoman territories, in Davutoğlu's view. Accordingly, the AKP government
tried to mediate between Afghanistan and Pakistan, between
the EU and Iran, between Israel, Syria, and the Palestinians,

8: Turkish Foreign Policy under the AKP Governments: **235**
An Interplay of Imperial Legacy, Neoliberal Interests and
Pragmatism

and between different groups in Iraq. This mediation role is in accord with Davutoğlu's doctrine of an active and balanced foreign policy. However, Ankara's new stance on Israel conflicts with Turkey's self-conception as an honest broker. Reconciling this aforementioned criticism of Israel with Turkey's role as a neutral mediator in the Middle East is currently one of the greatest challenges faced by Turkish foreign policy makers. Their relationship with Israel is deeply ambivalent.

However, it is not just over Israel that a gulf has opened up between ambitions and reality. Domestically, Erdoğan has failed to live up to his promise of being a "voice of the victims," as he proclaimed himself upon returning from Davos (Çandar, 2009). In view of the problems still faced by the Kurdish and Alevi populations in Turkey, it is clear that the AKP government, despite a number of reform initiatives, is not committed to long-term improvement in the rights of these groups. Although the AKP government plays the role of the guardian of the Palestinians, it does not show full commitment to the solution of the problems of Kurdish and Alevi groups (See Soyarık-Şentürk's contribution to this volume). Although the AKP initiated policies of "opening" (açılım) toward Kurds and Alevis, some of their basic problems still remain unsolved. For example, Kurdish is still named as an "unrecognised language" when spoken by Kurdish parliamentarians at the *Türkiye Büyük Millet Meclisi* (Turkish Grand National Assembly, TBMM) (Kaplan'dan bilinmeyen dile Kürtçe yanıt, 2010). Religion is still a must course in the schools (although Alevi groups repeatedly ask the government to lift it) and *Cemevleri*[134] are not recognised as official religious buildings by the Presidency of Religious Affairs (Tapan, 2010). This is an important indication of the divergence between its internal and external politics. The AKP's pragmatist approach is thus revealed in playing the falcon domestically, but the dove internationally.[135]

Apart from the policy based dimension of this divergence the change in the official stance on Israel has also affected Turkey's small Jewish minority who has been particularly affected by the changes in the country's stance on Israel. Jews have been present in the Anatolian lands since the Ottoman Empire accepted the exiled refugees from Spain in 1492. Although the government is at pains to dispel the impression that anti-Semitism is a problem in Turkey, it has further inflamed an already tense atmosphere with its harsh critique of Israel. With the lasting effects of the verbal attack on the Jewish minority during the Gaza war (Strittmatter, 2009), it remains to be seen what effect the harsh criticism of Israel will have on Turkey's Jews.

The Balkans offer the second example for Davutoğlu's neo-Ottomanist approach. The Balkans have not been on top of the AKP's foreign policy agenda until 2009, despite the emphasis of Davutoğlu on the region in his book *Stratejik Derinlik*, with concentration on Ottoman legacy. However, both the discourse and policies toward Balkans underwent a transformation at the time. Davutoğlu's opening speech in Sarajevo on 16 October 2009 was marked by the sanctification of the Ottoman sovereignty in the Balkans for centuries and the phantasy to reintegrate the Balkans, Middle East and Caucasus under the Turkish leadership. Calling the Ottoman centuries "success story" Davutoğlu argued that "we have to reinvent this success" through new cultural and economic means.[136] Davutoğlu's speech was full of clear neo-Ottomanist implications, hence it is worth of quoting at length:

> ... Anatolia belongs to you, our Bosnian brothers and sisters. And be sure that Sarajevo is ours... Yes, whatever happens in the Balkans, in Caucasus, in Middle East, it is our issue. when I sat in Ankara, I made a 1000 kilometers circle around my office. There are 23 countries. All of them are our

8: Turkish Foreign Policy under the AKP Governments: **237**
An Interplay of Imperial Legacy, Neoliberal Interests and
Pragmatism

relatives and they expect something from us... our
foreign policy aims to establish order in all these
surrounding regions, in the Balkans, Caucasus and
the Middle East. Because if there is no order then
we will pay the price. For a Western or another
diplomat from another part of the world, a Bosnian
issue is a technical issue to deal with, like a technical
diplomatic process. For us, it is a life and death
story. It is so important. The territorial integrity
of BiH for us is as important as the territorial
integrity of Turkey. The prosperity and security of
Sarajevo is as important as security and prosperity
in Istanbul. our history is the same, our destiny is
the same and our future is the same. Like in the
16th century, the rise of Ottoman Balkans as the
center of world politics, we will make the Balkans,
Caucasus and Middle East together with Turkey as
the center of world politics in the future. This is
the objective of Turkish foreign policy and we will
achieve this. We will reintegrate the Balkan region,
Middle East and Caucasus, based on this principle
of regional and global peace for the future, not for
all of us, but for all the humanity.[137]

As a sign of the launch of active Balkan policy in October
2009, Ankara initiated a trilateral negotiation framework among
Turkey, Serbia, and Bosnia-Herzegovina on the one hand and
Turkey, Croatia, and Bosnia-Herzegovina on the other. A series
of negotiations led to concrete results: the appointment of a
Bosnian ambassador to Belgrade (finally, after many years),
an apology from the Serbian Parliament over the Srebrenica
massacre of 1995 for the first time, and the Serbian President
Boris Tadic's attending of commemorations in Srebrenica in
July 2010. Turkish negotiations were aimed at contributing to

the maintenance of Bosnia-Herzegovina's territorial integrity in a response to increasing problems within the country. Considering that EU's long-lasting efforts have not yet produced any significant result, Turkey's latest initiatives were appreciated as seen in the remarks of Serbian Foreign Minister Vuk Jeremic: "Turkish mediation had done more for reconciliation in the Balkans than anything before it" (Quoted in Vogel, 2010). Although the AKP's Balkan initiative started relatively late, it bore its fruits in a short period of time.[138] It is also interesting to note that although Davutoğlu emphasises Bosniaks and Albanians as Turkey's closest partners in the region in *Stratejik Derinlik*, when it comes to reality, Turkey allies with Serbia as well, despite the background of thorny relations in the 1990s. Although the Serbian side is not one of Turkey's traditional friends in the post-Cold War era, when Turkey tries to increase its weight in Balkan politics, it does its best to start a rapprochement with the Serbian side as well. It proves that although the conceptual background of the AKP's foreign policy is based on neo-Ottomanism, it tends to be pragmatic whenever it seems necessary.

Another important Turkish policy in the Balkans under the AKP rule was the diplomatic recognition of Kosovo just one day after the declaration of its independence by the Kosovar authorities. This issue is interesting to explore in terms of minority rights in various contexts that directly or indirectly concern Turkey. To start with there is the yet to be resolved Kurdish issue. Second, it is also related to the non-recognition policy of those EU members which suffer from separatist demands in the case of Spain, Romania, and Slovakia. Likewise, it can be related to the Cyprus issue in the case of Greece and South Cyprus. Why then did Turkey prefer to recognise Kosovo though there was no international consensus over the issue at the time?[139]

First of all, it should be stated that the Turkish recogni-

8: Turkish Foreign Policy under the AKP Governments:
An Interplay of Imperial Legacy, Neoliberal Interests and
Pragmatism

239

tion of Kosovo did not represent a radical change in Turkish foreign policy, but rather a continuity. Turgut Özal's reception of İbrahim Rugova, leader of the Kosovo Albanians, in 1992, as well as the parliamentary debates in the 1990s indicate that Turkey sympathised with the Kosovar Albanians' cause from the very beginning. Second, Turkey was aware of the fact that Kosovo's independence process was irreversible and that there was no prospect for Kosovo returning to Serbian sovereignty. A stylistic change is that the Turkish Foreign Ministry ceased to emphasise Yugoslav territorial integrity by the 2000s. Turkey even took steps to promote the acceptance of the Ahtisaari Plan favoring independence of Kosovo by the UN Security Council in 2007 (Türbedar, 2007, p. 52-53). This has been in line with the changing position of the Western countries on the Kosovo issue, led by the US change of policies from supporting territorial integrity of Serbia to supporting independence demands of Albanians. Prior to Kosovo's declaration of independence, it was reported by the international press that US was encouraging its allies, including Turkey, to recognise Kosovo (*RFE/RL Newsline*, 2008). The AKP government likely did not want to remain indifferent to the newest state of Europe, as the recognition of Kosovo and the establishment of friendly relations between the two countries would increase the regional role of Ankara (Abazi, 2008, p. 4.). Kosovo would be a new partner for Turkey with regard to the security of both the Balkans and Europe. Besides, Kosovo has been the second country in the Balkans with a Muslim majority of more than 90 percent. Davutoğlu stated that Kosovo is a sister country to Turkey due to its specific geopolitical position, historical ties, and importance of its stability for the region ("Sayın Bakanımızın Kosova Dışişleri Bakanı İskender Hüseyni İle Ortak Basın Toplantısı", August 28, 2009). Furthermore, this can be shown as an example of the impact of neo-Ottomanism on Davutoğlu's approach to the region.

As mentioned above, the AKP's foreign policy under-standing clearly played a role in the recognition process, as it considers Turkey a central country and favors its active participation in regional developments (Davutoğlu, 2008). According to Davutoğlu, Bosniaks and Albanians are the most important people in the Balkans with regard to Turkish foreign policy. Therefore, if Turkey wants to establish a "sphere of influence" in the Balkans, it should first of all cooperate with these two groups, with which it has "historical and cordial closeness"[140] (Davutoğlu, 2001, pp. 316-317). Within this framework, it is supposed that the increasing regional role of Turkey would increase its position in global politics.

The interesting point here is that Turkey did not concentrate much on the problems of the Turkish minority in Kosovo when the matter of recognition was discussed in Ankara. The most signicant of these problems stems from the fact that Turkish is no longer one of the official languages of Kosovo. This dates back to the beginning of the UN Mission in Kosovo (UNMIK) administration, though it was one of the three official languages (in addition to Albanian and Serbian) during Yugoslavia. In effect, Turkish decision makers were careful to take care of the whole of Kosovo, not only the problems of Turks. According to Türkeş, the case of Turkish minority in Kosovo is a good example for understanding the increasing influence of global actors in the Balkans (Türkeş, 2008, p. 267-268).

In analysing AKP's approach toward the Middle East and Balkans, the impact of neo-Ottomanist discourse on the poli-cies must be taken into account as shown so far in this section. It should be noted that AKP's use of neo-Ottomanism is not just a rhetoric, but a discourse in line with Michel Foucault's use of the term. (Whisnant, "Foucault&Discourse".) In other words, by sanctifying and glorifying the Ottoman past the AKP tries to establish a Turkish sphere of influence in the

8: Turkish Foreign Policy under the AKP Governments:
An Interplay of Imperial Legacy, Neoliberal Interests and
Pragmatism

241

neighbouring, ex-Ottoman areas, through the use of various means with special emphasis on economics. The neo-Ottoman sphere is not seen as something given, but it is considered to be a site asking for establishment, based on common history. Davutoğlu's argument that "Anatolia belongs to you... And be sure that Sarajevo is ours"[141] as well as Erdoğan's message to injured Palestinians that "they are in the houses of their brothers and fathers"[142] are signs of that approach. The components of AKP's neo-Ottomanist approach are the glorification of the Ottoman past, existence of common religion and culture between Turkey and neighbouring countries, using of economic instruments to create Turkish sphere of influence as well as playing the facilitator role among the conflicting parties. Which component of the neo-Ottomanism would be emphasised is decided on a case by case basis. However, the underlying rationale behind this approach is the opportunity of playing the so-called "big brother" role in the ex-Ottoman territories. Davutoğlu's phantasy of the establishment of Ottoman Commonwealth under Turkish leadership by following the British example is another clear sign of this approach.[143]

The use of the neo-Ottomanist discourse in Turkish foreign policy can be traced back to the Özal era in which Turkish decision-makers, confronted with the sudden collapse of the bipolar system, tried to create a new state identity for Turkey. At the time, one of the factors influencing Turkish international relations was neo-Ottomanism since the old Ottoman territories were gaining their independence with the dissolution of the Yugoslav Federation and Ankara tried to establish cordial relations with these countries. Özal's discourse of the emergence of "the Turkic world from the Adriatic to the Chinese Wall" became popular at the time.[144] Neo-Ottomanist approach was used in order to legitimise Turkish interest in the ex-Ottoman territories. With the end of the Bosnian War, however, the influence of neo-Ottomanism seemed to wane till AKP came to power. Hence, it can be argued that AKP is a continuation of Özal style foreign policy not only because it instrumentalises economics, but also it has relaunched the neo-Ottomanist discourse. Since the issue of neo-Ottomanism was covered extensively in Davutoğlu's influential book *Strategic Depth* as well as in the discourses of AKP leadership, this section tried to deal with the subject rather extensively.

Pragmatism: A Sine Qua Non for the AKP's Foreign Policy

In addition to neoliberal and neo-Ottomanist approaches that characterise the AKP's foreign policy preferences one can note the decisive impact of pragmatism. In the post-Cold War era, the narrow understanding of foreign policy started to change as both actors and issues began to multiply. As a result, foreign policy no longer constitutes just state-to-state relations and it does not include only political or security matters. (Goldstein and Pevehouse, 2011, p. 93.) The emergence of alternative approaches in international relations theory has enriched Turkey's understanding of world politics considerably. In addition, the recurring crises of capitalism has led to the emergence of new political economy approaches as well.[145] Turkey is one of the countries that had an especially difficult transition from the Cold War to post-Cold War period, since its foreign policy had been then defined according to its geostrategic position. Turkish decision makers still have a tendency to assess the international politics from traditional perspective. In this respect, Davutoğlu's use of the traditional geopolitical theories is exemplary. In that framework, Turkey's approach to the new issues and concepts of the IR has been shaped via pragmatism under the AKP as it had been the case during the reign of previous governments as well. Issues of environment and

8: Turkish Foreign Policy under the AKP Governments:
   An Interplay of Imperial Legacy, Neoliberal Interests and
   Pragmatism   **243**

human rights can be appropriate case studies to prove this pragmatist side of Turkish foreign policy.

Admittedly, such environmental issues and human rights are not at the top of Turkey's foreign policy agenda. Indeed, Turkey for many years was not interested in signing the Kyoto Protocol. Then even when it signed it in 2009 due to pressure from the EU and international environmental organisations, it continued to ignore the requirements. Perhaps most significantly, Turkey did not pay much attention to demands to decrease its greenhouse gas emissions (Erdoğdu, 2010).

The same cautious approach can be observed in regard to the human rights issues in its foreign policy as well. One instance, of course, is the case of Darfur, which was discussed above. Although Turkish decision makers were vocal and tough in their criticism of Israel, they did not show the same sensitivity regarding the violence in Sudan. Another related example was the gross human rights violations in Iran in the summer of 2009, following the general elections, when security forces killed protesters who were demonstrating against the allegedly fraud election results. Turkish decision makers preferred to remain silent and did not raise their voice. These are all examples regarding how Turkish policy toward human rights is used selectively. The human rights discourse has been adopted in the case of Palestinians in Gaza, hovewer forgotten in the events of Darfur and Iran. The pragmatist dimension of the AKP's foreign policy is thus crystal clear in its approach to human rights.

Another important and recent example with regard to AKP's pragmatic approach to foreign policy is its attitude toward the Arab Spring that consisted of mass protests of people against the dictatorial regimes in the Middle East and Africa. The protest movements started at a time in which the AKP government established best ever political, economic and strategic relations with the leading cadres of many Middle Eastern and African countries ever since the establishment of the Republic of Turkey. When the rebellions started, the AKP remained at a crossroad in which it had to choose between the dictatorial regimes and peoples on the streets. Although many civilians were killed in this process, AKP's response was not as vocal as it might be expected. This fact drew the criticism that when it was the Muslim leaders who were killing civilian people, the AKP leaders' protest remained rather soft and cautious (İdiz, 2011). After a while, the AKP strengthened its support to the protesting masses as the movements spread all over the region and the Western governments made their position clearer. However, this time the AKP came across another dilemma in the case of Libya as to giving support to the NATO operation or not. Initially, Prime Minister Erdoğan declared the NATO operation as unnecessary and nonsense, however just after one month he stated his support for NATO operation. In addition, five Turkish warships and one submarine took part in NATO operation in order to monitor the UN embargo (Ergin, 2011). Hence, in the case of the Arab Spring, Turkish foreign policy under the AKP rule was rather cyclical, and in the end, it was harmonised with the pro-US policy preferences as could be foreseen in light of its pragmatist approach.

Concluding Remarks

The literature on the AKP's foreign policy has so far argued either for the importance of neo-Ottomanism or for the salience of commercial interests (Taspinar, 2008; Kardaş 2010; Kirişci 2009). This chapter's objective was to make a contribution by analysing the dynamics of neo-Ottomanism, neoliberalism and pragmatism in Turkey's recent foreign policy behavior. It can be argued that one of the

8: Turkish Foreign Policy under the AKP Governments: **245**
An Interplay of Imperial Legacy, Neoliberal Interests and
Pragmatism

main objectives of the AKP's foreign policy is to increase
Turkey's sphere of influence in the ex-Ottoman territorities,
hence creating some kind of wise, old brother role. In order
to reach this main target, it prefers to use economic means
provided by the neoliberal global order and cultural simi-
larities. The main assumption behind this is that as Turkey
develops its independent policy in its neighbourhood, it will
be capable of expanding from a regional power to a global
one. However, for the distant geographies, the emphasis is
mainly on geo-economics, as seen in the case of Asia where
both the aim and the means is geo-economics.

One can olso notice the impact of pragmatism on the
foreign policy behavior of the AKP. Turkey's relations with
Israel is a good example of this argument, since after each
crisis following a very harsh rhetoric, the period of normalisation began as soon as possible and channels for dialogue
were kept open. Moreover, Turkey's reluctance to embrace
new issues and concepts consistenly, especially in the realms
of the environment and human rights, is another indication
of its pragmatist worldview.

The major focus of the AKP's external behavior is the
ex-Ottoman territories, mainly the region of the Middle
East. In Davutoğlu's view it is through the establishment of
spheres of influence in the ex-Ottoman lands that Turkey can
become a global player in international politics. However,
this neo-Ottoman approach is then combined with neoliberalism, necessitating that Turkey use economic tools in order
to increase its influence worldwide. The increasing influence
of geo-economics in Turkey's African and Asian policies as
well as the utilisation of THY in furthering Turkey's foreign
ties can be considered important examples of how neoliberalism has become part of Turkish foreign policy. This uneasy
mixture of neo-Ottomanism and neoliberalism led to several
crises in Turkish foreign policy, as seen in its ties with Israel

and the US, which have led to the prevalence of pragmatism
from time to time.

8: Turkish Foreign Policy under the AKP Governments: **247**
An Interplay of Imperial Legacy, Neoliberal Interests and
Pragmatism

REFERENCES

Abazi, E. (2008). Kosovo independence: An Albanian perspective. *SETA Policy Brief, 11* (4).

AK Parti Seçim Bildirgesi, 2002. Ankara: AKP.

Altunışık, M. (2004). Turkey's Middle East challenges. In İ. Bal (Ed.), *Turkish Foreign Policy in post-Cold War Era* (pp. 363-377). Boca Raton, Florida: Brown Walker.

Altunışık, M. (2009). Worldviews and Turkish foreign policy. *New Perspectives on Turkey, 40,* 179-182.

Aras, B. (2009). Davutoğlu era in Turkish foreign policy. *SETA Policy Brief* (32), May.

Aktay, Y. (2010). Politics at home, politics in the world: The return of the political in Turkish foreign policy. *Mediterranean Quarterly, 21* (1), 61-75.

Başbakan Ağladı. (2009, January 13). Retrieved January 15, 2009 from http://www.haberajans.com/basbakan-agladi-haberi-76697.html

Başbakan Erdoğan'ın USAK'ta yaptığı konuşmanın tam metni. (2010, February 13). Retrieved July 26, 2010 from http://www.usak.org.tr

Bilgin, P. (2005). Turkey's changing security discourses: The challenge of globalization. *European Journal of Political Research, 44,* 175-201.

_____. (2007). Only strong states can survive in Turkey's geography: The uses of "geopolitical truths" in Turkey. *Political Geography, 46* (7), 740-756.

Brzezinski, Z. (1997). *The grand Chessboard: American Primacy and its Geostrategic Imperatives.* New York: Basic Books.

Criss, N. B. (2010). Dismantling Turkey: The will of the people? *Turkish Studies, 11* (1), 45-58.

Çalış, Ş. (2001). Hayalet bilimi ve hayali kimlikler, neo-Osmanlılık, Özal ve Balkanlar, Konya: Çizgi.

Çandar, C. (2009). Tayyip Erdoğan Ortadoğu'nun kimsesizlerinin kimi artık. *Radikal (Turkish daily),* January 31.

Çandar, C. (2010). Neo-Türkiye... *Radikal,* May 28.

Çelik, M. (2010). Turkey outdoes EU, US, raising hopes for peace in Balkans. *Today's Zaman (Turkish daily),* February 14.

Davutoğlu, A. (2001). *Stratejik derinlik. Türkiye'nin uluslararası konumu,* İstanbul: Küre.

_____, (2008). Turkey's foreign policy vision: An assessment of 2007. *Insight Turkey, 10* (1), 77-96.

Davutoğlu'nun hayali Osmanlı milletler topluluğu. (2010). *Milliyet (Turkish daily)*, December 7. Retrieved November 10, 2011 from http://www.milliyet.com.tr/davutoglu-nun-hayali-osmanli-milletler-toplulugu/dunya/haberdetay/07.12.2010/1323171/default.htm

Demirtaş-Coşkun, B. (2009 April). Kurswechsel mit Tücken. *Internationale Politik, 64* (4), 62-67.

_____. (2010). Kosova'nın bağımsızlığı ve Türk dış politikası (1990-2008). *Uluslararası İlişkiler, 7* (27), 51-85.

Dilek, B. S. (2009). Suriye ile entegrasyon adımı. *Cumhuriyet (Turkish daily)*, October 14.

Dinççağ, A. & Özkale, Ü. (2010). AB pazarındaki ihracat kayıpları. TEPAV, October 14.

Erdoğan: İsrail bir insanlık dramına imza attı. (2009). Retrieved from http://arsiv.ntvmsnbc.com/news/471128.asp

Erdoğan: İsrail insanlık yaşamına kara bir leke düşürdü. (2009). *Radikal,* January 7. Retrieved November 10, 2011 from http://www.radikal.com.tr/Radikal.aspx?aType=RadikalDetay&ArticleID=915782&Date=07.01.2009&CategoryID=78

Erdoğan'dan Suudi gazeteciye Ortadoğu tepkisi. (2009). *Milliyet,* January 6. Retrieved from November 10, 2011 http://www.milliyet.com.tr/erdogan-dan-suudi-gazeteciye-ortadogu-tepkisi/siyaset/sondakika/06.01.2009/1043439/default.htm

Erdoğdu, E. (2010). Turkish support to Kyoto Protocol: A reality or just an illusion. *Renewable and Sustainable Energy Reviews, 14* (3), 1111-1117.

Ergin, S. (2011). Erdoğan'ın Libya seyir defteri. *Hürriyet (Turkish daily)*, August 25.

Erkmen, S. (2005). 1990'lardan günümüze Türkiye-İsrail stratejik işbirliği. *Uluslararası İlişkiler, 2* (7), 157-185.

Gürcistan'a gösterdiğiniz hassasiyeti gösterin. (2009). *Hürriyet*, January 4.

http://www.akparti.org.tr

http://www.dtm.gov.tr/dtmadmin/upload/ANL/AfrikaDb/Sudan.doc

http://www.mfa.gov.tr

İdiz, S. (2011). AKP, Libya ve Suriye konusunda neden duyarsız? *Milliyet*, April 24.

İş dünyası artık dış politikanın öncülerinden. (2004 April-May). Ahmet K. Han's interview with Ahmet Davutoğlu, *Turkish Time*.

Interview with Ersin Özince, İki yılda Balkanlar ve Ortadoğu'da ciddi varlığımız olacak. (2010), *Milliyet*, August 25.

8: Turkish Foreign Policy under the AKP Governments: **249**
An Interplay of Imperial Legacy, Neoliberal Interests and
Pragmatism

İnat, K.,& Duran, B. (2006). AKP dış politikası: Teori ve uygulama. In
Z. Dağı (Ed.), *AK Partili yıllar* (pp. 15-70). Ankara: Orion.

Kanbolat, H. (2008). Turkey and Sudan: Darfur and trade. *Today's
Zaman,* January 29.

Kansu, H. (1998). *Kosova ikinci Bosna olmasın.* İstanbul: Yıldızlar.

Kaplan'dan bilinmeyen dile Kürtçe yanıt. (2010). *Birgün (Turkish daily),*
December 9. Retrieved March 12, 2011 from http://www.birgun.net/
politics_index.php?news_code=1291927223&year=2010&month=12
&day=09

Kardaş, Ş. (2010). Turkey: Redrawing the Middle East map or building
sandcastles? *Middle East Policy, 17* (1), 115-136.

Kibaroğlu, M. (2005). Clash of interest over Northern Iraq drives
Turkish-Israeli alliance to a crossroads. *The Middle East Journal, 59*
(2), 246-264.

Kirişci, K. (2009). The transformation of Turkish foreign policy: The rise
of the trading state. *New Perspectives on Turkey,* (40), 29-57.

Kosova'daki Türk Eşgüdüm Müsteşarı Volkan Türk Vural'ın açıklaması.
Kosova Radyo ve Televizyon Kurumu – RTK. 6:10 pm. News in
Turkish, August 16, 2007. Quoted in Türbedar, E. (2007). Kosova
düğümü çözülüyor mu?. *Stratejik Analiz* (89), 52-53.

Oğuzlu, T. (2007). Soft power in Turkish foreign policy. *Australian
Journal of International Affairs, 61* (1), 81-97.

Özkan M. & Akgün B. (2010, July). Why welcome Al Basheer?
Contextualizing Turkey's Darfur policy. *SETA Policy Brief* (45).

Goldstein J. S. & Pevehouse J. C. (2011). *International Relations.* Boston:
Pearson.

RFE/RL Newsline. (2008). Retrieved October 8, 2009 from http://www.
rferl.org/content/article/1144041.html

Sayın Bakanımızın Kosova Dışişleri Bakanı İskender Hüseyni ile ortak
basın toplantısı. (2009, August 28). Retrieved September 23, 2009
from http://www.mfa.gov.tr/sayin-bakanimizin-kosova-disisleri-
bakani-iskender-huseyni-ile-ortak-basin-toplantisi_-28-agustos-
2009_-ankara.tr.mfa

Speech by Ahmet Davutoğlu, on the opening ceremony of the
conference, Ottoman legacy and Balkan Muslim communities today
in Sarajevo (October 16, 2009) Retrieved March 1, 2011 from http://
www.ius.edu.ba/dzsusko/Davutoglu_transcript_dzs.doc

Strittmatter, K. (2009, January 31). Öl ins Feuer des Antisemitismus.
Süddeutsche Zeitung.

TBMM genel kurul tutanağı. 20th Period. 3rd Legislative Year. 67th Session. (1998, March 17). p. 60. Retrieved January 26, 2010 from http://www.tbmm.gov.tr/develop/owa/tutanak_sd.birlesim_baslangic ?P4=301&P5=B&PAGE1=60&PAGE2=&web_user_id=7268460

Tapan, B. (2010, December 5). AKP Alevi açılımını cami avlusuna bıraktı. Retrieved January 10, 2011 from http://bianet.org/bianet/azinliklar/126414-akp-alevi-acilimini-cami-avlusuna-birakti

Turkish Mfa confirms Davutoglu's meeting with Israeli Minister Eliezer. (2010). *The Journal of Turkish Weekly*, July 1. Retrieved July 15, 2010 from http://www.turkishweekly.net/news/103934/turkish-mfa-confirms-davutoglu-39-s-meeting-with-israeli-minister-eliezer.html

Taspinar, Ö. (2008). Turkey's Middle East policies. Between neo-Ottomanism and Kemalism. *Carnegie Middle East Center* (10), September. Retrieved March 12, 2011 from http://www.carnegieendowment.org/files/cmec10_taspinar_final.pdf

Türkeş, M. (2008). Türkiye'nin Balkan politikasında devamlılık ve değişim. *Avrasya Dosyası, 14* (1), 267-268.

Vogel, T. (2010). Real politik Turkish-style. *Internationale Politik, 11* (5) 35-39.

Whisnant, Clayton. (n.d.) Foucault & Discourse. Retrieved November 1, 2011 from http://webs.wofford.edu/whisnantcj/his389/foucault_discourse.pdf

Woods, N. (2011). International political economy in an age of globalization. In J. Baylis, S. Smith & P. Owens (Eds.), *The Globalization of World Politics* (pp. 246-261). Oxford: Oxford University Press.

Yanatma, S. (2010). Kuzey Irak'la ekonomik bütünleşme kararı. *Zaman (Turkish daily)*, June 4.

9

INTERNALISATION OF DEPENDENCY: THE AKP'S DANCE WITH THE GLOBAL INSTITUTIONS OF NEOLIBERALISM

Filiz Zabcı

Introduction

K arl Popper argues that we make use of the *trial-error* method in handling the problems that we face in the socio-political sphere. The experience that life offers us lies in our methods of solving the problems that we face, the lessons that we learn through the mistakes we make, and in our performance in reaching the technics that bring about solutions. Using the Popperian lenses, what then can be said about the nature of the political experience that the AKP has offered since it first came to power in 2002? What problems has the AKP faced and what kind of solutions has it tried to offer in the face of these obtacles? Has the party made mistakes? And, what lessons has it learned from these mistakes? Or, has it ever learned from these mistakes? If the AKP has had achievements in terms of solving certain political issues, is it indeed possible to consider a positive legacy that can be derived from its political experience?

In order to attempt to respond to all these questions we must accept the following presumption: The AKP governments have had an autonomous (or independent) structure that has enabled them to make decisions based on their own power and will. Yet, this presumption brings in other questions. How apt is it to read politics in *technical* terms and to argue that the different policy preferences of different governments arise from their own will, their own political stances? A brief look at the political space in Turkey over the past two decades renders a positive answer to this question difficult. In this respect, understanding the AKP years in Turkey requires taking dependency analysis as the background frame. This, in turn, involves the critical scrutiny of the asymmetrical relations between international financial institutions and the domestic bourgeoisie as well as the implications of this asymmetrical relationship on the policy outputs at the governmental level. Such an analysis promises to explicate the working of international agents through domestic means and actors in the unfolding of Turkey's integration into the neoliberal world order.

The AKP, which came to power in three subsequent general elections (2002, 2007, 2011) has not displayed a shift from the neoliberal policies that had formed the political parameters of previous governments. Rather, the party's policy preferences have been realised in accordance with the directives coming from the International Monetary Fund (IMF) and the World Bank. The AKP's *Acil Eylem Planı* (Urgent Action Plan) has, in turn, introduced a third partner into its dependency. Ultimately, the plan has required the implementation of neoliberal policies in line with the objective to speed up the process of Turkey's accession to the European Union (EU).[146]

In this chapter, I aim to reveal that the AKP governments have easily internalised these neoliberal policies. In so doing, I analyse two documents prepared by the World Bank. The World Bank and the IMF have been implementing structural adjustment programs (SAP) in perfect harmony. In critical studies on the policies that are derived from this joint endeavor, it is mostly the AKP's relations with the IMF that are analysed. This is because the IMF is more decisive in the running of the world capitalist economy. However, starting with the 1990s, the World Bank has re-shaped its mission and institution in relation to such issue areas as governance, poverty, and corruption, leading to an increase in its decisiveness, now comparable to that of the IMF. The documents on which I build my analysis on Country Assistance Strategies (CAS)–currently referred to as Country Partnership Strategies –show the grounds for the credits that the Bank extends to countries and the projects that it implements. I especially focus on Country Aid Strategy for the 2004-2006 period and then look over a document that assesses the assistance strategies (Country Assistance Evaluation, CAE) implemented in the period from 1993-2004 (World Bank, 2005).[147]

The Country Assistance Strategies of the World Bank

The CAS is a basic document, which regulates the policies toward each and every country that takes credit from the World Bank. This document contains both the World Bank practices in a country and the country-specific assessments made by the Bank. The documents of CAS, prepared on a three-year basis, are regularly submitted to the "assessments" of the countries concerned. Although the World Bank argues that this procedure ensures the participatory approach of the Bank, the countries involved do not have a say in the setting of the fundamental parameters of the strategy and the implementation plan.

What then, is the function of the World Bank's CAS? A clear answer to this question can be found in an interview by Gregory Palast with Joseph Stiglitz, the incumbent chief economist of the World Bank. Stiglitz states that the World Bank defines the CAS as an assistance program devised in accordance with country-specific "careful investigation" in poor countries (Palast, 2001). Yet, Stiglitz underlines that the "the Bank's investigation involves little more than close inspection of five-star hotels. It concludes with a meeting with a begging finance minister, who is handed a 'restructring agreement' pre-drafted for 'voluntary' signature" (Palast, 2001). In preparing the CAS, the Bank carries a detailed investigation of each and every country's economic dynamics and presents the finance ministers with a standard four-step program that involves privatisation, capital market liberalisation, market-based pricing, and free trade. The IMF enters into the picture especially in steps two and three. This liberalising-cum-marketisation process also testifies to the interplay between the collapse of the national economy and the requisites of neoliberal globalisation—in the form of the privatisation of public goods, state bankruptcy, and increases in poverty and social unrest (Palast, 2001).

CAS in the AKP years in Turkey

In 1990, the World Bank prepared two CAS for Turkey, which were followed by the 2000 and 2003 CAS. Additionally, the CAS have so far been accompanied by progress reports (2001, 2005). In other words, the AKP has failed to resist the conventional reliance on the CAS in Turkey. On the contrary, compared to previous governments, the AKP governments' relation with the Bank has displayed increased continuity; the Bank's structural reforms have been repeatedly reinforced under the AKP's policies. As is the case with the privatisation process in Turkey, "structural reforms" too have been accelerated since the AKP's coming to power. Today, as the economic policies have been implemented to a great extent, the pace of the reform process has decreased. One of the indicators of this development is the 2008-2011 Country Partnership Strategy document. This document emphasises Turkey's economic growth, especially in that the Turkish economy has become one of the twenty largest economies in the world. In this respect, it essentially focuses on mathematical assessments based on the precepts of neo-classical economics. Other themes that are considered in the document are human capital, social security, and the effective provision of public services (World Bank, 2008). A particulary interesting point is that the World Bank, contrary to its proposals made to past administrations, recommended a strategy for the strengthening of institutional structures instead of proposing transformative regulations.

To start with the CAE that covers the period between 1993 and 2004 one first has to note that this document evinces that fundamental policies have not experienced a major shift under the AKP's rule. Apart from the AKP's commitment to the CAS, the IMF and the World Bank have repeatedly expressed their positive approach to the AKP's coming to power on its own, which negated the risk of instability under coalition governments–one rule of the game in the 1990s. In other words, as a majoritarian government, the AKP has been viewed as the guarantee for economic stability. According to the CAE, the main topic of interest for the World Bank in Turkey in the period between 1993 and 2004 has been assisting in the implementation of reforms for macro-economic sustainability, required for the sustenance of growth and the reduction of poverty. In this period, the World Bank has tried to realise "structural reforms" in four spheres. First sphere concerns reduction in public deficits, involving the inclusion of extra budgetary funds or expenses to the budget; increasing the restrictions on the expenses of the State Economic Enterprises (SEE); accelerating the pace of privatisation. Second sphere is related to controlling the deficit in the retirement system, which requires intervention in the acquired rights of civil servants and public workers. Third is the reduction of input subsidies and price supports in the agricultural sector. And finally, guaranteeing the debt payment capacity of public banks defines the fourth sphere, which necessitates a thorough banking reform.[148]

In justifying its intervention into the economic sphere along the above listed themes, the Bank resorts to a familiar terminology: it employs the argument that populist policies lead to imbalance in public accounts and high inflation (World Bank, 2005, pp. 22-23). It continues in the same line of argument, stating that populist policies stand as a barrier to the "rapid growth" that was already actualised by the commercial liberalisation beginning in 1980.

The Strong Partnership of the World Bank with the IMF in Turkey

The coming to power of the AKP coincided with the change in the functions of the IMF and the World Bank in Turkey as part of the stage of neoliberalisation (see Goldman, 2005; Moore, 2007; Toussaint, 2008; Woods, 2006; Zabcı, 2009).[149] The change also meant to pre-empt backlashes in the projected "sucesses" of the two institutions. In Turkey there had already been what was considered a "successful example" of the IMF and the World Bank jointly-led programs for the 1983-1984 period. Turkey had received its first Structural Adjustment Loan (SAL) from the World Bank in 1981, which was followed by four more SALs over the next several years. In this respect, throughout the 1980s, the country received considerable support from the Bank and turned out to be the latter's *favorite*. Indicitive of this favoritism, in 1988, Turkey's portfolio in the Bank was the fifth largest (World Bank, 2005, p.5).

Yet, in 1989 this success story was interrupted, and in the period between 1989 and 1993, Turkey's portfolio became one of the weakest portfolios of the Bank. The Bank's account of this downfall was that the country had failed to display sufficient progress in structural reforms. By the currency crisis in 1994, the relations between Turkey and the World Bank reached a new threshold. In the midst of the crisis, the Bank prepared a long list of requisites for the extension of a new adjustment credit. However, these requisites were not deemed sufficient for the Bank's aspired expansion of its influence in the country. In the 1997-1999 fiscal years, new credits were extended; the Bank initiated a restructuration process in its portfolio and increased the capacity of country office in decision making processes as well as decentralisation in decision making processes.

The general division of labour between the World Bank and the IMF, which holds true for almost all the countries which fall within the sphere of intervention of these institutions, also holds for Turkey, especially in their policy implementations between 1993 and 1997. In this period, the IMF focused on taxation and the Bank on public expenditure. In 1997, the cooperation between the Bank and the IMF started to deepen, and the 1999 crisis ultimately resulted in the IMF's leadership (World Bank, 2005, p. 15).

One of the significant factors that expedited the relations between Turkey and the World Bank is the law on compulsory education that was amended in 1998, increasing the period of compulsory education from 5 to 8 years.[150] Afterwards, the 1999 Marmara Earthquake and the immediate response of the Bank to the government's demand for assistance helped to increase the Bank's public credibility. In the 1999 fiscal crisis, the Bank extended $760 million worth of Economic Reform Credit to the country. And, finally, the improved relations were further evinced in the inclusion of Turkey in the Bank's program with $5 billion worth of credit, contained in the 2000 CAS (World Bank, 2005, pp. 5-6). What marked the 1990s is the narrowing down of the space for the relative autonomy of the state policy making and the corresponding widening of the spheres of influence of the IMF and the World Bank in national economies.[151]

After the 2001 crisis, a new "reform package" was put into practice under the title of the *Güçlü Ekonomiye Geçiş* (Transition to Powerful Economy). Its architect, Kemal Derviş, was a technocratic figure appointed by the then in power *Demokratik Sol Parti (Democratic Left Party)–Anavatan Partisi* (Motherland Party)–*Milliyetçi Hareket Partisi* (Nationalist Action Party) coalition government as the state minister responsible for economy. Unsurprisingly, the new reform package had the blueprint of the cooperation between the World Bank and IMF. Turkey's particular significance is that it has been considered a "model" for this said cooperation. The ascription of the model status to Turkey was also related to the failures of the IMF-World Bank policies in many regions at the time, such as in a number of Asian countries and in Russia.

The amount of "assistance" increased incredibly in accordance with the reform program that was implemented in the aftermath of the 2001 crisis. "The Bank supported the Turkish program with $3.5 billion of new commitments in fiscal 2002" (World Bank, 2005, p. 6). This rate symbolised the highest amount of credit that the World Bank extended the same year. In the same period the IMF, too, supported Turkey's new economic program with $16,2 billion (World Bank, 2005, p.3). This significant amount of monetary support was one of the main reasons for the relative security experienced between 2002 and 2004.

As far as the sectoral distribution of the World Bank credits are concerned, the major liability is related to the "public sector adjustment". The Bank expresses liability for Programmatic Financial and Public Sector Adjustment

Loans (PFPSAL I and II) for the 2002 fiscal year. The second
sphere is the agricultural sector. In the same year, with the
approval of Agricultural Reform Implementation Program
(ARIP) and Social Risk Mitigation Program (SRIP), $3.55
billion of credit was extended. After the extension of the
second installment of the education adjustment credit in July
2002, the Bank stopped allocating credits to Turkey due to the
upcoming general election. In the coming years, the amount
of credits extended by the Bank witnessed a decrease (World
Bank, 2005, p. 10).

The World Bank Credits Have a Target:
The Public Sector

Changes in the fiscal administration of the public sector

Unsurprisingly, the World Bank has cited the cause of the fiscal
problems experienced in Turkey in the 1990s not as "the formal
budget deficit, but in the large number of extra-budgetary funds
(EBFs) and the use of the State Banks to finance unbudgeted
public transfers" (World Bank, 2005, p.19). For this reason,
in the first stage, the main aim was to include extra budgetary
funds in the budget and to subject expenditures to parliamentary supervision. The second stage, on the other hand, hosted
the softening or elimination of the "rigid" control mechanisms
that were considered to have led to extra budgetary funds in the
first place (World Bank, 2005, p.19).

The credits have been overwhelmingly oriented toward
the public sector. In the 2003 CAS, it is stated that the World
Bank considers public sector reform the most immediate
problem (World Bank, 2003, p. 22). Further, the realisation of
macro-economic stability—the first bulwark of the CAS—is
tied to reducing the role of the state. While such targets as
transparency and participation are emphasised in line with the

Bank's understanding of governance, at the same time, the institutional grounds for a considerable reduction in public expenditure is set. In this respect, the AKP governments have been committed to the Bank's established programs, as demonstrated in both the earlier documents, like the Urgent Action Plan, and related policy outcomes. The Urgent Action Plan–to which the Bank explicitly stated its support (World Bank, 2003, p. 23)—was in line with the transformation-cum-shrinking of the public sector.

The macro-economic stability part of the CAS involves the changes in the public sector targeted by the Bank within the scope of "structural reforms"–i.e., restructuring the state. In this vein, the Bank demanded the fulfillment of the two PFPSALs, noted above. The AKP immediately adopted the principles and the targets of the program and demanded that the Bank prepare a third PFPSAL operation. The resulting PFPSAL 3 required the strengthening of the conditionality in the fundamental spheres of the program, which the Bank deemed "problematic spheres" (World Bank, 2003, p. 23). These spheres are as follows: a. The enactment of a law that would institutionalise the Direct Income Support Program for farmers; b. The curtailing of the restrictions on the operational independence of the Banking Regulation and Supervision Agency (BRSA); c. The determination of a new road map for the privatisation of Vakıf Bank;[152] d. "The elimination of the system of earmarked revenues and expenditures" after the closing of extra budgetary funds (World Bank, 2003, p. 22).

Both of the PFPSALs were extended to support the restructuration of the public sector that was set in CAS for the 2001-2003 fiscal years. It was ensured that these credits were used in coordination with the IMF program. In this frame, the Bank focused on controlling the public expenditure and related this to the principle of governance. It is possible to observe that in these period budget reforms, fiscal transperancy, and accountability became the words of the day and consequently, legal and institutional regulations were put on the Turkish political agenda. Exemplary outcomes are the *Kamu Mali Yönetimi ve Kontrol Yasası* (The Law on Public Fiscal Regulation and Control (Law no. 5018, 2003), the *Kamu Finansmanı ve Borç Yönetiminin Düzenlenmesi Hakkında Kanun* (The Law on Public Finance and the Regulation of Debt Management) (Law no. 4749, 2002), the *Ulusal Yolsuzluk Karşıtı Strateji* (National Strategy against Corruption) (2001), and the *Kamu Yönetimi Temel Kanunu Tasarısı* (Draft Law on Public Administration) (2003) (World Bank, 2003, pp. 22-23). Here, one shall take note of the inclusion of these legal regulations within the scope of the EU adjustment laws. As Yeşilyurt-Gündüz in this book succintly elaborates, the EU has also functioned as a significant catalyst in the deepening of the neoliberal frame in Turkey. The EU accession process necessitated the radical re-shaping of the legal structure in Turkey. Although the mainstream literature has mainly emphasised those regulations and amendments that concerned human rights and liberties and which have not reached a sufficient level, the same process also necessitated filling the blanks in Turkey's adjustment to the neoliberal world economic system. Actually, the Bank has stated that one of the main aims of its programs in Turkey has been to support Turkey's EU membership.

Changes in the retirement system

One other topic on which the first PFPSAL concentrated was the distribution of public services. Among these, the institutional and structural reform of the social security and retirement systems are exemplary. As Özdemir and Yücesan-Özdemir elaborate in their contribution to the book, the social security system in Turkey has been radically revised under the AKP's rule, which in the final analysis nullified the *social* aspect. This is not surprising since the legal and institutional regulations oriented toward integration with the capitalist market, which form the bulwark of the World Bank's governance strategy, have formed the pivotal policy preferences of the AKP governments.

As for the retirement system, the Bank's diagnosis has been that the system has long been experiencing fiscal problems due to the populist policies of the governments. In the 1990s, in an attempt to compensate for the increasing deficits in the retirement system, a series of measures–such as a gradual increase in the minimum retirement age and decreasing the retirement pension–were added to the agenda. However, the deficits continued throughout the 1990s. For the Bank, the decisions of the Turkish courts regarding the invalidity of some of the amendments to the retirement system for existing participants had a significant effect on this continuity. Likewise, according to the Bank, despite the amendments that were enacted in 1999, retirement payments exceeded a rational amount, they continued for too long, and the retirement age was too low (World Bank, 2005, pp. 22-23)

In 2001, with the concern for the possibility that the civil servants would oppose the entire reform package, the DSP-ANAP-MHP coalition government did not include the issue of retirement within the scope of its structural reforms. Likewise, "steps to reduce the pension deficit were not included as part of the PFPSALs, apparently reflecting the view that their agenda was already large and the political balance so delicate that to do so might have put the whole package at risk" (World Bank, 2005, p. 23). It can be argued then that the AKP's rise to power allowed the World Bank to escape the anxiety surrounding Turkey's politico-economic instability. In order to achieve this, in 2005, the AKP gave its word to the IMF that it would see to the legalisation of social security reform in 2006, and it kept its promise by enacting the *Sosyal*

Sigortalar ve Genel Sağlık Sigortası Kanunu (Law on Social
Security and General Health Insurance) (Law no.5510) and
Sosyal Güvenlik Kurumu Kanunu (Law on Social Security
Institution) (Law no.5502). Additionally, the *Sosyal Yardımlar
ve Primsiz Ödemeler Kanunu Tasarısı* (Draft Law on Social
Assistance and Free Payments) is still waiting for parlia-
mentary approval (see Özdemir's and Yücesan-Özdemir's
contributions to the volume).

Reduction in agricultural subsidies

According to the World Bank, agricultural subsidies were
among the main sources behind the budgetary deficits. As a
result, agricultural policies have become key ingredients of the
neoliberal policy frame in the 2000s. In 2000, agricultural input
subsidies were decreased considerably and a new program
emerged under the title of Direct Income Support. This change
in the subsidies regime was realised as part of the Bank's
Economic Reform Loan, Agricultural Reform Implementation
Loan, and PFPSALs. In the AKP's discourse, on the other hand,
the change was linked to the Urgent Action Plan: [153]

> In relation to this issue we implemented a series
> of measures. … As you all know the agricultural
> policies that were implemented in recent years
> have affected our peasants in a very negative way.
> Agricultural supports extended to our producers
> who were in economic hardship were changed
> within the frame of "Agricultural Restructuration
> and Reform Program," agricultural credit subsidies
> and input support were abandoned, and system
> of intervention to product price was given up.
> These policies were replaced by direct income
> support independent of input use and based only

on processed land. The direct support practice will
be continued in 2003 in order to form a peasant
registry system and to ensure that the peasants
involved with agricultural production are least
affected by economic fluctuations.

Thus the AKP government shared the World Bank's claim
that the Direct Income Support program would ensure a more
egalitarian structure in the agricultural sector. This support
was limited to 500.000 square meters per person. In this
respect, for the Bank a balance would have been reached in
terms of support mechanisms to big land owners and small
and/or medium-sized landowners. However, the actual practice turned out to be different from the Bank's prediction.
Since the amount of payment is determined according to the
area of land owned, those involved in stockbreeding and/or
commercial growing of vegetables and fruits were provided
with an insignificant amount of support. And most importantly, the payments were abstracted from production, taking
the form of "social aid" (BSB, 2006, 85). The Direct Income
Support program, which has distrupted the balance of production and employment in the agricultural sector, and created an
inactive peasantry in the weakening agricultural associations,
was repealed in 2009.

Conclusion

It is certain that establishing dependency as the grounds for an
analysis, which involves taking the phenomenon of dependency
as an effective factor in the governments' policy outputs, necessitates integrating a critical approach to the process of reflection.
The international financial institutions, as important actors
in the functioning of the neoliberal world economic system,
occupy a decisive place in many country's decision-making

processes–including Turkey. Dependency works as a structural process, involving the workings of (neoliberal) capitalism at its different layers—local, national and international.

Assessing the policy preferences and outputs of any government in any time period without considering this multi-layered structural decisiveness risks insufficient explication of the neoliberal practice in different socio-political contexts. In other words, considering just this one layer might also lead to deficiency in the analysis and hamper the critical stance in another aspect. When the domestic factors are excluded from the analysis, the differences in terms of dependency among different countries turn out to be inexplicable. A related dimension is the internalisation of external decisiveness by the domestic decision-makers, which takes different forms in different national settings. Today, the nature of politics in Turkey is enmeshed with this feature and the AKP governments have so far presented model examples of this internalisation.

The AKP has been a desirious performer of the policies that internalise dependency. In this chapter, I tried to reveal the most important aspects of how this internalisation worked through the AKP's government-led legal reform process. It abided well with the arguments of the World Bank and the IMF in justifying the neoliberal measures. In this respect, it maintained the neoliberal monopoly over the problematisation of political tutelage, political patronage, and corruption - which actually concerns the public good–in neoclassical economic terms like efficiency and productivity.

Actually, such arguments as those for eliminating populist policies and separating economy from politics are part and parcel of class politics. Today, they are the ingredients of a *political* program that works to the advantage of foreign and domestic capital and to the detriment of labour. The end result is an ever-exploitative system that is reached through regulations that decrease public expenditure, collapse the retirement system, terminate subsidies in the agricultural sector, and eliminate public services that extend from the educational to health spheres (to the disadvantage of low income groups). Therefore, what lacks in the power structure in Turkey is a substantial opposition not only to particular neoliberal policies of the AKP governments, which actually work in a patchwork style (See Coşar's contribution to the volume), but also to the neoliberal frame that has seemed to determine the rules of the game.

REFERENCES

Bağımsız Sosyal Bilimciler. (2003). *2003 başında Türkiye ekonomisi ve AKP'nin hükümet programı üzerine değerlendirmeler.* Retrieved from http://www.bagimsizsosyalbilimciler/org

Bağımsız Sosyal Bilimciler. (2006). *IMF gözetiminde on uzun yıl, 1998-2008: Farklı hükümetler; tek siyaset.* Ankara: Türk Mühendis ve Mimar Odaları Birliği Y.

Başbakan Erdoğan'ın ulusa sesleniş konuşması. (2003, July 10). Retrieved from http://www.belgenet.com/2003/erdogan_100703.html

Goldman, M. (2005). *Imperial Nature: The World Bank and Struggles for Social Justice in the Age of Globalization.* New Haven: Yale University Press.

Moore, D. (Ed.) (2007) *The World Bank: Development, Poverty, Hegemony.* South Africa: University of Kwazula-Natal Press.

Palast, G. (2001). IMF's four steps to damnation. *The Observer,* April 29. Retrieved from http://www.stallman.org/imf-damnation.htlm,

Popper, K. (2006). Hayat problem çözmektir. In his *Hayat problem çözmektir: Bilgi, tarih ve politika üzerine* (pp. 203-211). (A. Nalbant, Trans.). İstanbul: YKY.

Toussaint, E. (2008). *The World Bank: A critical primer* (E. Anne et al., Trans.). London: Pluto Press.

Woods, N. (2006). *The Globalizers: The IMF, the World Bank and their Borrowers.* Ithaca and London: Cornell University Press.

World Bank. (2003). *Country Partnership Strategy with the Republic of Turkey 2004-2006, Report No. 26756-TU,* April 29.

World Bank. (2005, December 2). *The World Bank in Turkey, 1993-2004: Country assistance evaluation.* Report No. 34783. Retrieved June 1, 2009 from http://wwwwds.worldbank.org/external/default/WDSContentServer/WDSP/IB/2006/01/11/000160016_20060111114148/Rendered/PDF/34783.pdf

World Bank. (2008, January 25). *Country Partnership Strategy with the Republic of Turkey 2008-2011.* Report No. 42026-TR.

Zabcı, F. (2009). *Dünya Bankası: Yanılsamalar ve gerçekler.* İstanbul: Yordam Kitap.

10

THE EU AND THE AKP: A NEOLIBERAL LOVE AFFAIR?

Zuhal Yeşilyurt-Gündüz

*The problem is not that we run out of money occasionally.
The real problem is that we live our entire lives this way
and our children grow up into this too.
I don't see any progress since years. I have no future.*[154]

Introduction

These quotations do not come from people living in an *underdeveloped* or *developing* country. They come from people living in the most developed and most affluent countries of the world—those of the European Union (EU). Why then, does the EU have 80 million people (of 501 million) living in poverty and among them 19 million children (Euronews, June 1, 2010)? Why then, did the EU have to designate 2010 as the *European Year for Combating Poverty and Social Exclusion*?

The main reason for this poverty in affluence is the increasing currency of neoliberal policies in the EU and its member states. Notwithstanding the troubles the EU faces due to its neoliberal policies, which enrich a few immensely while pauperising the rest, it continues imposing neoliberal rules to other countries, especially those hoping to become members of this "very selective club," like Turkey. The governing AKP is a good catch for the EU's neoliberal desires. Although many policies and practices of the conservative AKP are at odds with EU principles, they have a *passionate* relationship.

This chapter tries to reveal the reason for this peculiar affair by unfolding the messages and ideals the EU wants to realise in Turkey–the implementation of IMF Structural Adjustment Programs (SAP), high-speed privatisation, accomplishment of corporate interests, and increase of foreign direct investment (FDI). In doing so, the chapter aims to disclose the deepening of the neoliberal agenda in the EU and in Turkey. It turns to the unavoidable consequence of increased pauperisation by providing data from the EU and Turkey. Then the EU's neoliberal demands of Turkey are presented by offering examples from Turkey's EU Progress Reports. Last but not least, the article intends to present the AKP's failed policies in "health" and "education" as concrete cases.

The EU: From Social Democracy to Social Exclusion

After the Second World War, Western European countries succeeded in finding "the social-democratic historical compromise that forced capital to adjust itself to the demands of social justice expressed by the working classes" (Amin, 2004). This European social model incorporated the quest for full employment, Keynesian policies for increasing demand, and the pledge for social welfare independent of the labour market. Until the middle of the 1970s, economic growth was based on industrial development, mass consumption, and social protection (Palier, 2006, p. 2). Neoliberalism was set in motion first in Chile in 1973. The U.S.-led coup against the elected socialist president and the establishment of a military dictatorship marked the beginning of the neoliberal model (Werlhof, 2008, p. 95). This shift from Keynesianism to monetarism and neoliberalism–assigned as "Reaganism" in the U.S. and "Thatcherism" in the UK–after the economic crisis of the mid-1970s, aimed to bolster capital accumulation. Other European states followed this trend of "American-style, antisocial liberalism" (Amin, 2004; Foster, 2005). At the heart of neoliberalism were ideas like privatisation, liberalisation, and deregulation" (Scholte quoted in Hout, 2006, p. 10). This reduced the control of the state on economics, and thus bid farewell to Keynesian principles that underlined regulation, planning, and management.

All of this was symbolised in the Washington Consensus from 1989 onwards, and spread by financial institutions like the IMF or the World Bank (Hout, 2006, p. 10-11). The Washington Consensus' promise to bring freedom, wealth, and economic development via deregulation, liberalisation, and privatisation has indeed come true–however, not for the people, but for the big corporations (Werlhof, 2008, p. 103). Europe's "social pact" between workers and capitalists, for which workers had fought for centuries, collapsed. This collapse worked through the IMF directed Structural Adjustment Programs (SAP).

Within the EU, it was the creation of the Single Market (1992), following the Single European Act, and the introduction of the common currency (2002), after the Maastricht Treaty, which deepened the "Americanization of the European economy under neoliberalism" (Girdner, 2005, p. 77). Deregulation, free competition, curbing the budget and state deficits, and low inflation were realised–all measures combined to build up a neoliberal economic system that was founded on monetarist supply-side economic policies, which support free competition (deregulation and labour flexibility) and conservative budgets (low debt, low interest rates and low inflation) (Palier, 2006, pp. 4-5). Notwithstanding their various social policies, over the last two decades most European countries have curtailed the welfare state in the name of "reducing social expenditure," by various means such as limiting entitlement for and levels of social benefits, initiating or raising charge for formerly free services, and detaching government's responsibility for social security to civil society (Palier, 2006, pp. 6-7). Besides, *"flexicurity,"* a peculiar combination of *flexibility* and *security,* was applied.[155]

All these measures combined had two impacts on social protection. Because of cuts in public social spending, responsibilities that once were considered to be the state's duties, were divided among the state, families, markets, and civil society. Additionally, retrenchment revealed that state spending for social protection was no longer considered to be a factor that would increase economic growth, but as a cost factor that needed to be lessened. The change of social protection from demand-side to supply-side policies was intended to reduce costs and was seen as a substitute for general social policies (Palier, 2006, p. 7). Social security was no longer regarded as a "fundamental *right*" of people but was conferred to some groups of people provided they complied with the given conditions (Özar, 2009). In so doing, social security payments were transferred from a "passive" to an "active" form, as the payments shifted "from a guarantee of replacement income outside of the market ('decommodification') to a strategy of providing incentives designed to promote a return to employment and of bringing people back to the labour market ('recommodification')" (Palier, 2006, p. 8).

The EU enlargements strengthened the pressure to reduce costs and boost productivity. Furthermore, the pressure of globalisation and global competition intensified. This led many EU states to force harsher working conditions, such as obliging workers to work more for less, or making severe cuts in welfare benefits. The result of this change in policy and vision in the EU is bleak. According to Eurostat statistics, (Eurostat, April 30, 2010) 23.311 million people in the EU were without employment in April 2010. When compared with data from 12 months ago, unemployment was found to have increased by 2.400 million people. The general rate of unemployment was 9.7 percent in April 2010, an increase of 1 percent since April 2009.

Neoliberalism's victory in Europe increases troubles like racism, discrimination, unregistered labour, workers' exploitation, and it endangers democracy and peace. (Bedirhanoğlu, 2009, p. 44) The death of the social state brings a desolate situation with a tiny amount of loyalty and trust and a massive amount of fear and hopelessness. The result is a diminished feeling of solidarity. (Nakay, 2010) A small group garners huge advantages, whereas all remaining, "the earth's human and non-human population, and the earth itself, suffer hardship to an extent that puts their very survival at risk." (Werlhof, 2008, p. 94). Claudia von Werlhof pleads: "Are there limits to the neoliberal politics that the European public will tolerate? How many more than 30 million unemployed or 70 [80] million who now live below the poverty line can Europe handle?" (Werlhof, 2008, p. 112).

Turkey and the EU: Europeanisation through Neoliberalisation

Turkey's political economy until 1980 was typified by state-led industrialisation, protectionism, and import substitution. This strategy brought high growth rates and rapid industrialisation. After the oil crisis, however, Turkey faced serious balance of payment problems that were deepened by high inflation, unemployment, and debt rates, turning Turkey to near-bankruptcy. In 1978 and 1979, the country was forced to accept the IMF Standby-Agreements out of necessity (Onder, 2007, p. 231-233). On January 24, 1980, the center-right *Adalet Partisi* (Justice Party) began a neoliberal program that built upon capital accumulation and export support, opened the Turkish economy, and transformed the state's role in economics. Intensified under the military rule (1980-1983) and under Turgut Özal (first as Prime Minister, 1983-1989; then as President, 1989-1993), Turkey developed its export-oriented economic policy, liberalised finance and trade sectors, and privatised state-owned businesses. International financial institutions increased their influence on Turkish policy processes–"even when there were no formal agreements" (Onder, 2007, p. 234). The economic crises of 1994, 1999, 2001, and 2008/9 revealed that liberalisation was destined to be a risky and unstable march. Surprisingly in those periods of crisis, neoliberal measures and liberalisations were rarely questioned; and even confirmed, thereby leading to a situation in which the neoliberal restructuring was being nourished by the very crises it produced itself (Bedirhanoğlu, 2008, p. 111).

Turkey's economy reveals two predicaments. The first one is the "perverse and rather premature neo-liberal development" (Eder, 2003, p. 223), which banged the door shut on balancing liberalisation with steps to reconcile its harsh effects with regulations and investment for development. The second trouble is Turkey's heritage of populism and patronage policies, which create hurdles to reforms that are difficult to execute and harsh in practice. Political crumbling, uneasy coalition governments, and recurrent elections also helped populist policies to augment. Thus, neoliberalism in Turkey started early, and was improved by the military regime and by Turgut Özal, and furthered—albeit on a slower pace–by all other governments. (See Coşar's contribution to this volume.) Its perfection, however, was realised by a party with Islamic roots–AKP. Whereas its predecessor, the *Refah Partisi*

(Welfare Party, RP) as an alternative to the Turkish economic model, framed its project "just order," the AKP was a "convert to neoliberal economics." (Onder, 2007, p. 241). As part of this transformation, the AKP went through two phases. The first was the break with its roots, in the *Millî Görüş Hareketi* (National Outlook Movement), by detaching itself from the anti-Western, statist/developmental, and nationalist visions of the movement and becoming more moderate. During the second phase, through building the historical bloc with Islamic sentiments (dubbed *new hegemonic bloc* by Uzgel, 2009, p. 12 and p. 25) together with liberal intellectuals and economic circles, the AKP began to erode Kemalist ideology–the official ideology of the Turkish Republic, named after the founding president Mustafa Kemal Atatürk—and its statist concept and those aspects of this ideology that are deemed to pose problems for Turkey's further globalisation. That is why, in order to transform Turkey, the AKP first had to go through a transformation process itself.

The AKP classified the role of the state as the facilitator of a liberal market economy and the guardian of private capital and removed the state from production activities, and pushed Turkey's economic integration into world markets. In its election campaigns, endeavouring not to dismay economic circles, the AKP pledged to continue the neoliberal reforms and the IMF's SAP. The AKP pursued the IMF program to the full consent of the business circles (Onder, 2007, p. 241). However, the AKP's addressee was not limited to the business circles. In its election campaigns it also had to appeal to the popular classes. In so doing, the AKP aspired to bring traditional values, including religion and the globalisation process, together. Although Islamism was no longer the main reference point, it still had a special role to play in the definition of the AKP's conservatism (Uzgel, 2009, p. 22). Therefore, the AKP represented not only the encounter point between Islam and democracy, but also between Islam and neoliberalism (Uzgel, 2009, p. 24).

This encounter also maintains the neoliberal love affair between the EU and the AKP; yet for the time being it has failed to offer definitive solutions to the increasing pauperisation in the country. Statistics offered by the *Türkiye İstatistik Kurumu* (Turkish Statistical Institute, TurkStat) in June 2010 revealed that the unemployment rate was (officially) 13.7 percent in March 2010. (TurkStat, June 15, 2010) The labour organisations, *Devrimci İşçi Sendikaları Konfederasyonu* (Confederation of Progressive Trade Unions, DİSK) and *Türkiye İşçi Sendikaları Konfederasyonu* (Confederation of Turkish Trade Unions, TÜRK-İş), state that the real percentage is higher–25 percent. (TÜİK Krizin Etkisini Küçük Gösteriyor, 2009). According to official statistics, the number of poor people in Turkey is 12.170.000 and the number of those living under the poverty limit is 1.400.000 (Turk-Stat, June 15, 2010) — a really desolate picture, indeed.

The EU's neoliberal stance in Turkey

It is strange but true that in many European countries the term neoliberalism simply does not exist. The reason for this puzzling disregard of a severe reality is this: "if there is no word for it, there is no problem, either. Unnamable, unspeakable, unthinkable: non-existing" (Werlhof, 2008, p. 95). Notwithstanding the ignorance in the terminology, neoliberalism is alive and kicking. In order to render the neoliberal vision widely accepted and successfully applied by its candidate countries, the EU uses means such as the accession conditions (Copenhagen Criteria), annual Progress Reports by the European Commission, and Reports by the European Parliament. The Copenhagen Criteria determine EU conditionality–all candidates have to meet them to become members.[156] The main problem with these conditions is that they are not concrete, but very fluid and open to inter-pretation–"making the Union a moving target for applicants. The conditions are not fixed and definite, and new conditions have been added and old ones redefined" (Grabbe, 2002, p. 251). The economic criteria, which require the "existence of a functioning market economy and the capacity to cope with competitive pressure and market forces within the Union," demand capital to be in private hands. This entails that those who *own* capital simultaneously *control* economic *and* political decisions. In this respect, big corporations are placed in deci-sion-making positions from where they are able to decide upon further capital accumulation (Girdner, 2005, p. 71-72). Indeed, the EU is firmly rooted in the neoliberal track. This becomes evident in the fact that privatisation and its priorities are of crucial importance among the conditions for membership. In light of this, big corporations get the chance to determine the EU's processes. As a further result, "satisfying the economic criteria for EU membership is inextricably linked with sticking to a neoliberal economic agenda" (Patton, 2006, p. 528).

One essential part of the economic criteria is full confor-mity with the IMF's SAP. Multinational corporations make their decisions about FDI in Turkey after reading the EU reports. Similarly, Turkey's credit position is decided upon after an evaluation of the cooperation between the AKP, EU and IMF (Patton, 2006, p. 528-529).

Progress reports–neoliberal demands

The EU–IMF cooperation is also evident in the EU's annual Progress Reports. A short analysis of these Reports provided by the European Commission highlights the EU's neoliberal track. Concerning the economic aspects of the Copenhagen Criteria, under the headlines of "functioning market" and the "capacity to compete," four topics (Eder, 2003, p. 234) stand out: a. Macroeconomic stability involving extreme public borrowing, political instability, and nonfunctional financial system are seen as reasons of macroeconomic instability; b. State withdrawal via privatisation, reform of state enterprises, and agricultural liberalisation; c. Price liberalisation and smoothing market entrance; d. Profit-making liberalisation and integration to the European and global markets.

All of these topics are in chorus with the IMF's SAP. Some of the economic reforms concern harmonisation with the EU's *acquis*, while nearly all were realised under the IMF's direction. All reveal a "market worshipping" character (Sönmez, November 09, 2007) with the IMF and the World Bank as reference points. Hence, while evaluating Turkey's *progress*, the EU considers the IMF and World Bank reports and its homework and gives its verdicts upon these reports. All Progress Reports have some particularities in common with the IMF demands.[157] The most conspicious points of commonality can be observed in the policies implemented for the neoliberalisation of the economic space. Thus, all of the EU Progress Reports honor the *privatisation* of state economic enterprises, criticise the *slow* speed in liberalisation and *privatisation*, and demand that Turkey ought to "finish" the "agenda". In an IMF-suiting manner, the reports also approve of fiscal control—although this means retrenchment in state spending on social security. Besides, in accordance with the IMF, is the current account deficit, which is *not* considered to be a problem. Following IMF-rules, another common topic is the reports' demand for more foreign direct investment and the termination of restrictions of free trade. Hand in hand with the IMF and World Bank programs, the EU Reports criticise the *high* degree of protection of agricultural goods and accentuate the necessity for extended agricultural liberalisation reforms. Further replicating the IMF's demands, the EU disparages all state subventions and calls for less state interference.

The EU's crocodile tears: Social rights

Yet, the progress reports also shed crocodile tears in response to the missing social rights in Turkey. One of these items is the desolate situation of trade unions in Turkey–no wonder, taking into regard the neoliberal positions since 1980. Accordingly, the EU criticises restrictions of trade union rights and the fact that the legal framework is not in line with the EU standards. Another crocodile tear is shed upon Turkey's high unemployment rate, which increased to 13 percent in mid-2009, and was especially high among the young (24 percent). The EU also highlights the very low female employment rate–only 24 percent.

Thus, another issue that attracts crocodile tears is the lack of gender equality. The Reports underline the problem of gender inequality, such as the still missing gender equality body as demanded by the *acquis*, the very low political representation of women at national and regional levels, the low participation of women in the labour market, and the extremely low access to education (lowest among the EU and OECD countries). However, it is not clear whether the EU *really* understands the dynamics behind this situation–since the AKP is a neoliberal, Islamist, and extremely conservative party that does not regard women's rights as a top priority (See Yeğenoğlu & Coşar's contribution to this volume).

The EU's stance on the issue of public services does not deviate from its neoliberal preferences. In this respect, especially regarding children and education, the EU criticism remains very limited. It slightly touches upon the increase in poverty among children and the low net enrollment rate of 58.5 percent in secondary schools. Thus, whereas the EU's criticism is mostly focused on economic liberalisation, when it comes to social rights, the critique becomes astonishingly silent and soft. The same can be said about health services.

Notwithstanding the many predicaments Turkey's health sector faces, the reports assess "good progress," again, totally disregarding the social rights (See Yücesan-Özdemir's contribution to this volume). This disregard has most recently been exemplified by the deaths of workers in jeans manufacturing factories, due to the stoning of jeans. Over 550 people suffer from silicosis disease and last year the forty-third person died of this practice–the whitening of jeans darkens and stops the lives of human beings (http://kottaslama.org/php/kt/wp). Unsurprisingly, these incidents could only attract a footnote-long acknowledgment from the EU.[158] Indeed, what we face here is the "footnotisation" of human life.[159]

The European Commission recommends that the experts "should redefine their budgetary priorities, in a medium-term perspective, in order to provide a sufficient level of investment in education, health, social services and public infrastructure across the country" (Report 2001, p. 45). However, it does not give a clue on where to take that money from–taking into account the exalted fiscal discipline! Consequently, Heather Grabbe calls these the "inconsistencies in the EU's advice (…) encourage to maintain fiscal and monetary discipline, and the Union stresses the need to control budget deficits while undertaking systemic reforms (such as pensions, healthcare (…)). But at the same time, the Union also demands major investments in infrastructure, (…), agricultural reform (…)." (Grabbe, 2002, p. 263).

As for poverty, a basic characteristic of the neoliberalisation process, the EU Reports, by mourning the increase of those at risk of poverty and the lack of progress in social protection, shed crocodile tears again. How could it simply be possible to follow the IMF / EU orders *and* simultaneously increase social rights and social protection? Thus, the EU's laments do not sound very convincing. Mustafa Sönmez underlines the "eclectic" character of the EU

Progress Reports, which on the one hand honor markets merits and praise IMF recipes, and on the other hand, reveal criticism about the anti-union character, regional disparities, increasing unemployment, and other troubles. However, they do so without underlining that this market-oriented, commercialised, fiscally disciplined, anti-social, privatisation-adoring, neoliberal economic system is the main source and reason for all of these predicaments. This eclecticism makes the Progress Reports–and thereby the EU itself–insincere, unconvincing, and even schizophrenic (Sönmez, November 09, 2007). In other words, this state of affairs attests to the EU's neoliberal tightrope: while requesting the implementation of the IMF programs, the EU simultaneously defends the social state and social protection.

The Draft Report on trade and economic relations with Turkey by the Committee on International Trade within the European Parliament, issued on May 12, 2010, again in an IMF-suiting manner, dealt with the further application of neoliberal economic policies. It asks for the removal of "remaining non-tariff barriers (...) Welcomes the positive conclusions of the latest WTO review on Turkey; urges the Turkish Government, however, to take the necessary measures to fulfil the recommendations therein and accelerate structural and legislative reforms." The report's "neo-liberal and right-wing economic outlook," and the fact that it "really wants a free-for-all, free-trade system (...) [and] calls for public services and public procurement [to] be opened to, of course, European major corporations" is a call for an increase in foreign direct investment and structural and institutional reforms that suit further investment. Any opposition to this call is read as letting politics mingle with economic affairs, and thus as undesirable.

The AKP's Practices in the Neoliberal World: Between *Progress* and Dissolution

Turkey once had a significant state sector. However, in accordance with the privatisation orders of the IMF, this sector dwindled. The public areas faded away and the *"res publica"* became *"res pivata."* It is crucial to remember that the word "privatisation" comes from the Latin word "privare," which means "to deprive" (Werlhof, 2008, p. 101).

Neoliberalising work: The TEKEL case

As an example *par excellance* the TEKEL strike should be seen as a breaking point—workers organising in a protest against the neoliberal policies of the AKP government and EU plus IMF-made "remedies". Concerning the labourers, the result of the neoliberal policies was an increased deunionisation, extension of informal sector (temporary, part-time or subcontract workforce), amplified international capital mobility, and increased unemployment. All of this meant a turn in the tide against workers (Onder, 2007, p. 242). As a striking example of the neoliberal economic policies of the AKP and the related EU's position, the TEKEL case should suffice. TEKEL was the previously state-owned tobacco and alcohol monopoly. In accordance with the IMF's privatisation demands, the AKP government decided to close twelve factories and announced preparations for the workers' relocation as temporary workers under the newly created "4C employment status." Under this status, TEKEL workers, who used to have a status as public workers (including the rights to strike and collective bargaining) and social security under the Labour Law, would have to turn into low-wage, temporary recruits in private companies for ten months and face unemployment after this period. Protests and strikes against these harsh plans began in December 2009 and intensified during the following weeks and months as the unbending determination of the (former) TEKEL workers increased. One commentator dubbed the images as "class warfare" (Updegraff, 2010).

The AKP obeyed the IMF orders like a pet pupil, by being enthusiastic to privatise state-owned companies, enhancing foreign direct investment, and setting Turkey's course towards a neoliberal market economy (Updegraff, 2010). Though TEKEL was not the first case of cruel privatisation in Turkey, the power of the protests was outstanding. In the TEKEL case the factual conflict between the AKP and the workers is revealed. Actually, the AKP has so far managed the conflict by covering class-based concerns with resort to a discourse based on identity politics. More briefly, the neoliberal assumption that class politics is over has been worked by underlining identity-based conflicts in terms of ethnicity and religion (For the colonisation of class-based politics by neoliberal identity politics see Yalman's contribution to the volume). On the one hand, the AKP's concern on identity politics can best be observed in its gender and citizenship policies (see Coşar's, Soyarık-Şentürk's and Yeğenoğlu&Coşar's contributions to the volume). On the other hand, the reflection of these policies in terms of the AKP's zeal to suppress class-based politics can best be observed in its social policy regime (see Yücesan-Özdemir's contribution to the volume). In this respect, the TEKEL case, which exemplified rights-based politics, forming the basis of solidarity among the workers, whom neoliberal discursive policies have been defined in identity terms was telling about the possibilities of a class-based opposition.[160]

Neoliberalising health

Whereas Turkey spent only 6 percent of its GDP on health in 2007, the average across OECD countries was 9 percent, with France (11.2 percent), Switzerland (10.7 percent), and

Germany and Austria (10.5 percent) ranking highest. Turkey has the lowest per capita health spending, $767, compared to the OECD average of $3.060. The neoliberalisation of the health care was not started with the AKP government. The initiator of the neoliberal program in Turkey, Turgut Özal's vision for health care three decades ago was to restructure health care and social security as "services whose price would be determined in the marketplace on the basis of the principles of supply and demand" (Akdur, 2003 quoted in Ağartan, 2007, p. 16). Erdoğan bolstered this vision by insisting that the private sector is more competent and skilled than state enterprises.

This very idea was revealed in December 2003 when the AKP announced the "Transformation in Health," with the aim of "establishing a qualified and effective health system to which everybody can have access" (p. 33) With this reform program the AKP made it clear that in the new system, health services would be offered by competitive profit-making delivery systems (Ağartan, 2007, p. 19). Based on decentralisation and privatisation, the reform included cuts in the list of cost-free drugs and the outsourcing of medical service staff in university hospitals. In short: "The essence of the changes in health sector lies in converting public health institutions into commercial enterprises, directing public health expenditures towards private sector and privatising all health services gradually" (Artvinli, 2007). Besides, the AKP has abandoned the notion of preventive health and reduced its percentage in public health spending. Disparaging, indeed life-threatening outcomes of the commercialisation of health are to be seen in fields like the control and treatment of tuberculosis, cancer, heart diseases, and others. In this respect, the "Transformation in Health Reform" brought a four-fold increase in total health spending as well as a huge rise in public health institutions' purchasing of health services provided by the private health sector (Yıldırım, 2009, p. 93). The result of this program was bleak: increase in infant mortality and subcontracting. From a neoliberal perspective, the program was a big success: the health care market grew and expenses for health care increased, while the government's expenses declined as many formerly free services were now being charged for. Those who could not afford those services had to face this harsh reality. Ultimately, the AKP's savings in health brings death to the people (Çakır, October 20, 2009).

So this much is certain, none of the AKP's health policies or reforms aim at improving the country's health conditions or solving Turkey's longstanding poor health conditions by taking into account public rapprochement or societal benefit values (Hamzaoğlu & Yavuz, 2009, p. 633). This is why the *Türkiye Tabipler Birliği* (Doctors' Union of Turkey, TTB), in their protests against these policies, claim that the *"AKP is destructive of health"* (TTB, 2007).

Neoliberalising education

Although education is a basic right and state schools are to provide free education based on equal opportunities, the reality is different. Of Turkey's 2010 budget, only 9.85 percent of the consolidated budget was spent on education (This ratio was 10.64 percent in 2009). This of course does not suffice to meet even the most urgent needs of this sector and is far away from the OECD standard. According to the OECD data, Turkey allocates $1.130 per primary education student and $1.834 per secondary education student. The average in OECD countries is $6.437 for primary school children and $8.006 for secondary school children (Türk-Eğitim-Sen, 2009). Whereas Turkey in 2008 allocated only 3.3 percent of its GDP to education, the average among OECD countries was 5 percent (Sönmez, July 28, 2009). As a comparison, in 1998, Turkey spent 2.94 percent of its GDP on education, whereas France spend 5.88 percent and Norway even 6.77 percent. Some 1.4 million children of elementary-school age do not attend school, 874.000 of them being girls. According to the United Nations Children's Fund (UNICEF), Turkey is among twelve countries globally that have not accomplished gender equality in education. Only 435.000 of over 4 million pre-school aged children obtain school training. On average, there are 50-60 students per classroom in big cities (Üstündağ, 2005).

Following neoliberal policies, education has become a commodity, a product to be delivered and sold to those who can afford it. Among the problems of the education sector are the low budget that is not enough to solve the problems of physical supplies and infrastructure; the educational content that becomes increasingly conservative, shifting away from democracy and employing capitalist logic in its curriculum; and the disparities in education levels between regions, provinces and schools (Çakır, September 07, 2009). Instead of collecting taxes, increasing the budget for education, building schools, hiring more teachers, and improving the education sector, the AKP relies on and continues to develop neoliberal ideas.

As a *solution* to the problems in the education sector, in the 2003-2004 academic year, the government announced that it would provide school books in primary public schools for free. This was a farce for the AKP. On the one side, the AKP did not provide for the basic needs of schools, citing budgetary restraints as the reason and coerced parents to make material contributions for their children's schools. On the other side, the AKP handed out free schoolbooks, which would have costed the families not more than 30 TL per student (İnal, 2009, p. 703) without even taking into account whether the families could have afforded these books or not. Worse, even three to four months after the academic year had started, the books still were not in students' hands. When they finally did receive them, the quality of the books was so bad that they soon fell apart (Güçlü, 2006; 2007; 2010).

Delighted by its *success*, in the academic year 2006-2007, the AKP widened this free-schoolbooks policy to secondary schools. According to the Turkish Ministry of Education, between 2003 and 2008 a total of 739.218.434 school books for primary and secondary schools were provided by the Ministry. Since 2003, state funds have been transferred to some AKP-affiliated publishing companies, adding to their capital accumulation. By providing school books for free, the AKP cover its unsocial behavior, which Yıldırım (2009, p. 92) calls "market populism." Another example of this version of populism are the conditional cash transfers to families forcing them to send their children to schools, while at the same time education costs for households have increased over 35 percent (Yıldırım, 2009, pp. 81, 91).

Political Islamists' "dance with money" (İnal, 2009, p. 716) has already become well known. What the AKP adds to this is a combination of *money* as capital and *religion* as identity, through which education is being constructed in line with the AKP's aspirations (İnal, 2009, p. 689). The AKP reveals that it is a capitalist conservative party by grouping education and money together–realising, private education for a fee (İnal, 2009, p. 716). Besides, parents who send their children to public schools are obliged to pay for registration, paper, report cards, chalk, banks, chairs, even water, electricity, heating and telephone costs of the school (Eğitimin Sorunu Neo-liberalizm, 2006). Those who can afford, pay. But those who *cannot* afford it are simply treated as second class citizens. More briefly, there turns out to be *two* different types of *public* school classrooms: those rooms, where the parents (in the hopes of providing better education for their children) are able to make donations and those in which they are not. In the former type, classes are provided with modest materials and educational needs, whereas those classrooms where the parents cannot make contributions are in a desperate situation in which even basic needs cannot be covered (Buğra, 2005). Even private establishments that prepare students for various exams and other creative companies are increasing, constructing not only a profit-raising "education industry" but also a very lucrative "exam industry" (Sönmez, July 28, 2009) with the willing assistance of the AKP. Now, have you ever read about this in the EU Progress Reports on Turkey?

Besides parents, it is also up to the charitable to ensure the education of Turkey's youth. With Law No. 4842, the AKP granted tax allowances and left it up to the philanthropic organisations and persons to offer basic education needs. Erdoğan also launched the "100 Percent Support for Education" campaign on September 11, 2003 (Üstündağ, 2010). The *Milliyet* newspaper provides another example, as it organised the campaign *Baba Beni Okula Gönder (Dad Send me to School)*. The grants provided via this campaign are used for the building of schools, dormitories, and classrooms and for scholarships for some 6.750 girls in fifteen cities in Southeastern Turkey. Another campaign– *Haydi Kızlar, Okula! (Come on Girls, to School)*–which was launched by the UNICEF and the National Education Ministry, aims at raising the number of girls attending school and supplying gender-equal education. That campaign was carried out in 53 cities in 2005 and ultimately created a 5.8 percent increase in the number of girls signing up for school. Actually, one can aptly name the *reformation* in the educational sphere as contracting the state's responsibilities to the benevolent.

This bleak reality in Turkey–smilingly overlooked by the EU–is never ending: in order to produce and sell more products with fewer costs and lower prices, big corporations either demand to pay fewer or even no taxes to the state and/or force employees to work for reduced wages. If workers do not accept these conditions, corporations threaten to close the companies and move to low-wage countries–as if Turkey is a high-wage country. So the workers' wages decrease, although they work for longer hours. Simultaneously, as to let taxes sink, the state limits its expenditures. The most convenient way to do this is by retrenchment in fields in which the state has responsibility. This means that in addition to coping with lower incomes, the working class must, at the same time, pay more for things that used to be provided for free by the state (Özar, 2009).

Concluding Remarks

The AKP years symbolise a new chapter in Turkey's political history, especially in terms of Turkey's integration into the neoliberal world order through globalisation. Integration-cum-globalisation involves increased interaction between the nation states and international organisations. So far as the IMF, World Bank and the EU are concerned, Turkey has proved to be a good student. Yet, there are other international organisations and regulations that Turkey has also been part of, which do not seem to be that effective. More briefly, while the AKP has been keen on doing its IMF-administered homework, the same cannot be said for that given by the UN, which requires respect for human rights, such as the right to work, the right to equal pay for equal work, the right to social security, the right to life worthy of human dignity, and the freedom of association (Articles 23 and 25, The Universal Declaration of Human Rights).

The year 2010 commemorates the twentieth anniversary of the United Nations' Development Program's annual Human Development Reports (HDR), which measure people's well-being by mixing measures of health, education, and wealth and "putting people first" (HDR, 2010). An analysis of the 2009 HDR (HDR, 2009) reveals that Turkey, with a GDP of nearly $13.000 per capita, has a human development rate of 0.806, placing it seventy-ninth out of 182 countries. Thus, Turkey's human development compared to her economic income is very low. Regarding infant mortality, Turkey ranks 86 out of 176, while in literacy it is seventy-seventh of 151 states. In the poverty index Turkey ranks 40 of 135. In gender equality, Turkey is placed 125 (!) of 155; in women's participation in economic and social life it ranks 101 of 109. The result is depressing: Turkey's development model is a neoliberal model heedless to humans and their needs (Türmen, June 02, 2010).

The AKP's so-called social policies do not amount to much more than providing school books, conditional benefit transfers, and social security reforms with cuts in security spending. The party's approach to handling social policy is to transfer the accountability to civil society and local administration. This it does through market populism, by the allocation of resources to the AKP's (potential) supporters. Moreover, the party has been keen on relocating *state* responsibilities to charitable and philantrophic associations. Actually, these strategies are totally in line with the IMF/EU line of neoliberalisation. In parallel with this understanding, the AKP government's gender policies do not aim to integrate women into the economic, social and political life, but to exclude and pauperise them (See Yeğenoğlu & Coşar's contribution to this vlolume). By putting in motion feelings of solidarity and altruism through the use of the Islamic ommunitarian means and integrating religious motives into its neoliberal applications, the AKP has been able to limit protests and resistance as much as possible (Yücel, 2008).

REFERENCES

Ağartan, T. (2007). Turkish health policy in a globalizing world: The case of 'Transformation of Health' Program. Paper for ISA Research Committee 19 Annual Academic Conference. Florence. Retrieved from http://www.unifi.it/confsp/papers/pdf/Agartan.doc .

Amin, S. (2004): U.S. Imperialism, Europe, and the Middle East. *Monthly Review, 56* (6), 13-33.

Artvinli, F. (2007). Open World Conference of Workers. In Defense of Trade Union Independence & Democratic Rights, Special Issue Bulletin n° 8: International Liaison Committee of Workers and Peoples, N° 231-232, April 17-24. Retrieved from http://www.owcinfo.org/ILC/NEWS/ILC_231_232.html

Austrian Presidency of the European Union (2006). 5th European Meeting of People Experiencing Poverty. How do we cope with every day life. May, 12-13. Retrieved June 3, 2010 from http://ec.europa.eu/employment_social/social_inclusion/docs/2006/pep_report_en.pdf

Bedirhanoğlu, P. (2008). Restrukurierung des türkischen staates im kontext der neoliberalen globalisierung. In İ. Ataç, B. Küçük & U. Şener (Eds.), *Perspektiven auf die Türkei: Geselschaftliche dis-kontinuitäten im prozess der Europäisierung* (102-126). Münster: Westfälisches Dampfboot.

Bedirhanoğlu, P. (2009). Türkiye'de neoliberal otoriter devletin AKP'li yüzü. In İ. Uzgel & B. Duru (Eds.), *AKP kitabı: Bir dönüşümün bilançosu* (40-65). Ankara: Phoenix.

Bringing Human Development into Focus. Retrieved June 30, 2010 from http://hdr.undp.org/en/reports/global/hdr2010/anniversary/

Buğra, A. (2005). *AB müzakere sürecinde STK'lar ve yoksulluk.* İstanbul Bilgi Üniversitesi Sivil Toplum Kuruluşları Eğitim ve Araştırma Birimi, Sivil Toplum ve Demokrasi Konferans Yazıları no 12. Retrieved from http://stk.bilgi.edu.tr/docs/bugra_std_12.pdf

Çakır, B. (2009). "Eğitim-Sen addresses the Ministry of Education for better education," *bianet.org*, September 7. Retrieved from http://bianet.org/english/english/116892-egitim-sen-addresses-the-ministry-of-education-for-better-education

Çakır, B. (2009). "Thousands of people protested AKP's health politics," *bianet.org*, October 20. Retrieved from http://bianet.org/english/health/117734-thousands-of-people-protested-akps-health-politics

Eder, M. (2003). Implementing the economic criteria of EU membership: How difficult is it for Turkey? *Turkish Studies, 4* (1), 219-244.

Eğitim-Sen. (2006). *Eğitimin sorunu neo-liberalizm.* Retrieved from http://ekutuphane.egitimsen.org.tr/pdf/4163.pdf

Eğitim ve insan kaynakları paneli (ara rapor). Retrieved October 27, 2010 from http://www.universite-toplum.org/text.php3?id=147.

European Commission. (n.d.). *Flexicurity.* Retrieved from http://ec.europa.eu/social/main.jsp?catId=102&langId=en

Foster, J. B. (2005). The end of rational capitalism. *Monthly Review, 56* (10), 1-13.

Girdner, E. J. (2005). A spectre haunting Europe: The European Constitution, the budget crisis, and the limits of neoliberal integration. *Uluslararası İlişkiler, 2* (7), 63-85.

Grabbe, H. (2002). European Union Conditionality and the Acquis Communautaire. *International Political Science Review, 07,* 249-268.

Güçlü, A. (2006). Ders kitapları hala yok. *milliyet.com,* November 1. Retrieved from http://www.milliyet.com.tr/ders-kitaplari-h-l--yok/abbas-guclu/turkiye/yazardetayarsiv/22.06.2010/176506/default.ht m

Güçlü, A. (2007). Ders kitapları? *milliyet.com,* November 13. Retrieved from http://www.milliyet.com.tr/ders-kitaplari-/abbas-guclu/turkiye/yazardetayarsiv/30.06.2010/222705/default.htm

Güçlü, A. (2010, May 12) EĞİTİM-SEN: *Ücretsiz* ders kitabı rant aracına dönüştü. Retrieved from http://abbasguclu.com.tr/haber/egitimsen_ucretsiz_ders_kitabi_rant_aracina_donustu.html

Hamzaoğlu, O. & Yavuz, C.I. (2009). Sağlıkta AKP'li dönemin bilançosu üzerine, In İ. Uzgel & B. Duru (Eds.), *AKP kitabı: Bir dönüşümün bilançosu* (633-659). Ankara: Phoenix.

Hout, W. (2006). The only game in town? European social democracy and neo-liberal globalization. *Internationale Politik und Gesellschaft, 2,* 9-23.

Europa Glossary Retrieved from http://europa.eu/scadplus/glossary/accession_criteria_copenhague_en.htm

kottaşlaMA! Retrieved June 3, 2010 from http://kottaslama.org/php/kt/wp/ .

Committee on International Trade (2010, June 29). Draft report on trade and economic relations with Turkey. Retrieved from http://www.abhaber.com/haber.php?id=30735

European anti-poverty campaign stresses collective approach. (2010, January 6). Retrieved from http://www.euronews.net/2010/01/06/european-anti-poverty-campaign-stresses-collective approach/

European Workers Liaison Committee (2007, April 17&24). We are raising a cry of alarm (Special Issue, Bulletin no: 8). *International Newsletter* (231-232). Retrieved from http://www.salutepubblica.org/uploadtest/Servizio%20Socio-Sanitario/Specialissue.pdf

İnal, K. (2009). AKP'nin neoliberal ve muhafazakar eğitim anlayışı, In İ. Uzgel & B. Duru (Eds.), *AKP kitabı: Bir dönüşümün bilançosu* (689-719). Ankara: Phoenix.

Nakay, Z. (2010, April 3). *Sade vatandaş olarak*. Retrieved from http://www.sadevatandas.net/yorum03042010.htm

OECD Health Data 2010. (2010). *How does Turkey compare*. Retrieved from http://www.oecd.org/dataoecd/46/5/38980477.pdf

Onder, N. (2007). The Turkish political economy: Globalization and regionalism. *Perspectives on Global Development and Technology*, 6, 229-259.

Özar, Ş. (2009, August 22). *Neoliberalizm ve yoksulluk*. Retrieved from http://www.bianet.org/biamag/kadin/116585-neoliberalizm-ve-yoksulluk

Palier, B. (2006). Is there a social route to welfare reforms in Europe? Paper presented at the annual meeting of the American Political Science Association, Marriott, Loews Philadelphia, and the Pennsylvania Convention Center, Philadelphia, PA Online <PDF>. Retrieved from http://www.allacademic.com/meta/p151310_index.html .

Patton, M. J. (2006). The economic policies of Turkey's AKP government: Rabbits from a hat? *Middle East Journal*, 60 (3), 513-536.

Sönmez, M. (2007): *İlerleme raporu: AB›nin referansı IMF. Bianet. org*, November 9. Retrieved from http://bianet.org/bianet/ekonomi/102829-ilerleme-raporu-abnin-referansi-imf

Sönmez, M. (2009). *Paran kadar eğitim. Bianet.org*, July 28. Retrieved from http://bianet.org/bianet/siyaset/116137-paran-kadar-egitim

The Universal Declaration of Human Rights. Retrieved from http://www.un.org/en/documents/udhr/index.shtml#atop

TTB. (2007). *Sağlıkta piyasacı tahribatın son halkası: AKP.* Retrieved from http://www.ttb.org.tr/kutuphane/saglikta_piyasaci_tahribat.pdf

Turkey 2009 progress report: Enlargement policy and main challenges 2009-2010. Retrieved June 4, 2010 from http://ec.europa.eu/enlargement/pdf/key_documents/2009/tr_rapport_2009_en.pdf

Turkish Ministry of Education (n.d.) Ücretsiz ders kitabı projesi. Retrieved June 3, 2010 from http://yayim.meb.gov.tr/ucretsizkitap.html

TurkStat Press Release. (2010). Household Labor Force Survey for March 2010. (106), June. Retrieved from http://www.turkstat.gov.tr/PreHaberBultenleri.do?id=6268

TÜİK krizin etkisini küçük gösteriyor. (2009). *bianet.org*, 16 April. Retrieved from http://bianet.org/bianet/ekonomi/113877-tuik-krizin-etkisini-kucuk-gosteriyor

Türk Eğitim-Sen Genel Başkanı İsmail Koncuk'un 2010 eğitim yılı bütçesiyle ilgili yaptığı basın açıklaması. (2009). Retrieved November 7 from http://www.turkegitimsen.org.tr/haber_goster.php?haber_id=2063

Türmen, R. (2010). *İnsan* merkezli kalkınma. *Milliyet*, June 2. Retrieved from http://www.milliyet.com.tr/insan-merkezli-kalkinma/riza-turmen/siyaset/yazardetay/02.04.2010/1219571/default.htm

Türmen, R. (2010). *İşsizler* birleşiniz. *Milliyet*, May 28. Retrieved from http://www.milliyet.com.tr/issizler-birlesiniz/riza-turmen/siyaset/yazardetay/21.06.2010/1243602/default.htm?ref=haberici

Türmen, R. (2010). TEKEL işçilerinin *öğrettikleri*. *Milliyet*, February 28. Retrieved from http://www.milliyet.com.tr/tekel-iscilerinin-ogrettikleri/riza-turmen/siyaset/yazardetay/11.02.2010/1196084/default.htm

UNDP. (2009). Human development report 2009. Retrieved from http://hdr.undp.org/en/media/HDR_2009_EN_Summary.pdf

Unemployment statistics. Retrieved June 30, 2010 from

http://epp.eurostat.ec.europa.eu/statistics_explained/index.php/Unemployment_statistics

Updegraff, R. (2010). Tekel, Neoliberalism, and the AKP [Web log message], February 9. Retrieved from http://turkishpoliticsinaction.blogspot.com/2010/02/tekel-neoliberalism-and-akp.html

Uzgel, İ. (2009). AKP: Neoliberal dönüşümün yeni aktörü. In İ. Uzgel & B. Duru (Eds.), *AKP kitabı: Bir dönüşümün bilançosu* (11-39). Ankara: Phoenix.

Üstündağ, E. (2005, June 16). Basic Education Up to the Charitable. Retrieved May 5, 2010 from http://bianet.org/english/politics/62483-basic-education-up-to-the-charitable

von Werlhof, C. (September 2008). The globalization of neoliberalism, its consequences, and some of its basic alternatives. *Capitalism, Nature, Socialism, 19*, (3), 94-117.

Yıkılmaz, G. and Kumlu, S. (Eds.) (2011). *Tekel eylemine kenar notları.* Ankara: Phoenix.

Yıldırım, D. (2009). AKP ve neoliberal populizm. In İ. Uzgel & B. Duru (Eds.), *AKP Kitabı: Bir dönüşümün bilançosu* (66-107). Ankara: Phoenix.

Yücel, Y. (2008, August 16). *Türkiye'de neoliberal devlet ve kadınlar.* Retrieved from http://bianet.org/bianet/ekonomi/107889-turkiyede-neoliberal-devlet-ve-kadinlar

5th European meeting of people experiencing poverty. (2006, May 12-13). *How do we cope*

with every day life? Retrieved June 3, 2010 from http://ec.europa.eu/employment_social/social_inclusion/dos2006/prp_report_en.pdf

CONCLUSION

HEARING THE SILENCE OF VIOLENCE

Simten Coşar & Gamze Yücesan-Özdemir

This edited volume can be regarded as an attempt to understand the AKP years in Turkey with specific reference to the articulation between neoliberalism and Islamist politics, which has created a modified version of the hegemonic ideology from the post-1980 period. Naturally, this ideological style is not static, but rather it changes according to the fluctuations in neoliberal politics at the global scale. The chapters in the book share the contention that the AKP's rule should be read in reference to the transformations within, and to the crisis of capitalism in neoliberal times, which necessarily involve different forms of suppression, oppression, and exploitation. All the different forms of suppression, oppression, and exploitation, which are revealed in the historical, class-based, and gender-based analysis of the economic, political, and ideological structures in the book, can be considered the reflections of neoliberal violence.

Turkey's years under the AKP governments can be read as the articulation of brute, violent neoliberalism with the silence of Islamist politics. Put differently, Islamist instruments such as Islamic life-worlds, beliefs, codes of conduct, and networks have been manipulated to domesticate and accommodate the exclusionary neoliberal practices embedded in economic, political, and ideological structures. The domestication of the brute violence of neoliberalism–presented as the flexible adjustment of neoliberal style to the domestic politics and policies–through Islamist politics is located in the very stitches of the texture of Turkish state and society. In this respect, the chapters follow up on this domestication process at the level of the state, law, civil society, citizenship, social policy, and gender. All these levels condition and are in turn conditioned by global power networks.

The brute violence of neoliberalism is most manifest in the marketisation and commodification of political and social spheres. All social and political *discoveries* under the AKP's rule have been made to conform to a neoliberal economic rationality, which is fixed on the goals of marketisation and commodification without regard to the real lives of real people suffering from exploitation, suppression, and oppression. Packaged under the banner of *liberality, and a democratic stance* based on the free-floating individual in the free-market, structural inequality is directly linked to the (neoliberal) globalisation process, which reproduces dependency at the local, national, and international levels–dependency on a functioning free market for survival. This package is publicised through the discourse on the free-market as a realm of freedom, equality, and individual and common utility. Yet, the market is not a set of abstract and static conditions, on the contrary, it is, in itself, a composite of social relations in which power is allocated. Given that we face the colonisation of life itself by market forces and/or the penetration of non-market spheres by market norms, as can be seen in the contributions to the volume, it is not freedom, equality, and utility that define the market, but exploitation, suppression, and oppression.

To start with the state level, the AKP's terms in office in Turkey have been marked by continuous debates regarding the party's political identity. In this respect, the AKP has variably named itself and/or has been identified as *conservative-democratic, (post-)Islamist,* and *conservative-liberal.* In this edited volume, as particularly clarified by Yalman in Chapter I, these labels are considered to share a commonality in that they invariably host the policies that lead to the elimination of class through state practices. The state restructuration, which started in the early-1980s, has initiated the steps for this elimination of class. Furthermore, the restructuration of the state is significant for understanding the violence of neoliberalism since it has implicated the response to the crisis of hegemony that the Turkish bourgeoisie had entered into in the late 1970s. Decisive in this response were the deconstitutionalisation of labour rights and ultimately the elimination of class as a political and explanatory actor. The accompanying legal structuration also enhanced the process of the elimination of class, by means of defining rights and freedoms in terms of bourgeois liberty. As Özdemir succintly explains in Chapter 2, the legal structuration has so far worked towards the suppression and oppression of labour by defining such critical themes as job security and workers' health and security in terms of *employers'* security and *work* health and security, respectively. This, ultimately, brings about the free-marketisation of law, and/or the designing of a market-friendly legal structure.

At the (civil) societal level, the elimination of class is also manifested in the AKP's perception of civil society. Briefly, and as expressed by Yılmaz in Chapter 4, the AKP's ideal model for civil society has been constructed with special reference to the bourgeois interests, which in the final analysis shows, has led to an exclusionary practice. However, here, the exclusion is not necessarily realised through legal means, though it does work through the discourse on state retrieval from the civil-societal sphere. In other words, ensuring the state's non-presence is understood as the cutting away of the state's financial involvement in the civil society, thus relating to the mainstream understanding of civil societal autonomy in terms of financial autonomy. In the (neo)liberal frame, this *autonomisation* is proposed to be the *sine-qua-non* for the free functioning of the civil societal actors–ultimately pointing at the free-marketisation of civil society. However, this design of the civil-societal sphere also hints at the violence of neoliberal politics by inhering authoritarian assumptions.

The *Erdoğanisation* of civil society, which derives from the production and reproduction of the party's identity on a leadership-basis–that is, personalistic politics–hint at authoritarianism as a definitive feature of the AKP. Indeed, the leader-based party representation is authoritarianism *par excellence*. In this respect, *Erdoğanisation* connotes the representation of the civilianising and/or liberalising of Islamist politics in the person of Erdoğan himself. Besides the authoritarianism displayed in such personalistic politics, arbitrary governmental practices in matters concerning the civil society also imply the party's authoritarianism. As also elaborated upon in this volume, though the AKP governments have repetitively declared their willingness to dialogue with civil societal actors, in practice they have acted selectively, excluding class-based and gender-based organisations deemed *radical* and/or *marginal*.

The exclusion at the civil societal level is also a manifestation of violence, which, in turn, is silenced through a resort to identity politics. The AKP governments have, for quite some time, pursued a committed program of liberalising official policies on identity issues concerning ethnic, religious, and gendered rights, which they have wedged into the discourse on Europeanisation, as discussed by Yeşilyurt-Gündüz in Chapter 10. Coupled with the dismissal of class-based politics from the public sphere, the AKP's *liberal* and *democratic* self-construction of identity politics has interpellated identity-based (ethnic, religious, and gendered) politics. This, in turn, has silenced claims against the dismissal of class-based rights. Though perceived as a *nouveaux* approach and/or a *revolution* in terms of state-society relations with special emphasis on *democracy, rule of law, tolerance, and* the *civilianisation of politics* within the AKP circles and/or the epistemic communities that ally with the party, as Coşar in Chapter 3 and Yalman in Chapter 1 underline, these policies have actually restricted discussions on the party's politics and policies regarding these topics in terms of identity issues.

Intersecting the state restructuration and civil societal restructuration in the dismissal of class-based politics is the AKP's citizenship regime. The identity politics of the AKP are crystallised in the party's policies on citizenship, which are delineated in Chapter 6 by Soyarık-Şentürk. From there, the inherent violence in the breakdown of the civil societal activism along identity lines is silenced by a call for unity through citizenship. In this respect, behind the party's four decade-long attempt to change the citizenship law, one can observe the silencing effect of the Turkish-Islamic synthesis—aside from the recognition of citizenship rights in terms of identity. Briefly, the party's citizenship regime, which prioritises Turkish-Muslimhood, interpellates the citizens to accommodate Islamist politics.

The realm of social policies is the seedbed for this accommodation of Islamist politics, which in turn silences neoliberal violence. Actually, the AKP's practices in the social policy realm, which Yücesan-Özdemir defines as a *social policy regime* in Chapter 5, evince the juxtaposition of the neoliberal, conservative, and Islamist roots of the party. In this respect, the AKP's social policy regime calls for the dismissal of the rights-based welfare regime and social citizenship. The functioning of neoliberal violence is then observed in the reproduction of precarious work, while Islamist mercy in the form of social assistance conceals this violence. On the one hand, precarious work denotes that the labour class is pushed into a deregulated and flexibilised market, which in the neoliberal order not only involves the worklife but also the life-world. Hence, the labour class, through precarious work, is forced into living in a risk society, which strips them of the basic needs for individual security, locking them into endemic insecurity. On the other hand, Islamist mercy mechanisms are then put to work through the family-charity nexus. The crucial point here is the dressing of precarious work with the essentialisation of the Turkish-Muslim family structure as the basic solidarity pattern.

The gender plane offers one of the most *precarious* and fragile examples of the harmonious dancing between neoliberal violence and Islamist politics. This dancing can be observed in the new mode of patriarchy, as described by Yeğenoğlu & Coşar in Chapter 7, which encompasses the AKP's neoliberal, conservative, and Islamist features. The neoliberal call for workers from the female labour force—flexible, insecure, and thus precarious—has been manipulated through an emphasis on the needs of the family, so as to fit into the religious-conservative essentials of Turkish society. This functions as an interpellation for women to adjust to the free-market conditions, without taking into consideration the additional burdens derived from the essentialisation of their familial responsibilities in the Islamist-conservative frame. At the same time, the flexibility that characterises the neoliberal version of the free-market also makes it easier for Islamist-conservative concerns to force the female labour force out of the market when the market and the family dynamics demand so. Here, the new mode of patriarchy works through gendered exploitation in the market, feeding into oppression in the familial sphere, the latter being defined with reference to Turkishness-Muslimhood. Thus, the silent demand that women submit themselves to the violence of the free-market contributes to the deepening of the patriarchal clutches on women's emancipation through Islamist-conservative policies.

The neoliberal restructuration of state-society relations at different levels in Turkey noted above, as elsewhere, has not functioned independent of the neoliberal globalisation process, and thus global power networks. In this respect, the transformations in the domestic sphere are directly tied to the deepening of dependency, internalised through the policies run under the hegemonic decisiveness of international organisations—the World Bank, the IMF and the EU. The *internalisation of dependency,* as Zabcı defines it in Chapter 9, is clearly irretriveable, embodying the *raison d'être* of the AKP. Neoliberal policy preferences have so far functioned as parts of the survival strategy for the AKP, putting the party at the very center of the global neoliberal agenda. Here, the party's tactical move to mask the violence of this neoliberal agenda is centered around its resort to Islamist politics through *neo-Ottomanism* and/or *middle-easternisation* in its foreign policy preferences, as discussed by Demirtaş in Chapter 8. Actually, the discourses on neo-Ottomanism can also be interpreted as an attempt to deter criticism coming from religious-conservative supporters of the party—that the AKP has surrendered to a *Western* neoliberal agenda. Yet, the tendency to revive the wise, old, big brother in the ex-Ottoman territories and in the Muslim East more significantly functions to silence the party's neoliberal violence.

All in all, the silencing of the violence of neoliberalism can work through Islamist politics in two veins. First, Islamist politics are manipulated in the domestication of neoliberalism through an appeal to Turkish-Muslim life-worlds, beliefs, codes of conduct, and networks. This strategy especially concerns the grassroots of the party–the religious-conservative electorate. Second, the Islamist politics have also been subjected to *liberalisation* by the AKP governments in order to appeal to a wider societal network for reasons of survival. In this respect, the neoliberal agenda is instrumentalised for the construction of a liberalised discourse on Islamist politics, which in turn domesticates both Islamism and also the mainstream secularist understanding of Islamism in Turkey.

(ENDNOTES)

1   Actually, it is open to discussion whether class-based politics had been decisive in the pre-1980 period, when the democratic rights and freedoms of the working class had been relatively recognised within the frame of 1961 Constitution.

2   In Gramsci's thought, passive revolution refers to a style of state politics that preserves control by a leading group on the one hand while instituting economic, social, political and ideological changes on the other. In other words, the concept encapsulates the means by which a dominant class maintains its hegemony by neutralising the pressures of various contending forces that might otherwise trigger profound structural transformations. Consequently, the defusing process is achieved without undergoing a political revolution that potentially could threaten the dominance of the leading group and the "modus operandi" of the system (Gramsci, 1971).

3   Articles 141 and 142 of the 1982 Constitution had been designed to prevent attempts to establish the domination of one social class over another. Article 163 had outlawed politically motivated religious activity and prohibited the establishment of religious organisations or political parties aimed at creating an Islamic Republic. Articles 141 and 142 were mainly anti-communist provisions and were used to restrict political activity by socialists and communists. Articles 141, 142 and 163 were abolished altogether on April 12, 1990. However, some of the provisions of these articles were reworded and incorporated into the Law on Struggle against Terror, which was adopted in 1991.

4   The DGMs were first founded by the 1973 amendment to the 1961 Constitution, in the aftermath of the 1971 military intervention, for considering those crimes that specifically aim at the security of the state. They were closed down in 1976. The DGMs were re-established in 1983 within the scope of the 1982 Constitution.

5   "The United Nations Alliance of Civilizations (UNAOC) is an initiative of the UN Secretary-General which aims to improve understanding and cooperative relations among nations and peoples across cultures and religions, and to help counter the forces that fuel polarization and extremism."

Silent Violence:
Neoliberalism, Islamist Politics and the AKP Years in Turkey

6   For an example of the academic research that interprets the AKP's understanding of the state in terms of service state see Yavuz (2006).

7   Here, as in other contributions to this volume, September 12 regime refers to two interrelated phenomena. First, it directly refers to the military *coup d'état*, and the interim regime between 1980 and 1983, which inscribed the turning point in the socio-political transformation in Turkey. Second, it refers to the setting of the structural requisites of the neoliberal frame that would characterise the following decades in Turkish political history.

8   According to a Turkish sociologist, Şerif Mardin, a major potential threat against the nurturing of a liberal environment in Turkey is "the neighbourhood pressure" (Çakır, 2007). With this term, Mardin sought to capture the unofficial, local, communal pressure on individuals to conform to religious-conservative norms in their everyday lives. Almost immediately, a lively debate began in Turkish newspapers and television programs on the concept of "neighbourhood pressure" and on its manifestations in Turkey.

9   For a critical assessment of this hegemonic discourse see Erdoğan (2009).

10   In Gramsci's thought, each successful political system requires the creation of an *historic bloc*, unified around an *hegemonic project*, in which the dominant class builds alliances beyond itself, and wins consent for its institutions and ideas (Gramsci, 1971).

11   For a critical reading of the religious orders in this process see Ayata (1996).

12   For an analysis of the AKP, which employs Gramsci's conceptual categories but which does not touch upon state transformation, see Yıldırım (2009).

13   Prior to 1961, there were no organs maintaining a similar function in the Turkish constitutional system. The main principle behind the logic of the 1921 and 1924 constitutions was the superiority of the national will, embodied in the *Türkiye Büyük Millet Meclisi* (Turkish Grand National Assembly, TBMM), and therefore articulated through the superiority of the will of the representatives of the nation. This principle was hardly convenient for the establishment of a system that was in harmony with the idea of the superiority of universal principles of law over national legislations.

14   The mode of regulation in the "golden age" of capitalism is characterised by the rights-based Keynesian welfare policies, which included the recognition of the workers' rights to unionise, to public services—health, education and social security—to unemployment benefits, and relatively high wages.

For the regime of capital accumulation this mode of regulation ensured the pre-emption of class-based opposition as well as an increasing tide in consumption patterns (Hardt & Negri, 1994).

15 Article 150 of the Constitution regulates annulment action as follows : "The President of the Republic, parliamentary groups of the party in power and of the main opposition party and a minimum of one-fifth of the total number of members of the Turkish Grand National Assembly shall have the right to apply for annulment action to the CCT, based on the assertion of the unconstitutionality of laws in form and in substance, of decrees having the force of law, of Rules of Procedure of the Turkish Grand National Assembly or of specific articles or provisions thereof. If more than one political party is in power, the right of the parties in power to apply for annulment action shall be exercised by the party having the greatest number of members."

16 The second way by which the CCT may control the constitutionality of parliamentary laws is through the application of Article 152 (1) and 152 (2) of the Constitution: "If a court which is trying a case, finds that the law or the decree having the force of law to be applied is unconstitutional, or if it is convinced of the seriousness of a claim of unconstitutionality submitted by one of the parties, it shall postpone the consideration of the case until the CCT decides on the issue. If the court is not convinced of the seriousness of the claim of unconstitutionality, such a claim together with the main judgment shall be decided upon by the competent authority of appeal."

17 Besides the CCT decisions-depending on the conjuncture-cases before the European Court of Human Rights (ECtHR) have also been a source of critical discussions in which the same parties are represented by similar faces.

18 The Court's ruling changed the articles 16 and 26 of the original package of reforms, which would redefine the process of electing members to the CCT and the HSYK. Under the original package of reforms, the president would have been able to appoint experts to the CCT with a background in economics and political science. The CCT cancelled this proposal. The CCT also cancelled a provision that would have allowed members of the HSYK and the CCT to choose only one candidate, rather than three as it is now.

19 One of the amendments required the creation of an ombudsman's office, yet the new ombudsman has not been empowered with a guarantee of autonomy. Similarly, the clause for affirmative action for women added just a rhetorical tribute to the previous provision. State employees are now granted the right to engage in collective bargaining, but they have no right to strike. The authority of military courts was curtailed slightly without touching the kernel of their powers. The provisional Article 15, which has provided irresponsibility and immunity from prosecution to all actors of the

military regime (1980-1983), is now repealed. But–unfortunately–
the repeal of this clause will not have an effect on the legal positions
of the generals, for the fact that it was an irresponsibility clause.
Opposition proposals to sharpen this provision were rejected by the
AKP leaders.

20   In the Decision No. 2006/112 dated October 15, 2006, the CCT
declared that the provisions concerning the retirement of public
officials must be regulated in a different manner from the other
employees. Based on this statement, the Court urged that the
provisions of the Act (No. 5510) covering civil servants and other
insured employees both be annulled. Therefore, the efforts aiming
to address the retirement facilities for the entire working population
under one single statute have become null and void for the time
being.

21   Turkey signed the ECHR on November 4, 1950 and ratified it on
May 18, 1954. The agreement entered into force on the same day.
The country granted the right of individual petition to the ECtHR,
just before its failed membership application in 1987. Turkey
accepted the jurisdiction of the European Court of Justice in 1990
with some reservations and then removed these reservations in 1992.
Turkey also ratified Protocol No. 11 to the ECtHR, establishing
a full-time court to replace the Convention's former monitoring
mechanism in 1997.

22   The government issued five decree-laws on the basis of Law 3987,
on labour compensation schemes as well as organisational issues.

23   The law did not, in principle, bring a novel idea. The previous
Kamu Ortaklığı İdaresi (Public Participation Administration) was
renamed the *Özelleştirme İdaresi* (Privatisation Administration).
The authority to make privatisation decisions, including decisions
to determine the companies to be privatised, means and methods of
privatisation, and finalising the sale, was granted to the *Özelleştirme
Yüksek Kurulu* (High Council of Privatisation, ÖYK). The ÖYK was
to be composed of Prime Minister, State Minister, Minister in charge
of Privatisation, Minister of Finance, and Minister of Industry and
Commerce.

24   2007 amendments required the president to be chosen by the popular
elections among the ones nominated by twenty deputies in writing.
In addition, the political parties, which obtained 10 percent or more
of the total valid votes cast nationally in the most recent elections,
are entitled to nominate a candidate for the elections (Article 101 of
the Constitution of Turkey).

25   1982 Constitution offers an example for the constitutionally
guaranteed elimination of collective rights of workers in Turkey.
The 1982 Constitution and the following legislations have been
functional in the elimination of any actual and/or potential

hindrances in the face of the articulation of Turkey into the neoliberal world order. In this respect, the liquidification of the collective rights of workers, as exemplified in the deunionisation process, has been an indisipensable requisite of neoliberal policies at the global scale (For the workings of neoliberal policies at the global scale with a view to deunionisation process see Hyman, 2000; Munck, 2002).

26 The Turkish government recently announced its third draft of the national program for the adaptation of *Acquis Communautaire*. The first two drafts of national programs were presented in 2001 and 2003 respectively. Media celebrated the declaration of the third draft as a signal for future developments in the realm of trade union rights. The third draft urges the government to initiate preparations to promulgate the proposal of laws that will change the existing legislation on trade unions, trade union rights, and strikes. However, the proposal of law brings no significant changes in the realm of trade union rights, including the right to strike. The third draft of the national program can be seen at the link http://www.abgs.gov.tr/index.php?p=42260&l=2

27 The revised European Social Charter was signed by the AKP government in October 2004. The AKP government put in reservations and the Turkish parliament refused to ratify the articles of the revised Charter regulating workers' rights.

28 On October 9, 2007, Ankara's 17th Central Judicial Court (following the Court of Cassations order), ruled to close *Türkiye Kamu Emeklileri Sendikası* (Retired Public Personnel Trade Union of Turkey, TÜRK Emekli-Sen) on the basis of Article 51 of the Constitution. However, this groundless verdict did not, in any sense, undermine Turkey's position in the accession negotiations with the EU, nor was it echoed in European labour circles.

29 This matter brings back memories of the case of the teachers' union, *Eğitim ve Bilim Emekçileri Sendikası*. The union has always been under severe pressure for its proposals on the necessity of education in one's own mother tongue. The authorities tried over and over again to close down the union on the basis of an annulled clause stressing the necessity of mother tongue in education, notwithstanding the fact that this demand and its formulation in the text was perfectly in line with the international legislation on human rights.

30 See Yeğenoğlu & Coşar's contribution in this volume.

31 The Standby Agreement enacted on January 2002 clearly states, "In support of these objectives, we will … [c]ontinue … to strengthen our debt position and rebuild market confidence."

32 In this first stage, the Bill (No. 4447) weakened the PAYG system in favor of private pension schemes. In 1999, the central government implemented a two-pillar system. The traditional

social security institutions acquired the role of first pillar under the 1999 reform. The second pillar is composed of private pension schemes. The attempts to 'support' the existing pension schemes by way of the private sector included the policy of keeping retirement earnings at low levels. Pension schemes managed by the private sector have become an optional second pillar of the Turkish system of social security, mainly after the 2002 regulation under the AKP's rule. The main goal of the 1999 reform was to shorten the benefit collection period and to enlarge the contribution period. For this purpose, the minimum entitlement age was elevated to 58 (for females)/60 (for the males). When considered together with the social security reform, it is safe to say that currently there is zealous encouragement to privatise the social security system in the long run.

33   The Turkish private pension law was drafted in 1999 and approved by the Parliament in October, 2001. However, the legal and institutional framework of the Turkish Private Pension System was completed in 2002. The route followed by the Bill (No. 4447) resembled the route proposed by the World Bank and supported by the Association of Turkish Industrialists and Businessmen. The World Bank proposed a three-tiered system of benefits. According to this system, the first pillar would consist of a minimum package of publicly-provided benefits. This mandatory first pillar covers minimum range of risks. The second pillar is also mandatory, but generally provided by the services of private sector and managed privately. Conversely, the third pillar is voluntary. The services included in this third stage aim to provide *high life quality* in return for high contributions.

34   2003 was the year in which the current social security reform was introduced to the general public.

35   For the strong criticisms raised by the *Türk Tabipler Birliği* (Turkish Medical Association,TTB), see http://www.turktabibleribirligi.com.

36   **Household Ratio with Real Deficit in Household Classes (%) (2003 and 2009)**

	2003	2009
Capitalists	19.44	18.93
Rentiers	57.93	39.60
Skilled Workers	16.80	18.76
Unskilled Workers	53.51	54.11
Unemployed	68.40	75.02

Source: Bahçe and Köse, 2010.

It is not easy to acquire available statistical data on income inequality due to the data collecting 'preferences' of the agencies dealing with data collection at national level and due to the complicated (internationalised) property structures of big companies (holdings). The mainstream analysis based on GINI coefficient disguise the real income inequality on social class basis. In this respect, the data on income inequality in the table is skecthed on the basis of real household deficits, which I believe reveals the inequality on social class basis. The real household deficit is calculated in terms of the difference between the total income and the total expenses of the household, considered as the unit of analysis. Here, the real deficit can be taken as an indicator of income inequality because the household emerges as the main unit of everyday survival. In this respect, the real deficit sheds light on the suffering in the reproduction of everyday life—i.e., in the reproduction of food, clothes, shelter, education, health. The data on labourer households disclose the increase in the real deficit on household basis in the years when the AKP has been in government. In parallel, the data also reveal that the rentiers' income has increased in the same time period. (We know that deficit of one category corresponds to the surplus of another.)

37 The main text of the Act can be accessed at http://www.sgk.gov.tr/sgkshared/dokuman/5510/5510_KANUN.doc   (in Turkish).

38 Some Articles of the Act foreseen to take effect beginning in 2007 were annulled by the CCT by the end of 2006. The Draft Law concerning the reorganisation of the annulled provisions was presented to the TBMM in November 2007. Following long discussions, the draft was approved on April 17, 2008 and entered into force in October 2008.

39 The minimum entitlement ages will start to increase biennially beginning in 2039, and continuing until the end of 2047. They will be set at 65 for both men and women entitled to retirement beginning in 2048. By the end of 2075, the minimum entitlement age will become 68 for both women and men. In the same vein, the Act enlarges the contribution period. Beginning in 2007, the minimum number of premium payment days increased to 100 days per year. In December 2008, the minimum number of premium payment days was 7 000. This amount will be 9000 days in 2026. To put it differently, the new Act requires beneficiaries to contribute for 2000 days more than the previous Act (No. 4447) required.

40 For example, the rate of monthly wage extension ranges between 3 percent and 2.6 percent per annum among different institutions for social insurance. Under the new legislation, these rates will be applied as 2.5 percent annually for all those insured between January 1, 2007 and December 31, 2015, and as 2 percent annually beginning January 1, 2016.

41 For those whose monthly incomes are under 175.71 TL (Turkish
Liras) (about $100), there will be means-tested access to health
services. In this case, the necessary contributions will be paid for
by the *Sosyal Güvenlik Kurumu* (Social Security Institution), a new
entity launched for the purposes of unifying different institutions
serving different groups of employed citizens, divided according to
their working status. Given that the *testers* will be chosen from the
state institutions, which are directly controlled by the government,
means-tested access to services of any kind creates the potential
danger of clientelism working for the party in power.

42 In this chapter and in the other contributions to this volume
Islamism and Islamist politics are considered in terms of the
political parties—and with their extensions in civil society—one
of the decisive ingredients of whose political identity is religion—
and in the Turkish context Sunni Islam. Political Islam, in this
sense, involves the aspiration for and/or actual state of acquiring
institutional and material power. In this respect, Islamist politics in
Turkey also signifies the transformation of the state structure and the
decisive locus of Islam in the new state form.

43 *Millî Nizam Partisi* (National Order Party; 1970-1971)-*Milli
Selamet Partisi* (National Salvation Party; 1972-1981)-*Refah Partisi*
(Welfare Party, RP; 1983-1998)–*Fazilet Partisi* (Virtue Party, FP;
1997-2001)-*Saadet Partisi* (Felicity Party, SP; 2001-).

44 In this chapter and in the other contributions to this volume
neoliberalism is used as the economic and political structure,
involving both policy preferences, policy practices as well as the
discursive strategies that are designed to promote the global flow
of finance capital. Neoliberalism is considered in terms of the
dissolution of the public into the private through individualisation
of each and every social right and through communitarianisation
of the society. Decisive in the individualisation and the
communitarianisation of *the social* is the categorical prioritisation of
the market, despite the society.

45 The new Citizenship Code reflects the AKP's endeavour to adjust the
Turkish legal system to the EU stipulations. In this respect, Soyarık-
Şentürk (in this volume) argues that the new code was tailored in
accordance with the European Convention on Nationality. Thus, it
includes articles that address the elimination of discrimination in
naturalisation and in compulsory military service–at least partially.

46 Kemalism, throughout the republican era, has been subjected to
different interpretations academically and politically. Here, I use the
term to refer to the six arrows of the early-republican state party, the
Cumhuriyet Halk Partisi (Republican People's Party), and especially
with reference to its understanding of modernisation, namely, a
state-directed socio-political transformation through nationalism,
corporatism, and authoritarian secularism (Parla, 1995, p. 323).

Kemalism has until recently, signified the basics of the republican establishment. As it is argued in this volume, the republican establishment has been experiencing a transformation in the last decade.

47 For a succint account of the different facets of Turkish nationalism during the early-republican era, see Yıldız, 2001.

48 Here, one should note Yıldız's (2009, p. 55) conclusion that the AKP's pro-Western foreign policy preferences are more to do with the structural dynamics of the current era, to which the new generation of *Millî Görüş* parties had to concede to an extent.

49 In this chapter and in other contributions to this volume the term "neo-Ottomanism" is used to underline the culturalist preference in the political realm. Briefly, while the established republican culture politics had opted to distance the country and the populace from the Ottoman past *via* directly adopting a pro-Western stance, the neo-Ottomanist discursive strategy signifies a preference for a cultural policy that is based on the continuity between the Ottoman Empire and the Turkish Republic. Here, Sunni Islam and communitarian practice of ruling stands out as the main bond between the two political entities. Neo-Ottomanist foreign policy preferences, on the other hand, work through discursive strategies based on a claim to historical hegemony over the lands over which the Ottoman Empire ruled—including the Balkans, Central Asia, the Middle East and North Africa—to be materialised through alliances built on financial and security concerns. Ultimately, neo-Ottomanism involves the historico-culturalist transformation of the state structure.

50 The AKP, by getting involved in a pro-EU and pro-US–and thus Israel-friendly–policy, faces the risk of losing a considerable support base that emanates from its religious conservative supporters. In this respect, it has to level this risk by a well-tuned religious-nationalist discourse at the domestic level. The reaction of Erdoğan to the President of Israel in 2009 in Davos and the domestic repercussions of this situation attest to this strategy.

51 On the connection between the "Anatolian tigers" and the capital of İstanbul, see Sönmez, 2009.

52 Article 301 of the Turkish Penal Code was devised to address those who openly insult Turkishness, the Republic and the Turkish Grand National Assembly, the government, the judiciary, and the security forces. Recently, there have been amendments to the article (April 2008), which standardised the period of imprisonment for those who are convicted guilty from six months to two years and dropped "Turkishness" from the article.

53 The Law on Struggle Against Terror (No. 3713) was first enacted under the ANAP government in 1991, replacing the infamous Articles 141 and 142—related to "crimes of thought." Though presented by the

ANAP government then as a positive step toward the improvement of individual rights and liberties, the article was met with criticism along the same lines (see for example İnsel, 2002). Likewise, the law was amended in 2006 under the second AKP government. The AKP was keen on linking the amendment to the process of Turkey's accession to EU. However, despite the official rhetoric of liberalisation, the law included new acts within the scope of "deeds of terrorism," like "disaffecting people from military service" and "resisting public officials." In addition, the trial of children between 15-18 years of age was excluded from the mandate of Children Courts and put under the authority of the Criminal Courts. These changes displayed a rather ambiguous stance, rather than a ready liberal and/or democratic one. For a detailed analysis of the new Law on Struggle, see Ermiş (n.d.).

54 Here, one shall note the ambivalence between the integrationist practice of citizenship in Turkey regardless of one's ethnicity and the discursive essentialisation of ethnic Turkishness.

55 For an example of the adoption of a Hayekian approach in the replacement of social rights with acts of charity, see Akdoğan 2004. For a criticism of reading the AKP's policies that lead to the negation of social rights in terms of Islamic charity, see Bakırezer and Demirer, 2009, pp. 173-176.

56 AKP's trials in the centre space signified a dual process of transformation—that of the space and the actor itself. Briefly, the authoritarianism of the centre space, which initially was symbolised in the rather traditionalised pattern of military's involvement in civilian political sphere was handed over to the civilian governments; the Turkish-Islamic synthesis was banalised in AKP's discursive policies, and the AKP by relying heavily on this banalised version of the synthesis has evolved from a pro-Islamist to a religious-nationalist political party.

57 Here, I borrow the term "banal" from Michael Billig (1995). In his analysis of nationalism in the United States, Billig refers to the term "banal nationalism" to underline the hegemonisation of nationalism through everyday use of nationalistic motifs that happen to go unnoticed (see Coşar, 2011).

58 See, for instance, the edited volumes by Cizre (2007) and Yavuz (2006b).

59 The Turkish electoral system in effect today combines the D'Hondt version of proportional representation with an exceptionally high 10 percent national threshold. This hybrid system tends to produce severe vote-seats ratio distortions principally to the advantage of bigger parties. The AKP has been a major beneficiary of this electoral arrangement, allowing it to obtain two thirds of the parliamentary seats by receiving only one third of all the votes cast in the 2002 general election.

60 For more on the importance of political learning in the moderation of Islamist parties, see Wickham's (2004, 2006) "complex learning" thesis. For an empirical critique of Wickham based on the Jordanese case, see Clark (2006).

61 For a general overview of the economic as well as cultural determinants of democracy see Clark *et al.* (2008) and Lipset (1994).

62 See, for instance, Bollen (1979), Helliwell (1994), Lipset (1959), and Przeworski *et al.* (2000) for cross-national statistical evidence on the positive association between economic development and democracy. For contrasting results, see Landman (1999).

63 Other intervening variables identified by historical-comparative analyses of the emergence of democracies included the timing and character of economic development, the nature of the state and its relation to social forces, and international factors such as wars and crises (Landman, 2003).

64 In addition to a strong bourgeoisie, Moore (1966) has argued that the presence of a revolutionary break with past political institutions distinguishes France, Britain, and the US from the fascist and communist states in his study.

65 For an alternative formulation of this point as private capital's "fear" of democratisation, see, Bellin (2000).

66 Other business associations with a conservative membership basis include, among others, the *Türkiye İşadamları ve Sanayiciler Konfederasyonu* (Confederation of Businessmen and Industrialists of Turkey, TUSKON), the *Anadolu Aslanları İşadamları Derneği* (Association of Anatolian Businessmen, ASKON), and the *İş Hayatı Dayanışma Derneği* (Business Life Cooperation Association, İŞHAD).

67 For the Association's membership figures between 1990 and 2004, see "AKP'nin Ampulünü" (2004).

68 The contribution by the rival TÜSİAD to gross national income was around 35 percent in 2006 (Berberoğlu, 2006).

69 In a mini-poll conducted by the daily *Milliyet* in 1996, only 25 percent of the MÜSİAD members said they supported the RP, while 50 percent indicated no party affiliation. In the same vein, Erol Yarar, the founding president of MÜSİAD, in response to poll results stated that MÜSİAD cannot be considered as an organisation under the RP umbrella even though a significant part of its members support the party ("Onlar Refah'ı", 1996).

70 For more on the impact of the February 28 decisions on the political Islamist movement, see Cizre-Sakallıoğlu & Çınar (2003) and Yavuz (2000).

71 In addition to the 1st and 2nd presidents of MÜSİAD, Erol Yarar and Ali Bayramoğlu respectively, several other MÜSİAD member businesses were tried before the State Security Courts for financing illegal Islamist networks. Both Yarar and Bayramoğlu were found guilty, in 1999 and 2000 respectively, under article 312 of the Turkish Penal Code for "publicly inciting hatred and hostility among people by pointing to differences in religious beliefs," and received one year prison sentences.

72 Internal factions formed within the political Islamist movement before the onset of the February 28 process. Yet, the RP's highly hierarchical organisational structure dominated by Erbakan's charismatic leadership managed to keep a tap on these earlier factional struggles. For more on this point, see Çakır (2004).

73 Erol Yarar, then president of MÜSİAD, was involved in the internal affairs of the RP to such an extent that there were rumours in late 1997 that he would candidate himself for the leadership of the new party to be established by reformists with a "Muslim democrat" identity ("Refah için", 1997). To retaliate MÜSİAD's siding with internal dissidents, Erbakan commissioned the establishment of a rival business association, ASKON, in November 1998 hoping to attract the members of MÜSİAD once the State Security Court dissolved the Association ("MÜSİAD'ı tasfiye", 1998).

74 For more on the concept of "conservative democracy" by a prominent AKP ideologue, see Akdoğan (2006).

75 To be sure, the disproportionate emphasis placed on religious and economic freedoms is not a novelty in the history of democratic opposition to the Republican regime in Turkey. Especially after the transition to multi-party politics in 1950, the violations of these freedoms have become the most important element of the regime critiques voiced by right-wing political parties. For more on this point, see Keyder (1987).

76 For a detailed account of the Turkish-Islamic Synthesis, see Buğra (2002b) and Toprak (1990).

77 This is a recurrent theme in annual economy reports published by MÜSİAD since its inception.

78 TÜSİAD's discourse of democracy, while coached in a much more universalistic language, bore the marks of the intra-capital conflict as much as MÜSİAD's did. To illustrate, TÜSİAD, while adopting a surprisingly open-minded approach to the solution of the Kurdish problem, carefully refrained from challenging the authoritarian measures taken against Islamist constituencies including MÜSİAD in the context of the February 28 process. See, Öniş & Türem (2002).

79 On the state-business relations front, the two actors' conversion to democracy had quite different motives. The big industrialists

represented by TÜSİAD have always been close partners of the Turkish developmental state that catered to the needs of secular and Western-oriented private capital as much as possible, as part of its modernization drive. Their state-dependent character led to the adoption by TÜSİAD of a complacent attitude towards authoritarian state policies for at least the first two decades of its existence. However, starting in the early 1990s, big business reached a certain level of autonomy *vis-à-vis* the Turkish state, "maturity" in Harris's (1987) words, thanks to the new market and financial opportunities created by economic liberalisation policies (Öniş & Türem, 2002). For more on state-business relations in Turkey, see Buğra (2004), Heper (1991), and Keyder (1987).

80 For more on the impact of flexible production processes on the informalisation of the Turkish labour force in the post-1980 period see Buğra (2003).

81 MÜSİAD fiercely opposed the passing of the Job Security Act placed on the parliamentary agenda in 2002 by the tripartite coalition government that preceded the AKP ("İş Güvencesi," 2002). It failed to prevent the act's passage, but managed to postpone its implementation until June 2003 by pressuring the AKP government. Likewise, it fully endorsed, in May 2003, the enactment of a new labour code increasing labour market flexibility and trimming the Job Security Act in a more business-friendly direction despite the harsh opposition from all trade unions (Yıldırım, 2006).

82 The Association previously cited the EU's pressure on Turkey for a political solution to the Kurdish problem as one of the reasons behind its objection to EU membership (MÜSİAD, 1995).

83 See, also Özdemir (2004) on the MÜSİAD's generally hostile attitude towards unionisation at the workplace.

84 From a more critical perspective, Coşar & Özman (2004) describe this mixture as "neoliberalism with a Muslim face."

85 For the strong criticisms raised by the *Türk Tabipler Birliği* (Turkish Medical Association, TTB), see the association's website: www. turktabibleribirligi.com

86 The Social Risk Mitigation Project will alleviate the impact of the recent economic crisis on poor households, and improve their capacity to withstand such risks in the future. The components will achieve this through: 1) an adjustment portion, as a rapid relief response to vulnerable groups through existing channels. Financing will be available for public, and private sector import requirements of the balance of payments against a negative list, and, the Government will make use of the Turkish Lira counterpart loan funds, to finance priority actions for immediate relief. Disbursements for assistance programs include school materials, and textbooks; pharmaceuticals, and medical supplies; and, expansion

of social assistance programs. The component's tranche release
will be conditional to a satisfactory macroeconomic framework,
and program progress as defined in the Letter of Sector Policy;
2) an investment portion to build the institutional capacity of the
government agencies providing coverage, and targeting social safety
nets for the poor. This includes policy research, monitoring and
evaluation, information technology development, staff development
and training; 3) conditional cash transfers (grants) to finance an
expanded social safety net targeted to the poorest six percent of
families with children, with the proviso of positive family behavioral
change with respect to education and health; 4) local initiatives, by
strengthening and financing key programs proposed by the provinces
and local communities, to enhance employment opportunities
aimed at poverty mitigation. Such programs are income-generating
sub-projects supported by technical assistance, employment training,
adult literacy, and small business practices (Zabcı, 2009, p. 119).

87 For a discussion of Islam and social policy, see Heyneman (2004).

88 For more information about the *Deniz Feneri Derneği*, see their
website http://www.denizfeneri.org.tr

89 Recently, a German court revealed that the German affiliation of the
Deniz Feneri collected donations from Turks living in Germany. It
was stated by the German court that 17 million Euros of an overall
41 million Euros in donations were illegally transferred to Turkey.
Beneficiaries include a company owned by pro-government Kanal
7 television channel. The *Deniz Feneri Derneği* of Turkey has no
official link to *Deniz Feneri* e.V. in Germany. However, the *Deniz
Feneri Derneği* (Turkey) has also received 8 million Euros of the
transferred money. The money transfers to Turkey are received
in cash by way of couriers, whose identities are also interesting.
German jurists portrayed the president of the Supreme Board of
Radio and Television (RTÜK) as a courier for the Lighthouse e.
V. in Germany. The president was the AKP nominee for RTÜK
presidency. There were also allegations of a link between the AKP
and the *Deniz Feneri Derneği* (Turkey), perhaps because the *Deniz
Feneri Derneği* (Turkey) was given the Eminent Services Award of
the Turkish Parliament under the AKP's rule. Further, the AKP is
accused of protecting accomplices in the *Deniz Feneri* e.V. case.

90 The informal economy refers to activities and income that are
partially or fully outside government regulation, taxation, and
observation. The main attraction of the undeclared economy is
financial. This type of activity allows the self-employed to increase
their take-home earnings or reduce their costs by evading taxation
and social contributions.

91 In the post-1980 period, especially during the 2000s, despite rapid
growth and a significant surge in exports, Turkish economy could
not generate jobs at the desired rate. This phenomena is called

"jobless growth" (Yeldan and Ercan, 2011). On the one hand, it is argued that the inadequate job creation of the economy is due to the excessive regulatory framework and the tax burden. On the other hand, the *structuralist* tradition sees the problem as one of *"joblessness"*, and regard it as a global phenomenon of the deflationary environment under the finance-led global economy (Yeldan and Ercan, 2011).

92   In Turkey, the coalition of the 1960 coup, including the new industrial bourgeoisie, the intelligentsia and both civilian and military bureaucracies, laid the foundations for a new regime of accumulation, with its social policy, political balances and administrative mechanisms. It had been accepted by the coalition that this new regime of accumulation, 'import substituting industrialisation' (ISI), which was also supported and advocated by the world hegemonic power, would be developed through state-directed plans. Turkey implemented four five-year plans between 1963-1983. The common characteristic of these plans was sustainable economic growth with a heavy emphasis on industrialisation. A highly restrictive trade regime was instituted in the form of import and export licensing, quotas, high custom duties and various surcharges.

93   The import substitution strategy was restored by a reduction in government involvement in productive activities, by an increased emphasis on market forces and by the replacement of an inward-looking strategy with an "export-oriented strategy of import substitution" (Kepenek and Yentürk, 2011).

94   The military take-over in September 1980 aimed at stabilising the political turmoil and hostile industrial relations by banning all trade union activities, ending all ongoing strikes and imprisoning trade union leaders. The 1982 Constitution, the Labour Law adopted in 1983, the Trade Unions Act (no. 2821) and the Collective Agreements, Strikes and Lockouts Act (no. 2822) led to severely restrictive labour legislation. Under the provisions of the constitution and the laws, the right of association is guaranteed except where associations are closed down by a court order or by the Minister of Internal Affairs. The rights of collective bargaining and strike are guaranteed. However, trade unions are not allowed to pursue political ends and unions are not be authorised to negotiate unless they represent 10 per cent of the workers in the industry or more than 50 per cent of the workers in the workplace. The internal affairs of unions and their financial sources are closely regulated. To form international affiliations trade unions require official approval.

95   In the post-1980s, facing the changing nature of industrialisation policies, unions confront new challenges and constraints. In the public sector, unions are concerned about the increasing use of contractual workers, who do not benefit from the rights of the

collective agreements signed in the enterprises. Most of the unions remain critical of the privatisation of the state enterprises, for it means job losses and de-unionisation for the working class. In the private sector, the main issues of concern for unions are the flexible use of workers such as an increasing number of temporary, contractual and subcontracted workers and easy fire and hire policies of the companies (Koray, 2000). These forms of employment lead not only to a growing number of workers without any rights but also cause the unions to loose power. Hence, unions in Turkey in the course of the 1990s, are no different from their counterparts in other countries who are facing changes in the structure of employment such as the growth of subcontracted, contractual and temporary workers and a marginal workforce in unstable employment, against a restricted socio-economic, political and legal environment.

96 According to the Turkish Statistical Institute (TÜİK), in 2008, the top-earning 20% of the population earned 47% of the country's income, while the bottom 20% earned 6%. 59% of the population eat meat or fish rarely; 46% cannot buy new clothing; 39% cannot heat their homes properly. The numbers have not changed: In 2007, as in 2008, the difference between the top 20% and bottom 20% in income was 8-fold. The top group earned on average 19,559 TL ($12,937) a year, the bottom group 2,426 TL($1,538). This is higher in the west and lower in southeast Turkey. 17% of the population is at risk of poverty (as it is formally defined) — 15% in cities, 14% in rural areas (TÜİK, 2009).

97 The post-2001 growth had indeed been high. Annual rate of growth of real GNP averaged 6.5% over 2002-2008 (Yeldan and Ercan, 2011). According to Yeldan and Ercan (2011: 3-4), "the *main* characteristic of the post-2001 era was its *jobless-growth* pattern. Rapid rates of growth were accompanied by high rates of unemployment and low participation rates. The rate of unemployment rose to above 10% after the 2001 crisis, and despite rapid growth, it has not come down to its pre-crisis levels (of 6.5% in 2000)... Over 2001 the GDP contracted by 7.4% in real terms, whole sale price inflation soared to 61.6%, and the currency lost 51% of its value against the major foreign monies. The burden of adjustment fell disproportionately on the labouring classes as the rate of unemployment rose steadily by 2 percentage points in 2001 and then another 3 percentage points in 2002. Real wages fall abruptly by 20% upon impact in 2001 and could not recover since."

98 This part of the chapter is mainly based on the paper, *"Türkiye'de Sosyal Yardımlar: İktisadi, Siyasi ve Kültürel Yapılar Üzerine Bir Çözümleme"* by Gamze Yücesan-Özdemir and Denizcan Kutlu, presented at Uluslararası Yoksullukla Mücadele Stratejileri Sempozyumu, İstanbul, October 13-15, 2010.

99 The SYDTF was established in May 1986 with the enactment of Act No. 3294. The act stated that the institution should assist citizens in absolute poverty and other persons that have been admitted to Turkey. One of the major projects introduced by the SYDTF is the Green Card program. The objective of the Green Card program, enacted in 1992 following a protocol(agreement?) between the SYDTF and the Ministry of Health, was to provide health services to poor people that were ineligible for social security and that had a monthly income of less than one-third of the minimum wage amount. In 2006, approximately ten million people were entitled to "green cards" (WTO, 2006).

100 Benefits provided by the SYDTF are distributed in two forms. The first form is in-kind benefits, which include food, coal, clothing, productive projects of small sizes, fuel, and medicine. Benefits are also distributed in cash, which encompass grants and scholarship programs and emergency situations.

101 The Conditional Cash Transfer (CCT) includes pregnancy allowances to poor families, as well as allowances given to poor families on the condition of regular health controls for preschool aged children, and school attendance for school-aged children. The project is implemented by the local foundations of the General Directorate of Social Assistance and Solidarity (SYDGM) (SYDGM, 2007, p. 59).

102 The modernisation efforts in the Otoman Empire started in the nineteenth century. The underlying aim was to hold the Empire together with a move towards a relatively secular order and renewed administrative system. The *Tanzimat* Edict of 1839 was the first significant step in that sense. The Edict aspired to modernise the state affairs and to hold the Empire together against the rising nationalistic claims with the introduction of an "Ottoman" identity that would surpass the religious and ethnic cleavages. Those attempts were intensified by another edict, The Reform Edict of 1856, which among other things introduced the notion of citizenship for the subjects of the Otoman Empire. The legal regulations on citizenship were issued by a citizenship law in 1869. The modernisation attempts continued with the transition to constitutional monarchy in 1876, which turned out to be ill fated since the constitution was shelved between 1877 and 1908. All in all, the mid-nineteenth century witnessed the modernisation and Westernisation efforts that will continue until the fall of the Empire. Those efforts laid the grounds for the new Republic as well. In this respect, the state-run modernisation process, which first and foremost aimed at the institutional restructuration process form the axis of parallelism between the late Ottoman and Republican contexts. The context of nation-state construction *via* integration to the then world capitalist system and the passifisation of religions as an asset in the shaping of the new citizen forms the

axis of differences between the two contexts. For further inquiry see, Davison, 1963; Berkes, 1964; Ortaylı, 1995; Üstel, 2004.

103 A quotation from one of the republican public intellectuals exemplifies the sensitivity regarding manners: "a person, who pushes his fellow citizens while getting on a street car is not a citizen in the real sense of the term" (Nermi, 1928/ 1992, 488 as cited in Soyarık, 2000, p. 101).

104 Recep Peker was the General Secretary of the CHP between 1931-1936. The quotation is taken from his statement concerning the new Labour Code, adopted in 1936.

105 It might be argued that citizenship studies as a new area started to emerge by the second half of the 1990s in Turkey. See for instance İçduygu, 1996; İçduygu, Çolak and Soyarık, 1999; İçduygu & Keyman, 2000.

106 The AKP's victory in the 2002 general elections was significant not only because it came out of the Islamist movement, but also because it represented the first single party majority government in almost a decade.

107 The Alevis are the members of a sect in Islam, which resembles the Shiite faith, and they constitute a minority in the Sunni dominant population. Therefore, they demand recognition and non-discrimination, officially recognised places of worship, and to be exempt from the compulsory religious courses in schools.

108 The MGK was established in 1962 in line with the 1961 Constitution. It was composed of the Prime Minister, Chief of the General Staff, Deputy Prime Minister, Ministers of National Defence, Internal Affairs, Foreign Affairs, Finance, Transportation, and Labour as well as the Chief of Staff and Commanders of the Army, Navy, Air Forces and Gendarmarie under the chairmanship of the President. It was formed as an advisory body, but by the memorandum of 1971 firstly, and then with the 1982 Constitution following the 1980 military coup d'état it was turned into a more influential board. Consequently, its recommendations were to be given high priority in government affairs. The MGK could be viewed as part of safeguarding the military's significant role in Turkish politics. In the refrom pacakges of 2001 and afterwards, it was relegated into an advisory board with increased civilian participation and a decreased military presence; Heper, 2006, p. 363).

109 However, this change was not a smooth one. In the parliamentary discussions there was a reaction from the opposition parties on the grounds that military service is a holy duty, and that this would raise further problems. This objection from the opposition was to do with the situation of the concentious objectors in Turkey. Their causes are rejected officially and they fall into a vicious cycle of trials and imprisonment, but this law does not still recognise them.

110 The early republican motto was very similar as it stated "common culture, common language, and common ideals." This stress on a common language at that time was carried out with campaigns such as "Citizen, speak Turkish!" against the non-Muslim minorities. The emphasis on Turkish-as-mother tongue was strong not only in the early Republican period, but during the 1980s as well. For instance between 1983 and 1991 a law banned "the use of a language other than the official languages of those states recognized by the Turkish Republic for expression, dissemination and publication," which referred specifically to the Kurdish language (see Yeğen, 2006, pp. 67-68). Also in line with the EU reforms, currently the official Turkish Radio and Television Broadcasting has TV channels broadcasting in Kurdish (TRT 6) and Arabic (TRT *Arapça*). Therefore, the emphasis on a common language among the basic traits of the country is not as evident currently. However, this does not mean that the conflicts over education in mother tongues have been resolved.

111 Here, we do not mean that the only reason behind the improvements was the accession process. On the contrary, the main leitmotiv has been the active lobbying by the women's rights organisations, while the international dynamics functioned as catalyst. On the juxtaposition of the effects of international dynamics and women's activism in Turkey see Aldıkaçtı-Marshall, 2009, pp. 358-378.

112 In Turkey, in general elections, the party decision making cadres do not list the women candidates at those ranks and consitituencies, which would increase the possibility of their election. The party authorities use the pretense of 10 percent electoral threshold when approached and questioned by the women's rights activists for not pursuing a gender equal candidate listing procedure. Aside from this systemic working of sexist politics, feminist political perspective highlights the fact that without a gender equal participatory perspective it is impossible to opt for a participatory democratic practice.

113 The falsity of the liberal assumption was revealed by the reproduction of patriarchal premises in liberalised political contexts (Eisenstein, 1981).

114 In this alliance, what differentiates the gendered perspectives of the allies originates from their approach to those issues directly related to the rights over the body—traditionally considered as issues of privacy—like abortion, contraception, and debates about marital rape. For the neoconservatives the liberal gains of the feminist movement that improved the individual rights of women in the private sphere mean moral ills that devastate the society. In curing these ills the neoconservatives have opted for the increase in the public effectiveness of religion so as to reinstitute social morality. They, in turn, criticised the neoliberals for their permissiveness

in letting the principle of individual liberty to extend beyond the borders of the free market and into the society at large (Wilson and Kelling, 2004).

115 The fact that even the nationalist coalition government of the *Demokratik Sol Parti* (Democratic Left Party, DSP), *Anavatan Partisi* (Motherland Party, ANAP), and the MHP (1999-2001) prioritised the accession process gives an idea about the spirit of the times. This prioritisation gains more significance when the MHP's Euroskeptic stance is taken into account (Öniş, 2007, p. 249).

116 In Turkey most of the political parties do not include gender quota in their bylaws. Among the exceptions are *Barış ve Demokrasi Partisi* (Peace and Democracy Party, BDP) and *Özgürlük ve Dayanışma Partisi* (Freedom and Solidarity Party, ÖDP).

117 Technically, the current AKP government is the third government formed by the party. The first AKP government was formed immediately after the landslide victory of the party in 2002 general elections. In this government, the party chairperson and current Prime Minister, Recep Tayyip Erdoğan could not participate due to the fact that at the time of the general elections he had been banned from political activity. In 2003 the ban on his political participation was lifted up and the second AKP government was formed under his Prime Ministry.

118 One such recent symbolic outcome of this alliance has been the dissolution of the State Ministry Responsible for Women and Family and its replacement by the State Ministry Responsible for Family and Social Policies. The name of the new ministry is telling about the neoliberal-conservative alliance in liquidifying the social into the "private", identified not only with the market mechanism but also with the family as the basic unit of society in conservative practice.

119 For a pioneering work on the issue see D. Campbell. (1992). Writing Security. United States Foreign Policy and the Politics of Identity. Machester: Manchester University Press.

120 A. Davutoğlu. (2001). *Stratejik Derinlik. Türkiye'nin Uluslararası Konumu*, İstanbul: Küre. 69th edition of *Stratejik Derinlik* has been published as of November 2011, which is not common for academic works on international relations in Turkey.

121 Interview with Davutoğlu, *Turkish Time*, 2004.

122 For example, with regard to the problems between Turkey and its Middle Eastern neighbours in the 1990s Davutoğlu refers to the possible role of increasing economic relations in the solution of the disputes. See Davutoğlu, 2001, pp. 181 and 404.

123 Author's own translation.

124 *Türkiye İş Bankası* is the first national bank of Turkey established in 1924.

(Endnotes)

<u>**323**</u>

125 *Milliyet*, August 25, 2010.

126 Başbakan Erdoğan'ın USAK'ta Yaptığı Konuşmanın Tam Metni, February 3, 2010.

127 Regarding geographical determinist approach see P. Bilgin. (2005). Turkey's Changing Security Discourses: The Challenge of Globalization. *European Journal of Political Research, 44*, pp. 175-201.

128 I benefitted from my previous study on the issue in writing this part: B. Demirtaş-Coşkun. (April 2009). Kurswechsel mit Tücken, *Internationale Politik, 64* (4), 62-67.

129 In 1996 Turkey and Israel signed two important military agreeements: Military Education and Cooperation Agreement and Defence Industry Cooperation Agreement. The agreements consisted of cooperation in the education of military officers, modernisation of Turkish tanks and fighter planes, and the purchase of unmanned aerial drones (Heron) by Turkey as well as intelligence cooperation.

130 For further discussion of this issue see Coşar's and Yeğenoğlu & Coşar's contributions to this volume.

131 Gürcistan'a gösterdiğiniz hassasiyeti gösterin, 2009; Erdoğan: İsrail insanlık yaşamına kara bir leke düşürdü, 2009; Erdoğan'dan Suudi gazeteciye Ortadoğu tepkisi, 2009.

132 "Başbakan Ağladı", 2009.

133 "İsrail ile ilişkilerde tarihi karar!..", Retrieved November 1, 2011.

134 "Cemevi" is a building in which Alevi population of Turkey perform worship.

135 See Coşar's contribution to this volume.

136 Speech by Ahmet Davutoğlu, on the opening ceremony of the conference "Ottoman legacy and Balkan Muslim Communities today" in Sarajevo, October 16, 2009.

137 Ibid.

138 For a comment on the issue see M. Çelik. (2010, February 14). Turkey Outdoes EU, US, Raising Hopes for Peace in Balkans. *Today's Zaman.*

139 For a comprehensive discussion see B. Demirtaş-Coşkun. (2010). Kosova'nın Bağımsızlığı ve Türk Dış Politikası (1990-2008), *Uluslararası İlişkiler, 7* (27), 51-85. This part is based on the article mentioned above. The author would like to thank the editors of the *Uluslararası İlişkiler* Journal for their permission.

140 It is interesting to note that Davutoğlu is not the first who named Bosniaks and Albanians as people who have "historical and cordial closeness to Turkey". The same discourse was used by some of *Fazilet Partisi* (Virtue Party-FP) parliamentarians before. Hüseyin

Kansu, MP from the FP used the same terms for these two Balkan people: Hüseyin Kansu, *Kosova İkinci Bosna Olmasın*, İstanbul, Yıldızlar, 1998, p. 27. Similarly, Davutoğlu's description of Kosova as the "life vein" of Turkey's policy toward Balkans was previously stated by the FP parliamentarians Mustafa Baş and Hüseyin Kansu: Davutoğlu, *Stratejik Derinlik*, p. 317; Mustafa Baş's speech, TBMM Genel Kurul Tutanağı, 20th Period, 3rd Legislative Year, 67th Session, March 17, 1998, p. 60, Retrieved January 26, 2010; Kansu, *Kosova İkinci Bosna Olmasın*, p. 30.

141 Speech by Ahmet Davutoğlu, on the opening ceremony of the conference "Ottoman legacy and Balkan Muslim Communities today" in Sarajevo, 16 October 2009,

142 "Başbakan Ağladı," 2009.

143 "Davutoğlu'nun Hayali Osmanlı Milletler Topluluğu", Milliyet, December 7, 2010, Retrieved 10 November 2011.

144 For a comprehensive analysis of the emergence of the neo-Ottomanist discourse in Turkish foreign policy under the leadership of Özal, see Ş. Çalış. (2001). *Hayalet bilimi ve hayali kimlikler, neo-osmanlılık, Özal ve Balkanlar.* Konya: Çizgi.

145 For a discussion on traditional and new approaches to the international political economy see N. Woods (2011). International political economy in an age of globalization.

146 For an assessment of the AKP governments' policies and *Acil Eylem Plânı* see Bağımsız Sosyal Bilimciler (2003).

147 My analysis mainly takes into consideration the structural reforms related to public administration, while the reforms related to social rights—health, education, and social security—are covered in Gamze Yücesan-Özdemir's contribution to the book.

148 The banking reforms require a decisive liberal attitude for the sustenance of open capital accounts.

149 Starting with the 1950s, the World Bank and the IMF shifted their financial assistance to the Third World due to political transformation through independence movements. In the 1970s, both institutions started to handle problems related to SAPs. The SAPs worked through two axes: a. Macro-economic stability; b. Structural adjustment. Strategies that involve the social aspects of the SAPs–like the strategy to decrease poverty-developed by the the World Bank, are essentially connected with the efficient resource allocation policy. At the same time, through these *socially sensitive* policies, the Bank attempts to forge legitimacy for the SAPs. This, in turn, has resulted in the rapid expansion of the Bank's sphere of influence. The Bank made its first moves in this direction in the 1980s, *via* initiatives in matters like the environment and some social policy issues. In the 1990s, it would eventually take the initiative in matters

concerning financial aid to countries that experience civil war, the protection of environment, reduction of poverty, and in developing joint programs with civil society organisations.

150 The Bank gives weight to educational problems in developing coutries since it regards education as an indispensable part of making people economically productive, that is, rising the level of human capital. According to the Bank, human capital, which includes the knowledge, skills, and experience of people, can be increased by investing in education.

151 The 1998 Staff Monitoring Program with the IMF is a case in point. The Programme signified those IMF conditionalities, which endowed the institution with the power to veto domestic policy making, ensuring the prioritisation of local and international finance capital.

152 Vakıf Bank, which was founded in 1954, was the fourth largest bank in Turkey according to a 2006 report of the Bank's Association of Turkey.

153 Başbakan Erdoğan'ın ulusa sesleniş konuşması. (2003, July 10).

154 5th European Meeting of People Experiencing Poverty. (May 12-13, 2006) *How do we cope with every day life?*, Brussels, Retrieved from http://ec.europa.eu/employment_social/social_inclusion/docs/2006/pep_report_en.pdf

155 Described by the European Commission as "attempts to conciliate employers' and workers' needs, flexibility and security, by ensuring the worker safe transitions inside the labour market, while maintaining and improving competitiveness of the companies and also preserving the European social model."

European Commission; Employment, Social Affairs and Equal Opportunities GD,

156 To join the EU, a new member state must meet the following conditions in three spheres: political: stability of institutions guaranteeing democracy, the rule of law, human rights and respect for and protection of minorities; economic: existence of a functioning market economy and the capacity to cope with competitive pressure and market forces within the Union; acceptance of the Community *acquis*: ability to take on the obligations of membership, including adherence to the aims of political, economic and monetary union.

157 All Progress Reports can be found at the EU's official web site.

158 "The incidence of accidents is highest in manufacturing of metal products (except machinery). Fatal cases of silicosis caused by poor working conditions in jeans sandblasting workshops continued to occur." (Report 2009, p. 63).

159 I would like to thank Simten Coşar, who formulated this term while discussing the topic.

160 For an analysis of the TEKEL resistance see Yıkılmaz& Kumlu, 2011.

ABOUT THE
AUTHORS

Simten Coşar is professor of political science, Başkent University, Ankara, Turkey (Ph.D. in Political Science, Bilkent University, Ankara, Turkey, 1997; MA in Political Science, Bilkent University, Ankara, Turkey, 1991; BA in Political Science and International Relations, Boğaziçi University, İstanbul, Turkey, 1990). Her areas of interest are political thought, political thought in Turkey, political parties in Turkey, and women in political thought. She is the author of various articles in *Journal of Political Ideologies, Contemporary Politics, Feminist Review, Journal of Third World Studies, South European Society and Politics,* and *Monthly Review.*

Birgül Demirtaş is associate professor of international relations, TOBB University of Economics and Technology, Ankara, Turkey (Ph.D. in Political Science, *Freie Universität* Berlin, Germany, 2005; MA in International Relations, Bilkent University, Ankara, Turkey, 1999; BA in Political Science and International Relations, Boğaziçi University, İstanbul, Turkey, 1995). Her studies concentrate on the Balkans, Turkish foreign policy, German foreign policy, EU foreign policy and International Relations theories. She is assistant editor of the Journal of *Uluslararası İlişkiler* (*International Relations*) published by Turkish International Relations Council. She is the author of following books: *Turkey, Germany and the Wars in Yugoslavia: A Search for Reconstruction of State Identities?* (Berlin: Logos Verlag, 2006), *The Vlachs: A Forgotten Minority in the Balkans* (London: Frank Cass, 2001). She is the co-editor of *Neighborhood Challenge. The European Union and Its Neighbors* (with Bezen Balamir-Coşkun, Boca Raton, Florida: Universal Publishers, 2009). She has articles published in *Internationale Politik*, *WeltTrends*, *Perceptions*, and *Insight Turkey*.

Zuhal Yeşilyurt-Gündüz is associate professor at the Department of International Relations at TED University, Ankara, Turkey (Ph.D. in Political Science and International Relations, Bonn University, Germany, 2000; MA in Political Science and International Relations, Bonn University, Germany, 1995). Her field of interest covers topics like Turkey-EU integration, women and gender issues, Euro-Mediterranean Partnership, economisation and securitisation of migration, securitisation of HIV/AIDS, securitisation of Islam, Xenophobia and Islamophobia in the EU. She has published articles in Journals like *Perceptions, Internationale Politik, WeltTrends, Turkish Review of Balkan Studies, International Policy Analysis, Journal of Muslim Minority Affairs,* and *Monthly Review.*

Ali Murat Özdemir was born on 21 April 1968 in Ankara, Turkey. He received his Bachelors degree in Law from the Faculty of Law, Ankara University, Ankara, Turkey, received his M.A. degree in international commercial law from the Centre for Legal Studies, Sussex University, UK, and his doctorate degree from the Department of Political Science and Public Administration, Middle East Technical University, Ankara, Turkey. He has published widely on the sociology of law and political economy in general and on the political economy of the Turkish legal system in particular both in English and Turkish. He has a forthcoming book on the political economy of labor law (*Political Economy of Labour Law: the Case of Turkey*, Roman Books), and some of his articles are published in *South East Europe Review* and *Economic and Industrial Democracy*.

Gamze Yücesan-Özdemir is professor of social policy, Ankara University, Ankara (Ph.D. in Development Studies, University of Sussex, Brighton, UK, 1998; MA in European Studies, University of Reading, Reading, UK, 1993; BS in Management, Middle East Technical University, Ankara, Turkey, 1992). Her areas of interest are labor process, social policy, labor markets, labor politics, and trade unions. She is the author of various articles in *Economic and Industrial Democracy, Capital and Class, Turkish Studies, South East Europe Review,* and *International Union Rights*.

Nalan Soyarık-Şentürk is assistant professor in the Department of Political Science and International Relations, Başkent University, Ankara (Ph.D. in Political Science, Bilkent University, Ankara, Turkey, 2000; MA in Political Science, Bilkent University, Ankara, Turkey, 1994; B.Sc. in Political Science, Bilkent University, Ankara, Turkey, 1993). Her areas of interest are citizenship studies, Turkish politics, and globalisation.

Galip Yalman is associate professor of political science, Middle East Technical University, Ankara, Turkey (Ph.D. in Political Sciences, University of Manchester, Manchester, UK; M.Sc. in International Relations,

University of Southampton, Southampton; B.Sc. in Political Science and Public Administration, Middle East Technical University, Ankara, Turkey). His areas of interest are state theory, comparative political theory and political economy of Turkey. He has given papers to *Historical Materialism Conferences*, *International Political Science's Association Congresses*, and *United Nations Conferences*. He is the co-editor of the book, *Economic Transitions to Neoliberalism in Middle-Income Countries: Policy Dilemmas, Economic Crises, Forms of Resistance,* London: Routledge.

Metin Yeğenoğlu is a PhD candidate in the Department of Sociology at Middle East Technical University (MA in Politics and Social Sciences Program, Hacettepe University, Ankara, Turkey, 2005; and MA in Gender and Women's Studies, Middle East Technical University, Ankara, Turkey, 2006; BA in Political Science and International Relations, Başkent University, Ankara, Turkey, 2006). His areas of interest are political thought, feminist political theory, and Turkish politics. He is the author of articles on Turkish politics in Turkish and English. He has published in *South European Society and Politics and Monthly Review.*

Berna Yılmaz is a PhD candidate in political science at the University of Milan, Graduate School in Social, Economic and Political Sciences, Milan, Italy (MA in International Relations, Bilkent University, Ankara, Turkey, 2004; BA in Political Science and Public Administration, Middle East Technical University, Ankara, Turkey, 2001). Her areas of interest are party politics, religious mobilisation, and civil societal organisations.

Filiz Zabcı is associate professor of political science, Ankara University, Ankara (Ph.D. in Political Science, Ankara University, Ankara, Turkey, 1997; MA in Political Science, Middle East Technical University, Ankara, Turkey, 1990; BS in Public Administration and Political Science, Faculty of Political Sciences, Ankara University, Ankara, Turkey, 1986). Her areas of interest are political theory and political economy. She is the author of various articles on the state, non-state actors, war and private military companies in the global capitalism and a book on World Bank.

www.ingramcontent.com/pod-product-compliance
Lightning Source LLC
Chambersburg PA
CBHW030639270326
41929CB00007B/135